MARGUERITE YOURCENAR
READING THE VISUAL

# THE EUROPEAN HUMANITIES RESEARCH CENTRE

## UNIVERSITY OF OXFORD

The European Humanities Research Centre of the University of Oxford organizes a range of academic activities, including conferences and workshops, and publishes scholarly works under its own imprint, LEGENDA. Within Oxford, the EHRC bridges, at the research level, the main humanities faculties: Modern Languages, English, Modern History, Literae Humaniores, Music and Theology. The Centre stimulates interdisciplinary research collaboration throughout these subject areas and provides an Oxford base for advanced researchers in the humanities.

The Centre's publications programme focuses on making available the results of advanced research in medieval and modern languages and related interdisciplinary areas. An Editorial Board, whose members are drawn from across the British university system, covers the principal European languages. Titles include works on French, German, Italian, Portuguese, Russian and Spanish literature. In addition, the EHRC co-publishes with the Society for French Studies, the British Comparative Literature Association and the Modern Humanities Research Association. The Centre also publishes *Oxford German Studies* and *Film Studies*, and has launched a Special Lecture Series under the LEGENDA imprint.

*Enquiries about the Centre's publishing activities should be addressed to:*
Professor Malcolm Bowie, Director

*Further information:*
Kareni Bannister, Senior Publications Officer
European Humanities Research Centre
University of Oxford
47 Wellington Square, Oxford OX1 2JF
enquiries@ehrc.ox.ac.uk
www.ehrc.ox.ac.uk

# Marguerite Yourcenar
## *Reading the Visual*

❖

NIGEL SAINT

## LEGENDA

European Humanities Research Centre
University of Oxford
Studies in Comparative Literature 5
2000

*Published by the*
*European Humanities Research Centre*
*of the University of Oxford*
*47 Wellington Square*
*Oxford OX1 2JF*

*In association with the British Comparative Literature Association*

*LEGENDA is the publications imprint of the*
*European Humanities Research Centre*

*ISBN 1 900755 39 4*
*ISSN 1466-8173*

*First published 2000*

*British Library Cataloguing in Publication Data*
*A CIP catalogue record for this book is available from the British Library*

*LEGENDA series designed by Cox Design Partnership, Witney, Oxon*
*Printed in Great Britain by*
*Information Press*
*Eynsham*
*Oxford OX8 1JJ*

*Chief Copy-Editor: Genevieve Hawkins*

# CONTENTS

❖

For Vernon Sewell

and

In memory of Stafford Saint

# ACKNOWLEDGEMENTS

❖

Many people have helped me from time to time with my work on Yourcenar and I would like to thank the following: Kajsa Anderson, Chris Barlas, Marie-Claire Barnet, Françoise Bonali-Fiquet, George and Sylvie Bowden, José Jesus Cabello, Colin Davis, Vicky Dicopoulou, Peter Dietl, Frederick Farrell, Camillo Faverzani, Yannick Guillou, H. R. Hoetink, Peter Jackson, Walter Kaiser, Richard Maber, Elizabeth McGrath, Ana de Medeiros, Ann Moss, Rémy Poignault, Manuel Lucas Sánchez Villalón, Carla Singh, Tom Smith, Alice Staveley, Alexandre Terneuil, Jeremy Thurlow, Michael Tilby, Gennaro Toscano, Kelle Truby, Sally Wallis, Peter Whyte, Michael Worton, Adrian Wright and Alexander Zahar. I would also like to record my gratitude to the late Louis Allen, Edith Farrell, David Wallace-Hadrill and Tony Whitehouse.

For many years now, Valerie Mainz has helped me to study art-historical questions and she remains unfailingly supportive. I am also very grateful to Stephen Bann and Eddie Hughes for their stimulating comments during my PhD exam. Throughout the project Patrick ffrench made suggestions and sorted out word-processing difficulties. Roland-François Lack read an early chapter of my thesis and was always ready to offer advice.

This study of Yourcenar owes very much to my PhD supervisor, Annette Lavers, whose enduring enthusiasm for the subject and skilful guidance of my research allowed me to find the focus for my work. Her critical attentiveness and intellectual brilliance continue to be illuminating. This book is being published thanks to the keen interest of Stephen Bann, Malcolm Bowie, Elinor Shaffer and the EHRC. I am extremely grateful to my godfather Vernon Sewell and to the Department of French at Royal Holloway, University of London, who have contributed towards the publication costs.

My work on Yourcenar could not have even begun without the financial assistance of my parents, Nicholas and Pamela Saint, who have also patiently performed the many roles usually assigned to parents during the writing of a thesis and first book. My sister, Charlotte, helped with the illustrations.

# ABBREVIATIONS

❖

Most references to Yourcenar's works will be to the two Pléiade volumes: *Œuvres romanesques* (Gallimard, 1982) and *Essais et Mémoires* (Gallimard, 1991). The abbreviations used in the text and notes follow the form standardized by the *Bulletin de la Société Internationale d'Etudes Yourcenariennes* (henceforth *Bulletin de la SIEY*) in June 1994:

| | |
|---|---|
| CL | *La Couronne et la Lyre* |
| EM | *Essais et Mémoires* |
| LYO | *Les Yeux ouverts* |
| MCA | *La Mort conduit l'attelage* |
| ON | *L'Œuvre au noir* |
| OR | *Œuvres romanesques* |
| PE | *En pèlerin et en étranger* |
| QE | *Quoi? L'Eternité* |
| SBI | *Sous bénéfice d'inventaire* |
| TGS | *Le Temps, ce grand sculpteur* |
| VC | *La Voix des choses* |

# PREFACE

❖

Since the publication of *Mémoires d'Hadrien* in 1951, the work of Marguerite Yourcenar (1903–87) has attracted widespread admiration from many different audiences. Yourcenar had the rare distinction of seeing a volume of her work appear in the prestigious 'Bibliothèque de la Pléiade' during her lifetime, thus achieving a sort of double immortality, since two years before, in 1980, she had been the first woman elected to the Académie française. Election to the Académie royale belge de langue et de littérature françaises in 1970, an interview by Bernard Pivot in his 'Apostrophes' series in 1979, regular repeats of interviews and readings on France-Culture, posthumous publications and many critical studies all bear witness to Yourcenar's status as a major modern writer.

In Yourcenar's fiction, essays, drama and family memoirs, the historical process, the interaction of individual and collective consciousness, the function and potential of myth, and the inquiry into the legitimacy and durability of values, all determine the way each text represents the world. Yourcenar's vision of the world is conveyed in fictional works set in the past (*Le Coup de grâce*, *Mémoires d'Hadrien*, *L'Œuvre au noir*, *Anna, Soror...* and *Un homme obscur*), in rewritings of myths and tales where the time-scale shuttles between past and present (*Feux* and *Nouvelles orientales*), in novels with contemporary settings (*La Nouvelle Eurydice* and *Denier du rêve*), in plays exploring the myths of Electra, Theseus and Alcestis, in essays on diverse subjects from Bede to Borges, from the Solstices to the Sistine Chapel, from Homer to slaughterhouses, and in translations of James Baldwin, Cavafy, Hortense Flexner, Mishima, Negro Spirituals and Greek poetry from Homer to the ninth century CE. Finally, in the unfinished trilogy *Le Labyrinthe du Monde* (1974–88), family, cultural, political, social and ecological histories overlap in a narrative stretching from '"Avant la naissance du monde"' to the 1970s.

This book argues that the key to assessing Yourcenar's achievement as a writer is provided by the engagement in her work with the visual in all its guises (cultural, social and individual). Rather than concentrating primarily on her approach to the writing of the historical novel or her avowed aesthetics, this book attempts to recontextualize her essays and fiction from an art-historical and theoretical perspective. Questions of memory, cultural survival and historiography are investigated in order to open up the practice of reading the visual, leading to a greater understanding of how the writing represents the world. The visual emerges as the topic which most enables the reader to approach the lasting contribution of the Yourcenarian project.

If a publication in the series 'Le musée retrouvé' (Paris: Stock) were to take on all the visual sources and interests of Marguerite Yourcenar, the completed volume would be enormous and contain hundreds of images. But such a publication would run the risk of fixing and delimiting the life and writing of a prodigiously well-travelled, versatile and erudite writer. For Yourcenar, the sculptures, buildings and paintings of the past act as an open archive for the novelist researching the Roman Empire of the second century or Europe in the sixteenth and seventeenth centuries, and for the essayist writing on diverse subjects including Böcklin, Chenonceaux and Tyrolean religious art.

The visual productions of the past provide initial access to the central figures represented: the heroes of myths and historical narratives. They also provide unique access to the world inhabited by Hadrien, Zénon and Nathanaël, whose hold on their surroundings is problematized and increasingly weakened in Yourcenar's work. Questions of background and detail are particularly challenging and fertile. The reader's role is revitalized during the discovery of the dislocations experienced by the texts as they encounter alterity, defeat and the workings of memory.

Since her election to the Académie française, Yourcenar has received a good deal of critical attention, notably in Belgium, Canada, France, Italy and the USA. There have been over a dozen international conferences devoted to her since 1990, with a regular flow of conference proceedings, monographs and articles, but until now there has been no book-length study of her from the UK. The aim of this book is to contribute to the existing body of studies working 'against the grain' of received accounts of Yourcenar's work, in this case by employing visual theory to examine her writings on the visual arts and by subsequently looking at her treatment of the visual in her fiction.

# LIST OF ILLUSTRATIONS

❖

# INTRODUCTION

❖

In hospital in Maine in 1985, Marguerite Yourcenar was handed a small piece of malachite, black-grey, smooth and cold. She considered its age and provenance, marvelling at the route which had brought the stone from the mountains to her hands. Weak from fatigue, she lost hold of the object, which fell to the floor and broke into further, less even pieces. 'La voix des choses' was the response of her companion, reiterated and reported to us by Yourcenar herself (*VC*, 7). For a writer so passionately preoccupied by the visual in all its guises, this equanimity is distinctive and engaging. In her search for a voice as a writer, Yourcenar wrote regularly on the visual arts, eager to establish her vision and independence. In the study of her voice presented in this book, the hold of writing on the visual is assertive, liberating, poignant, and at times possessive and insecure.

There are many essays by Yourcenar on the visual arts and they are treated as a corpus of texts in this book. The range of her interests is extensive. She wrote about the Innsbruck Hofkirche, Michelangelo, the mosaics of Ravenna, Poussin, Piranesi, Dürer, Ruisdael and Rembrandt. These essays form the core of her writings on the visual arts and will therefore be discussed in detail in this book. While the presence of the visual arts in her work has been widely acknowledged in Yourcenar studies, the uses of art, architecture and sculpture in her fiction and non-fiction have in fact received little critical attention. The essays on the visual arts have been studied in terms of thematic development and a start has been made on looking at the connections between her essays and her fiction, including the employment of the visual arts in the latter. This book attempts to make up for this neglect and also to follow in the wake of the more adventurous examples of criticism on questions of history, silence, solitude, narcissism, maxims and violence in Yourcenar's work.

Recognizing the modernity of Yourcenar's engagement with the visual arts led to a consideration of how the visual may be understood

more broadly in the context of her fiction, primarily here the
historical novels *Mémoires d'Hadrien*, *L'Œuvre au noir* and *Un homme
obscur*. This enquiry involves, among other topics, the study of the
articulation of historiographical perspective, encounter, memory and
disappearance. It enables the reader to produce new and creative interpretations of Yourcenar's major texts.

The essays on the visual arts are studied in the second chapter of
this book. The diversity of Yourcenar's interests is reflected in the large
number of books on art which she kept at her home in Maine,
making up most of the entries in the inventory of her library from
no. 343 to no. 799.[1] The collection includes general art books,
monographs, exhibition catalogues and masses of postcards and other
reproductions. This context provides an introduction to Yourcenar's
writings on art. An idea of the influences on her may be deduced
from the presence of books by Bernard Berenson, Kenneth Clark,
Roger Fry, Elie Faure and Erwin Panofsky. The outlook of these and
other art historians whose books feature in Yourcenar's library may
broadly be termed humanist. According to Rensselaer Lee,[2] in the
humanist aesthetic, which was elaborated as a theory during the
Renaissance and Classical period, the artist produces an ordered,
elevated, unifying vision of the world on his canvas. The spectator
admires this superior arrangement of the world and reads the account
of the world represented according to its pictorial unity and its
depiction of significant actions, noble sentiments and decipherable
symbols. In her essays, Yourcenar can be seen, in part, to articulate this
view.

Only in part, however, since this would be to overlook the modern
cast to her perspective: the humanist iconographical framework never
quite covers the ambition of Yourcenar's response, nor that of some
of her guides mentioned above, nor other guides she had, such as
Roberto Longhi and André Malraux. We are able to trace the different
formulations of her engagement as a spectator with painting, leading
increasingly away from received iconographical readings to an openness
to the power of visual phenomena. The desire to articulate her personal
investigation into the pictorial leads her to negotiate the fragmentary
and disruptive as the modern condition of the work of art. Throughout
her writings on the encounter with the visual, Yourcenar returns to
how to account for the direct visual impact of the work of art.

We will see, therefore, that analysis of the essays cannot occur with
reference only to humanist art history. To reach an initial awareness of

what is at stake in each essay, some initial categories are investigated in order to acquire a working methodology. In the case of the essay on Poussin, reference naturally has to be made to the art-historical and theoretical context in order to gain the terminology for an understanding of the concerns of an essay written in 1940 about a seventeenth-century artist. Then the tradition of French writing on Poussin needs to be considered in order to locate Yourcenar's contribution, especially in the period surrounding her essay. Next there is the essay's particular engagement with the paintings. All these categories interweave, of course, and they are only divided here for the purposes of seeing the different concerns at work in the essay. After this groundwork has been done for all the essays, in varying degrees, it is necessary and central to the whole critical enterprise to point out the distinctive areas of the essay which may elude the above categories, examining how they articulate Yourcenar's voice and provide the focus for the study of where the visual impact of Poussin on Yourcenar's writing may be located and how it may be interpreted.

By adopting the methodology outlined above, it is possible to indicate the boldness in Yourcenar's positions, which soon depart from any attempt to find in art reassuringly ordered representations of the world. Representation itself is questioned in terms of its dynamics, strategies and durability. This shift in her work is manifested in the essays on Piranesi, Ruisdael and Rembrandt. No longer the guarantor of cultural permanence, the pictorial work is interpreted according to its representation and negotiation of figures of disruption and dispersal: the pictures discussed are interpreted as sites of ephemeral passage, cataclysmic testimony, sombre visions and vanishing corpses. There is a constant challenge to the humanist cultural and metaphysical significance attributed to the art object.

The purpose of this reading of the essays on Innsbruck, Ravenna, Poussin, Dürer, Ruisdael and Rembrandt is, therefore, to discuss the issues involved in Yourcenar's written responses to the visual. Starting with the essays, we are able to follow the way she presents, questions and reworks her perspectives during her discussion of the artists concerned. It is now necessary to set out the theories used to explore the territory—art theory, representation and the question of visualization—into which this study of the visual leads us.

For the contemporary philosopher and art historian Georges Didi-Huberman, the encounter with the work of art must involve the risk of a challenge to received ideas. The ideal form of attention to a work unpacks the baggage of art-historical interpretation. Drawing on Freud and Lacan, whose analytical practice he discusses in relation to his own project, Didi-Huberman proposes to allow a work to exercise its power over the spectator:

Quelque chose comme une attention flottante, une longue suspension du moment de conclure, où l'interprétation aurait le temps de s'éployer dans plusieurs dimensions, entre le visible saisi et l'épreuve d'un dessaisissement. Il y aurait ainsi, dans cette alternative, l'étape dialectique—sans doute impensable pour un positivisme—consistant à ne pas se saisir de l'image, et à se laisser plutôt saisir par elle: donc à *se laisser dessaisir de son savoir sur elle.*[3]

Reacting to the neo-Kantian and humanist model worked out by the art historian Erwin Panofsky, Didi-Huberman proposes that the visual arts are far more disruptive than the account offered by a chronological and pragmatic mode of inquiry would suggest.

He argues that the humanist theory that artistic inspiration is located in the work of the intellect (*disegno*) and then communicated to the canvas or the stone by intuition allows art history to present its discipline as a science of art. In Panofsky's elaboration of a method of interpreting the objects represented in painting as symbols within the framework of a depicted story, we pass from the object to the idea to the work of art and back again; Didi-Huberman suggests that Panofsky was aware that he had not got round the problem of his modern theory's similarity with classical mimesis. He acknowledges and learns from the erudition and rhetoric of Panofksy's arguments, but wishes at the same time to question the stability of the bases of the theory and its points of reference. He proposes a Lacanian link between the humanistic discipline practised by Panofsky and a time of European cultural crisis:

Il faut cependant tenir compte du fait que Panofsky prêtait là à un autre glissement, une autre dénégation: il s'interdisait—et interdisait à l'histoire de l'art—de voir ou plutôt d'*affronter ce moment où les images font violence*, sont elles-mêmes des actes de violence. Une partie de l'art médiéval et même renaissant répond pourtant à cette sombre contrainte. Mais à cela Panofsky tournait le dos, quitte à *désincarner* une partie des objets qu'il étudiait.[4]

Hence Didi-Huberman, discussing Panofsky's reading of Titian's *Allegory of Prudence*, points out that barely any attention is given to the visual impact—starting with the bold and heavy colour—of the painting. Panofsky states at the end of his second essay on the painting that he specifically wishes to avoid divorcing 'form' from 'content', distancing himself from art history that concentrates on 'the distribution of colour and lines, light and shade, volumes and planes'. Such pictorial features, 'however delightful as a visual spectacle, must also be understood as carrying a more-than-visual meaning'.[5] For Didi-Huberman, Panofsky thereby avoids incorporating the visual fully in his project, describing it problematically as a 'delightful spectacle', while neither 'form' nor 'content' is necessarily the stable category denoted by Panofsky. In her reading of Poussin, as we will see, there comes a moment when Yourcenar faces up to the violence or disruption inflicted by the work of art on the spectator.

For Didi-Huberman, it is problematic to neglect the visual for the sake of a theory uniting the visible (imitation) and the readable (iconography). He takes as an example of this problem the ways of interpreting the area of white between the Angel and the Virgin in Fra Angelico's *Annunciation* of 1440–1, an interpretation elaborated in his book on the artist.[6] In *Devant l'image*, he argues that the terms visible and invisible do not adequately cover both the lack of a specific depiction and the presence of something. He prefers to use the term 'visuel' to clarify what it is that is seen in the painting.[7] The confrontation with pictorial spaces that cannot be described in a pragmatic manner leads Didi-Huberman to be suspicious of both the idea of the detail and the practice of producing verbal 'descriptions' of the visual.

The interpretation of details runs the risk of making simplistic deductions from the whole of the picture to its constituent parts. Looking for details posits an act of looking that can encapsulate the visible, if only on the reduced scale of the detail.[8] Following Sartre, Didi-Huberman reminds us that the pictorial instead refutes reality.[9] Thus when it comes to thinking about the description of the pictorial in writing, Didi-Huberman indicates that we need to revise our terminology and to speak instead of writing in its own terms. In his discussion of Bergotte's encounter with Vermeer's *View of Delft* in *A la recherche du temps perdu*, he distinguishes between writing and description: 'Corrélativement, Proust ne cherchait pas dans le visible des arguments de *description*, il y cherchait la fulguration de *rapports* [...] L'énoncé comme la pratique de Proust nous enseignent ici à quel point écrire est le contraire de décrire.'[10] Didi-Huberman proceeds to discuss the celebrated 'petit pan de mur jaune' and explains how the visual impact of the patch of yellow disrupts any attempt to gain an overall unifying view of the picture and instead presents (borrowing a term from psychoanalysis) a pictorial 'symptom' to the spectator. This symptom indicates the explosive potential of representation. Such potential, this time in verbal form, may be located in the account given in *A l'ombre des jeunes filles en fleurs* of Elstir's painting *Le port de Carquethuit*, where the charging and volatile phrases convey the visual arrangement of land, sea and figures in the imaginary picture.[11]

In an interview given in 1986, the theorist Louis Marin also called for an exploration into the traces, indices and symptoms of painting.[12] He argued that the Freudian model of psychoanalysis challenged art history to explain the function of these effects on the spectator. Marin is fascinated by the way in which classical (meaning, primarily, seventeenth-century) theories of representation can be understood with reference to the modern inquiry of psychoanalysis. In particular he looks to theory to open up the encounter with the visual, to explain the many permutations of looking that can be discovered when the positions of the spectator, of the represented figures and of artistic theory interact. This book aims to adopt this project of opening up the discourse of writing on the visual. The resultant lines of inquiry can possess the energy of Didi-Huberman's notion of 'rapports'.

At the same time, the question of subjectivism is considered by Marin. The basis for his inquiry into the visual is, he explains, neither spurious nor arbitrary, since the search for a discourse of plurality reflects the awareness of this danger. In a paper on Giorgione's *Tempest*, he argues for this plurality as a way of tackling the question of the subjectivity and potential narcissism of the gaze at a picture: 'Ecrire le tableau, d(écrire) le tableau, c'est d'abord chercher du regard, des regards multiples, pluriels, secrets, scellés dans la texture et les figures de l'œuvre peinte, parce que les regards sont des traversées pures, génératrices d'espaces pluriels et singuliers'.[13] During the round-table discussion after a paper given at Cerisy in 1981, Marin pointed to the search for a way around the problem of the implication of the spectator in the interpretation of a painting: 'c'est d'essayer de montrer comment sortir du narcissisme, c'est-à-dire du rêve impossible de voir son propre regard'.[14] The approach being outlined here by Marin aims to pay full attention to the surface of the painting, encouraging the encounter with the pictorial to be as open and unfixed as possible, exploring all patterns of looking in a work, here described as 'pluriels', 'singuliers', 'secrets' and 'scellés'. This investigative model of inquiry, this openness to the different discourses at work, is applied in this book to the encounter with the pictorial in Yourcenar's essays and is extended to the non-pictorial in her fiction in order to pursue, for example, the multiple directions of Zénon's researches in *L'Œuvre au noir*, enabling us to explore Yourcenar's articulation of the visual.

This openness to the negotiation of complex visual exchanges may nevertheless lead to an impasse for the reader. Following W. J. T. Mitchell's argument,[15] we will see that this difficulty locates the recognition and place of alterity. The passage across from spectator to object may be interpreted in terms of the figure of the threshold: the place of the encounter may be a point beyond which the interpreter cannot pass. In *Ce que nous voyons, ce qui nous regarde*, Didi-Huberman discusses the distance between spectator and object as an unstable process of aspiration and defeat. The threshold stages a limit and an opening out. The act of looking occurs in the space of a site: 'Les images—les choses visuelles—sont toujours déjà des lieux: elles n'apparaissent que comme des paradoxes en acte où les coordonnées spatiales se déchirent, s'ouvrent à nous et finissent par s'ouvrir en nous, pour nous ouvrir et en cela nous incorporer.'[16] The sites of the encounter with the visual will be studied here, as well as the corporeal exchange between spectator and image. The painting, for example in the reading given here of Yourcenar's essay on Rembrandt, is the bodily surface of blood and skin; it is experienced as an exchange and site of limit. Thus, what emerges from this investigation into notions of multiplicity and exchange is an inquiry into the visual that operates and fuses both a symptomatic and a canonical reading of the texts.

In Yourcenar's fiction, visual traumas dominate the early texts: in *Alexis ou le traité du vain combat*, Alexis struggles in vain in the web of narcissism; spectres and mirrors in the streets of Rome perplex the characters in *Denier du rêve*; fixed images of the self and others confront the mythological figures in *Feux*; and Eric in *Le Coup de grâce* is confounded when he cannot accept the difference between his image as constructed by introspection and the image of himself he sees in the mirror, while he is also disturbed by the memory of a starfish that haunts his sexual obsessions. Reference will be made to these works, but this book concentrates on later works, taking as its corpus of fiction *Mémoires d'Hadrien*, *L'Œuvre au noir* and *Un homme obscur*, where there are comparable problems in visualizing the self and others, but where a loosening of the visual hold on the Other can also be seen to operate. Disruption and difference are accepted as the experience of looking. Merleau-Ponty discusses this visual operation in *L'Œil et l'Esprit*: 'La vision n'est pas un certain mode de la pensée ou présence à soi: c'est le moyen qui m'est donné d'être absent de moi-même, d'assister du dedans à la fission de l'Etre, au terme de laquelle seulement je me ferme sur moi'.[17] For the corpus of Yourcenar's texts discussed in this book, the act of tracing the negotiation of disruption and limitation by her principal characters, whether explicitly a part of the discourse or instead detected in the writing, allows the reader to work behind the lines of the received accounts of Yourcenar's work that posit homogeneous progressions in the lives of her heroes.

It should be noted that the trilogy *Le Labyrinthe du monde* is not discussed in any detail here. There is ample material in the study of the essays and fiction for a full exploration of the problematic of the visual and this book hopes to contribute to the current debate on its chosen corpus of texts. Meanwhile, Yourcenar's early poems after sculptures and paintings have been studied in depth by Camillo Faverzani in his doctoral thesis, 'Marguerite Yourcenar et la culture italienne'.[18]

Drawing on the above theories, we are able to explore the problematic of writing's approach to the visual and the verbal strategies and resources implicated in its representations. But in order to develop the notion of the potential of the verbal-visual inquiry, we also attempt to allow the connections that may be made between the concerns of the written text and the features of the work of art in question to interact and offer new directions for reading Yourcenar. Throughout, however, every effort is made to keep in mind W. J. T. Mitchell's warning about the problem of privileging the verbal over the visual. This criticism is addressed at the claim that a semiotic approach to interartistic comparison achieves an unbiased transdisciplinarity. Mitchell is doubtful: 'The challenge is to redescribe the whole image/text problematic that underwrites the comparative method and to identify critical practices that might facilitate a sense of connectedness while working against the homogenising, anaesthetic tendencies of comparative strategies and semiotic "science".'[19]

Let us outline some examples of the interconnections which lead to new readings of the texts. One example occurs in the discussion in Chapter 3 of her essay 'Le cerveau noir de Piranèse'. This essay on Piranesi and the reference to his etchings of Hadrian's Villa in 'Carnets de notes de *Mémoires d'Hadrien*' encourage us to look at Piranesi's etchings when reading the novel. This is partly to follow the preoccupations of Yourcenar's account of this artist, but it is also an opportunity to see if any aspects of her reconstruction of the emperor Hadrian may be traced by the reader in Piranesi's etchings of the emperor's Villa; such tracings can then supplement Yourcenar's comments in the 'Carnets'. (The English name Hadrian is used to refer to the historical emperor independent of Yourcenar's text; Hadrien is used for Yourcenar's version of the emperor.) In this investigation into connections between Yourcenar's writing and Piranesi's etchings, the latter are studied first from the point of view of Hadrien's comments in the *Mémoires*; then an attempt is made to draw attention to aspects of Piranesi's *Views* of the Villa which either are only elliptically referred to by Hadrien or whose relevance for reading his discourse in the *Mémoires* emerges only as the result of the inquiry into the visual. This is particularly crucial in view of Yourcenar's reconstruction of Hadrien's life through memoirs, since both the lapses and the power of memory are central to any discussion of the text. The etchings are therefore one place to look for echoes of the obsessions of Hadrien's memoirs, whether as the identifiable sites or as independent connections, which are detected by the reader and open up analysis of the activity of the text.

The inquiry into parallels between Yourcenar's writings and the visual arts in this book wishes to avoid simplistic assertions of equivalence between text and image. As Mitchell argues, there may be equivalent concerns in different media, but it is necessary to be very specific about what is involved (*Picture Theory*, 160). Hence, for instance, the suggestion made by several critics of a direct link between Piranesi's *Prisons* and Zénon's prison in *L'Œuvre au noir* is treated sceptically in Chapter 4: there needs to be more of a basis for discussion than the word 'prison' alone.[20] There are, however, connections which must be traced, even if the readings thereby proposed are demanding and intricate. Chapter 4 looks at the section of Yourcenar's essay dealing with Piranesi's *Views of Rome*, plots the configurations of Zénon's enquiries in the chapter 'L'Abîme' and considers the function of colour at the end of the novel, with reference to the critical context of interpretations of the function of alchemy in *L'Œuvre au noir*. These topics all help to bring fresh interpretations to the texts concerned.

Again, concerning new ways of reading Yourcenar, Mitchell's location of alterity (*Picture Theory*, 28) in the distance between 'speaking Self' and 'seen Other' assists our reading of the elusive passage of

Nathanaël through the text of *Un homme obscur*. Examining the visual helps to indicate the otherness of Nathanaël from his surroundings and from the reader as we see him appear and disappear from the surface of the text, move 'vertically' and 'horizontally' within it, while he engages with the spectacle of society and the arts. The visual paradigm provides a fertile approach to the novel whose analysis is aided by an 'interactive' reading of the essay on Rembrandt. We are able to articulate Nathanaël's experience of wonder and limitation, perceived by him through a structure of symptomatic realizations.

The methodology used in the book is therefore built upon the way Yourcenar's writing articulates visualization and the visual. The theoretical apparatus adopted has to be open-ended, where the reader follows the reverberations between text and image. The visual does not represent the content of the text, nor vice versa. The two media are acknowledged to be unavoidably different, but the negotiations involved in questions of the visual have their textual counterparts. These can seem elusive, but they in fact constitute a study of the limits and power of representation. The processes at work in these interactions illustrate and negotiate the otherness of the visual. The disruptive and dangerous course by way of the visual can make many contributions to Yourcenar studies.

## Notes to the Introduction

1. Yves Bernier, 'Inventaire de la bibliothèque de Marguerite Yourcenar' (unpublished typescript, 1988).
2. Rensselaer Lee, *'Ut picture poesis': The Humanistic Theory of Painting* (New York: W. W. Allen, 1967).
3. Georges Didi-Huberman, *Devant l'image: question posée aux fins d'une histoire de l'art* (Paris: Minuit, 1990), 25 (author's italics).
4. Didi-Huberman, *Devant l'image*, 144.
5. Erwin Panofsky, 'Titian's *Allegory of Prudence*: A Postcript' (*c*.1954), in his *Meaning in the Visual Arts* (London: Peregrine, 1970), 205.
6. Georges Didi-Huberman, *Fra Angelico: dissemblance et figuration* (Paris: Flammarion, 1990).
7. Didi-Huberman, *Devant l'image*, 26.
8. Didi-Huberman, *Devant l'image*, 291.
9. Jean-Paul Sartre, *L'Imaginaire*, 229–42 (Paris: Gallimard, 1948).
10. Didi-Huberman, *Devant l'image*, 291.
11. Marcel Proust, *A l'ombre des jeunes filles en fleurs* (Paris: Laffont, 1987).
12. Louis Marin, 'Le concept de la figurabilité, ou la rencontre entre l'histoire de l'art et la psychanalyse', in his *De la représentation* (Paris: Gallimard/Seuil, 1994).

13. Louis Marin, 'Les fins de l'interprétation, ou les traversées du regard dans le sublime d'une tempête', in *De la représentation*, 185.
14. Marin, 'Les fins de l'interprétation', 202.
15. W. J. T. Mitchell, *Picture Theory* (Chicago: University of Chicago Press, 1994), esp. 172–3.
16. Georges Didi-Huberman, *Ce que nous voyons, ce qui nous regarde* (Paris: Minuit, 1992), 194.
17. Maurice Merleau-Ponty, *L'Œil et l'Esprit* (Paris: Gallimard, 1993), 81.
18. Camillo Faverzani, 'Marguerite Yourcenar et la culture italienne' (Université de Paris III–Sorbonne Nouvelle, 1990), 72–134.
19. Mitchell, *Picture Theory*, 87–8.
20. See Georgia Hooks Shurr, 'Yourcenar et Piranèse: une relation artistique', in *Marguerite Yourcenar et l'art. L'art de Marguerite Yourcenar*, ed. J.-P. Castellani and R. Poignault (Tours: SIEY, 1990), 175–86, and Ingeborg Kohn, 'The Castle and the Prison: Verbal Architecture in the non-fiction of Marguerite Yourcenar' (unpublished paper, MLA Convention, New York, 1981).

# CHAPTER 1

❖

# Essays on the Visual Arts

Beginning with Yourcenar's response in essay form to art and artists enables us to unravel the issues at work in her writing when it addresses questions of looking at and interpreting the visual. A way of reading the functions of the visual across Yourcenar's work will arise from examining the content and context of a particular essay; the engagement with the preoccupations of art history; the position vis-à-vis accounts by other writers of the work or artist in question; and lastly the distinctive voice of Yourcenar's writing on the visual arts.

This chapter begins with a brief discussion of Yourcenar's reflexions on the tomb of Maximilian I in the Hofkirche in Innsbruck. Then the essay on Poussin is analysed within the contexts mentioned above, working towards a view of both Yourcenar's critical independence as a writer on painting and the outline of a dramatic new aesthetic discovered, as much as invented, at a time of personal and public crisis. The outcome is next seen at work (with qualifications) in the short essays on Dürer and Ruisdael, where the encouragement to the reader to interpret with similar independence can lead to developments of Yourcenar's accounts. When the essay on the Château of Chenonceaux and its owners is studied in the last section, both the interests of Yourcenar and the possible responses to her writing are investigated by focusing on the orientation of historical perspective and personal engagement. This reading of the essay looks ahead to the following chapters, proposing a framework for reading Yourcenar's engagement with the visual.

## From Innsbruck to Ravenna

'L'improvisation sur Innsbruck' (1930; *EM*, 450–9) stands out among Yourcenar's early essays as the most personal of her reflections on cultural history. While 'Diagnostic de l'Europe' (1929; *EM*, 1649–55) discusses the cultural climate in Europe and 'La symphonie héroïque'

(1930; *EM*, 1656–67) reflects on the passions of mythological and literary heroes and heroines, 'L'improvisation sur Innsbruck', which is equally polemical, concentrates on the interaction between the writer and the cultural icon. The large tomb of Maximilian I (1459–1519) in the Hofkirche in Innsbruck involves a complicated arrangement of larger than life statues of real and imaginary ancestors, smaller statues of family saints and busts of Roman emperors. The tomb and statues are described and illustrated in Jeffrey Chipps Smith's *German Sculpture of the Later Renaissance*.[1] Yourcenar's essay consists of a wry analysis of the historical context and aesthetic qualities of the tomb. The structure of this early essay may owe much to Montaigne: Yourcenar feigns a nonchalant approach to the history of the Holy Roman Empire, problematizes any engagement with images of the past, appears to digress into a discussion of folk art, rebuilds a fractured framework for historical inquiry and finally argues forcefully for an ongoing, unending encounter with history. This section of Chapter 1 proposes that the essay on the Hofkirche, previously read by critics as a sign of Yourcenar's desire to broaden her historical vision of the present, also introduces us to some of the preoccupations of her later writings on the visual.[2]

With a heavy dose of irony, Yourcenar suggests that civilizations come and go because mankind is restless. In the early part of the essay, Yourcenar is negotiating her anxiety about the purpose of historical inquiry. She is aware of the twin dangers, at a time of political uncertainty and 'fascinating fascism' (as in the title of Susan Sontag's essay on Leni Riefenstahl), of being mesmerized by a death-instinct she detects in the rulers of the past: 'Ces malheureux, et c'est de nous que je parle, font songer à Chatov: il avait besoin du suicide pour se prouver qu'il était libre; les hommes, pour se prouver qu'ils existent, ont besoin de se crucifier. Nous avons tous si peur de la paix que nous la prenons pour la mort' (452). On a more personal level, she argues, there is another danger: that of becoming trapped in mirror-images of self-scrutiny while investigating appealing historical figures. Yourcenar wanders in her essays and in the museums of Europe as an 'amateur d'âmes': 'Il vient malheureusement un soir où la sympathie paraît presque aussi vaine que l'amour: il faudrait pourtant éviter que l'amateur d'âmes, errant amoureusement dans tous les musées du monde, ressemble à l'ivrogne qui se figure avoir rencontré un ami, parce qu'il trébuche contre la glace d'une vitrine' (453). The quest is understood as an amorous engagement with the past, even if it is figured here as hopeless; the emphasis on desire indicates the commitment of Your-cenar's approach. In this essay, Yourcenar is mindful of slipping into simplistic and comfortable identification with the past, a pitfall which she envisages in the guise of narcissistic self-mythologization. At the same time, Yourcenar is not content to settle for a detached study of aesthetic form, even if that would permit her to avoid the two pitfalls already mentioned, in other words the ephemerality of the glory of the figures and the illusion of gaining access to the lives of the figures in statues and paintings. In *L'Œuvre au noir*, as we will see in Chapter 3, the platonism which privileges form over historical contingency is considered problematic in a conversation between Zénon and Henri-Maximilien. Instead of settling for an unhistorical variety of aestheti-cism, 'L'improvisation sur Innsbruck' chooses to avoid its converse—a rigidly historical interpretation of the statue group in the Hofkirche—and sets off in pursuit of the origins and context of the art of the Tyrol, only returning to the statues in Innsbruck to illustrate how the impasse of narcissistic historical writing has been avoided.

Yourcenar considers the impact of eighteenth-century Baroque art, the imagery of the Catholic Church, the cultural beginnings of the nascent Austria and the humbling perspectives of folk art. As she acknowledged later on in her endnote of 1982 to 'Diagnostic de l'Europe' (*EM*, 1655), the early essays have their limitations, which may be detected in 'L'improvisation sur Innsbruck' in the way she pronounces on the attitude of the common people to religion and explains the cultural deficiencies of Austria in terms of the absence of a cultivated bourgeoisie and the consequent lack of 'la rigueur d'une tragédie de Corneille' (457). None the less, the discussion of non-nationalistic, trans-European folk art, particularly its treatment of human perspective, leads her to review the position and role of the spectator:

Cet art anonyme, à ras de sol, nous ramène à la modestie des origines; déjà, ces paysages de montagnes nous disposaient à une idée plus juste des proportions humaines, sur une planète trop grande pour n'être que le support de l'homme. Seuls, les peintres d'autrefois, les Brueghel, les Dürer, surent éviter l'orgueil dans le tracé des perspectives: de petits êtres rampants combattent ou s'étreignent dans un coin du paysage, au bord de fleuves sans cesse écoulés, mais pourtant plus fixes qu'eux-mêmes, au pied de montagnes qui changent si lentement qu'elles paraissent ne pas changer. (458)

Placing pre-individualistic folk art in its European context allows

Yourcenar to demonstrate the potential combination of the writer's personal investment in the interpretation of works of art and an openness to transnational perspective. Meanwhile, the importance attributed to the position of the spectator is reduced in response to the fixed and distant gazes of the figures in the statue group with their 'glorious' past.

With the odd wayward turn, Yourcenar has worked towards an approach which opens up the historical perspective and incorporates a fragmentary but energized personal involvement in the study of the images of the past: 'Je m'efforce en attendant de fixer, en quelques images précises, le double enseignement de spectacles qui passent et d'un Moi non moins passager' (459). The elaboration of a method of approach also signals the presence of Valéry, who explores methods of speculation and invention in an early essay: 'Il faut donc placer celui qui regarde et peut bien voir dans un coin *quelconque* de ce qui est'.[3] As in the case of Valéry's text, Yourcenar's essay 'L'improvisation sur Innsbruck' is not concerned with fixing a method of inquiry, but is interested in exploring the idea of a working method. The essay led her to unravel the rhetoric of the cenotaph to Maximilian I, where the devout and benedictory poses of the figures do not convince her, since their grandeur exaggerates the human perspective. History's written and visual evidence provides instead the space for Yourcenar to develop 'notre monologue intérieur' (458).

In the 'improvisation' on the mosaics of Ravenna, 'Ravenne ou le péché mortel' (1935), Yourcenar closely allies the visual to the verbal.[4] The Basilica of San Vitale was built between 524 and 547 CE, while the mosaics were completed in 548. The period in question is therefore that of Justinian (527–65) and the Later Roman Empire; the historical outlook at work here is discussed in Chapter 2. In our present context, the assertive alliance of word and image leads to a dynamic reading of the surfaces of San Vitale: 'L'hyperbole et la parabole sont ici les deux sésames mathématiques des absides, les deux formes de la courbe auxquelles obéit la pesanteur des pierres. Grammatical ou géométrique, leur emploi éclate à chaque page de ces livres de verre et d'or' (485–6). In its interest in the description of space by arch and mosaic, this essay is concerned with the interaction between the inner and the outer world. Both the mosaics and the historical figures are figured moving from the immobile surface of the walls in a direction that is a movement within, secretive and embedded in the mosaic: 'L'un des secrets de Ravenne, c'est que l'immobilité confine à la vitesse suprême: elle mène au vertige' (486–7). Yourcenar is fascinated by the representation of inner secrecy and disappearance, but following the conclusion to the Innsbruck essay, she cannot accept the renunciation of the external world exemplified by Ravenna.[5] She improvises her own way out by calling up the ghost of Byron to voice his boredom with inaction and his sense of estrangement from the world.

While she may be aware of the dangers of mythologizing the past when she looks at its images, she does not shy away from indulging in knowing self-mythologization, although the function of the invocation of Byron here is rather to evoke a flight from complacent and excessive introspection: 'Le sublime Lord est las d'errer au fond de lui-même, parmi les fresques écaillées de ses rêves, et les inscriptions presque effacées de ses souvenirs' (105). Byron is about to act by going to fight in the Greek War of Independence. What is at stake in Yourcenar's personal engagement is indicated by this reference to Byron: her interpretation of the mosaics retains an ambivalence, since she experiences the need for detachment as well as the desire to inquire into the images on display. Another way of explaining the method of inquiry is to note that some degree of aesthetic judgement precedes a thorough engagement with issues of representation.

By avoiding hasty and rigid conclusions Yourcenar has recuperated her own role in the interpretation of images and staked out her claim for critical independence. In her brief elaborations on the icons of Innsbruck and Ravenna, she argues for an openness of perspective within a historical inquiry into the function of images. This approach considers the rhetoric of the visual and the readiness of the spectator to respond and invest in the encounter. As Yourcenar shows, these features of the act of looking have to be acknowledged and analysed. The nature of Yourcenar's personal investment in her essays is confirmed, after these early examples, by further examples of her writing on the visual, which continues to be committed and ambitious.

## The Writer in Exile: 'Une exposition Poussin à New York'

The brief foray into the mosaic paintings of Ravenna referred in passing to Kandinsky, and in Chapter 2 we will hear André Suarès on the same subject. This context constitutes another aspect of writing on the visual arts, namely the tradition of writing on a given artist. As Philippe de Chennevières-Pointel observed, Poussin is the

paradigmatic case in French culture: 'Il n'est, dans notre pays, écrivain
d'art, se respectant quelque peu lui-même, qui n'ait cru se devoir
d'écrire sur Poussin une notice ou un éloge.'[6] Writing on Poussin is
thus resonantly palimpsestual, fitting neatly into Genette's third
category of textual parentage, 'métatextualité'.[7] Yourcenar's essay on
him, written following an exhibition in New York in 1940, in turn
provides us with a clearly defined example of her engagement with
other writers on a specific painter, especially as the essay is situated
between received views of Poussin and her own attempt to find an
original voice with which to write on the artist. In order to outline
her approach, this section will consider the following issues: the essay
and the context of the exhibition; Poussin criticism and the situation
of other writers; the manifestations of exile; and the distinctive
contribution of Yourcenar's essay to responses to the visual power of
Poussin, with the potential developments that this section will suggest.

'Une exposition Poussin à New York', published posthumously in
*En pèlerin et en étranger*, was written after Yourcenar saw an exhibition
of eleven Poussins from American collections, plus one on loan from
France, at the Durlacher Gallery (*EM*, 468–73). The exhibition closed
in mid-April 1940, but it may not be possible to determine whether
the essay was written before or after Yourcenar heard the news of the
fall of France. In the first paragraph she mentions 'cette sombre année
1940' and the final sentence of the essay looks ahead to darkness: 'Il
ne reste plus ensuite qu'à explorer la seule nuit.' The essay offers her
an opportunity to examine the threatened position of the cultural
legacy of the high art represented by Poussin. Yourcenar is therefore
writing from the opposite end of the war to Gide, whose essay on
Poussin was written in March and April 1945, according to Maria van
Rysselberghe's notebooks.[8]

The paintings assembled by the Durlacher Gallery allow Yourcenar
to discuss a selection of Poussin's works which is fairly representative
of his output. The emphasis was on mythological (mixing the sacred
and profane) and biblical subjects, from early pictures focusing on
small groups of figures to a late landscape. Thus the combination of
religious and secular themes, which Poussin scholars since 1940 have
certainly emphasized, was represented at this exhibition. On the other
hand, the Durlacher Gallery's selection reflected tastes in 1940 by
omitting several areas of Poussin's *œuvre*: works from the 1620s; the
*Sacrements*; and history paintings. Yourcenar partly makes up for this
by her references to the *Sacrements* and to two of the *Saisons*.

The exhibition was not accompanied by a catalogue, but the journal *Art News* carried an article by the Poussin scholar Walter Friedländer entitled 'America's first Poussin show'.[9] Yourcenar does not acknowledge Friedländer's piece, which she follows very closely and occasionally copies. Evidence for the claim that Friedländer is doing part of the looking for Yourcenar may best be provided by the two details which he picks out and which Yourcenar mentions in her third paragraph. A detail of Moses breaking the tablets from *Le Veau d'Or* is reproduced in Friedländer's article (p. 8); Yourcenar also selects this detail and even refers to 'l'agrandissement photographique' (470).[10] Although he does not include a reproduction, Friedländer focuses on the classical tripod in *La Sainte Famille Whitcomb*, as does Yourcenar.[11] Although Yourcenar finds many of the commonplaces in literature on Poussin in the article, she does appear to lift several aspects of Poussin's work directly from Friedländer, especially when the latter writes, '[Poussin's] position in the history of French art is analogous to the positions in philosophy and literature of his contemporaries Descartes and Corneille', and 'his work defies such cut and dried classifications as the blanket terms *classicism* and *rationalism*'. However, Yourcenar then elaborates her own contemporary and personal interpretation of Poussin.[12]

In the essay, Yourcenar addresses some standard topics of debate concerning interpretations of Poussin: the artist as both classicist and pre-romantic; painting and poetry as sister arts; Poussin and 'le réel'; music and the ancient Greek modes. In the long third paragraph Yourcenar sets out to justify her initial claim that Poussin lies at the heart of the French tradition of the arts: 'Mais tandis que Raphaël est situé au centre de la seule peinture, c'est toute la pensée, toute la sensibilité française qui a chez Poussin ses équivalences ou ses signes' (469). Placing Corneille, Racine and La Fontaine alongside Maurice de Guérin, Chénier, Hugo and Vigny lends support to the claim that Poussin needs to be read as both romantic and classical, and the paragraph intricately interweaves classical and romantic artists and writers. However, the parallels drawn do indicate problems with assertions of equivalence or similarity.

This is an approach common to many of the writers discussed by Richard Verdi in 'Poussin's Critical Fortunes'. The basic formulation of Yourcenar's position at the beginning of her essay establishes her perspective: 'Toute l'œuvre de Poussin atteste le romantisme profond contenu dans cette aspiration classique vers l'absolue beauté, et le

classicisme toujours présent en France au milieu des fougues
romantiques, comme le mors à la bouche des chevaux d'Apollon'
(470). The comparison in the same paragraph between *La Sainte
Famille Whitcomb*, on the one hand, and Racine's Andromaque and
Corneille's Sabine, on the other, asserts a connection between two
artistic forms of the same classical period. When Yourcenar then
suggests echoes of specific lines from Racine, this does not carry any
clear notion of comparison specific to Poussin: reading the slightly
comical opening of Racine's *Iphigénie en Aulide*, it is at first hard to
see the connection with Poussin's *L'Education de Bacchus* (see below,
fig. 4). Asserting a link with our memory of the lines can be a very
elusive proposition, but if we follow Louis Marin's discussion of
sleeping figures in some early mythological paintings by Poussin,[13] we
could adapt Yourcenar's suggestion and consider a link between
Poussin's early pictures and the landscape of dreams. However, in
terms of the suggestion that the Hartford *Crucifixion* (fig. 2) can be
considered as the image of Christ in the mind of Polyeucte or Pauline
in Corneille's *Polyeucte*, the visual force of the painting seems to
surpass any imagined psychological parallel.[14] As a way into writing
on Poussin and to underline his openness to many modes of
interpretation, Yourcenar perhaps overmilks the classical *ut pictura
poesis* ('as in painting, so in poetry') conceit, a problem whose many
manifestations are traced in the seminal study by Rensselaer Lee. In
her desire to nuance this traditional organizing parallel, at this point
in the essay Yourcenar combines a well-worn written response,
amplified by some rhetorical flourishes, with genuine insight and
appreciation.

  The second aspect of the essay to be discussed here concerns
Poussin and 'le réel' or, as Yourcenar puts it, '[le] réalisme' (471).
Yourcenar's discussion of realism in Poussin is brief and ambitious, but
involves at the same time her own ideas about aesthetics, the defiance
of art-historical terminology and the engagement with other writers
of her generation. Prominent among her ideas was the conviction that
historical reconstruction should achieve as high a degree of accuracy
as possible, avoiding exoticism and formulaic structures. This
approach is outlined and defended in relation to Sainte-Beuve,
Flaubert, Proust and Valéry in her lecture 'L'écrivain devant l'histoire'.
In Poussin Yourcenar detects, albeit in an art form different from hers,
a precision of observation allied to timeless vision. The avoidance of
stridency is, for Yourcenar, a key element in this achievement: 'Mais

ce réalisme n'est pas pittoresque; il n'insiste pas; il est fait de scrupuleuse exactitude et non des résultats d'une lyrique à rebours' (471). Yourcenar's fascination with Poussin's means of achieving his pictorial vision reflects her desire to unpack the methods of the artist and to learn from his working practice. Yourcenar looks at *La Sainte Famille à la Baignoire* and works from the mathematical structure and formal arrangement of the figures via the family at play to the sense of the eternal and general.

The last two terms in a sentence from a letter to Constantin Dimaras of July 1951 illustrate Yourcenar's attempt to link the concrete to the abstract in her construction of a theory of exactitude: 'j'ai fini par éprouver pour l'exactitude une espèce de passion sèche' (*Lettres à ses amis et quelques autres*, 90). Especially in her works of the 1930s, culminating in the essay on Poussin, Yourcenar may be seen as a writer vacillating between the two positions outlined by Gertrude Stein in *The Autobiography of Alice B. Toklas*:

> Gertrude Stein, in her work, had always been possessed by the intellectual passion for exactitude in the description of inner and outer reality. [...]
> It was this conception of exactitude that made the close understanding between Gertrude Stein and Juan Gris.
> Juan Gris also conceived exactitude but in him exactitude had a mythical basis. As a mystic it was necessary for him to be exact. In Gertrude Stein the necessity was intellectual, a pure passion for exactitude. (228)

In *Feux*, for example, Yourcenar has the intellectual passion and the interest in myth. Exactitude and metaphysics become closely and explicitly aligned in her later work. In the early 1980s she wrote an essay about Henry James ('Les charmes de l'innocence : une relecture d'Henry James', *EM*, 556–63), with particular reference to his novel *What Maisie Knew*, which she had translated in the winter of 1938–9: 'Comme il arrive très souvent dans de très grandes œuvres, et précisément dans celle de Marcel Proust, une irréalité et une étrangeté irréductibles, assez pareilles à cette "étrangeté de proportions" que Léonard croyait toujours découvrir dans tout bel objet, s'installent au centre du réalisme le plus sec et des *rapports de relation* les plus exacts entre les personnages' (562). The essay on James was written in the aftermath of her Académie française address on the work of Roger Caillois, which discussed ideas of symmetry and dissymmetry: 'L'homme qui aimait les pierres' (*EM*, 535–55). In her approach to Poussin's *Déluge*, we will see how Yourcenar may be compared with

Bachelard in her attempt to forge a combination between 'étrangeté', strict realism and exactitude.

The search for a definition of 'le réel' among the writers of the generation preceding that of Yourcenar focused on Poussin in the aftermath of the first public showing of *L'Inspiration du poète* at the Louvre in 1911. Marc Fumaroli's account of the debate from 1895–1945, published before the appearance of Yourcenar's essay, suggests that Yourcenar was only one of many writers who attempted to define 'le réel' in Poussin: 'Et cette poétique leur a paru accordée avec la leur, dans la mesure où, indifférente au réalisme mimétique, à l'effet théâtral ou décoratif, elle visait au cœur du réel, à ce qui dans le réel chante' (23).[15] Poussin was the hero of the hour. Fumaroli recounts how Paul Desjardins, Jacques Rivière, André Lhote, Cocteau and Picasso, amongst others, found in Poussin an economy of form, moral autonomy, prodigious intelligence and a freedom which differed from *fin-de-siècle* art. This is most clearly articulated in Desjardins's *La Méthode des classiques français* (especially 172–3). Fumaroli also cites Valéry's metaphor of the horse and rider, whose united prowess represents the power of invention and mental agility possessed by the great artist, by 'le Possible d'un Léonard', Valéry's phrase in a marginal note added in 1930 to 'Note et Digression' (1919), the second of his meditations on Leonardo (*Introduction à la méthode*, 77). As Fumaroli notes, the aesthetics discussed by writers in connection with Poussin were very much their own.

While Poussin was seen as an *exemplum*, Fumaroli notes that this did not mean that a close analysis of his paintings took place, since the admirers enthused 'sans s'embarrasser d'exactitude historique ni mythologique' (23). This criticism reflects the preoccupations of Poussin studies since the time of Yourcenar's essay. Yourcenar and others were concerned to articulate and define the secrets of Poussin's art. 'Une exposition Poussin à New York' attempts to explain how the intuition of a general and eternal order works when looking at *La Sainte Famille à la Baignoire* (fig. 1).[16] In Yourcenar's view, the spectator discovers the pyramidal shape of the composition, the spatial arrangement of the figures and the background landscape, before noticing the familiar everyday scene of the two infants in the story, the one unruly and the other alarmed. Poussin has transposed realistic elements onto this monumental setting: 'Aucun détail humain ni local n'est sacrifié: ce village est un vrai village italien, cette Sainte Famille est une vraie famille, mais l'art de Poussin consiste à dégager de tout cela le général,

Fig. 1. Poussin, *La Sainte Famille à la Baignoire* (1650)
Oil on canvas, 100×132 cm
Fogg Art Museum, Harvard University

l'éternel' (472). The accuracy of the representation of these details is asserted in this aesthetic formulation, whereas such a statement about verisimilitude would be contested by later writers on Poussin. Yourcenar's essay, however, is determined to pursue its intuitive search for an explanation to account for Poussin's sense of the eternal.

The relation of the intuition of this sense of the eternal to Poussin's depiction of real objects is also discussed by Yves Bonnefoy in *Rome 1630*. Bonnefoy locates the intuition not in the physical object, but rather in a process of passage or mediation which he identifies with the Baroque:

Artistes en conflit, je l'ai assez souligné; mais au-delà de leurs différences, un point commun se révèle: et c'est chez tous une remarquable distance à l'égard de ce que plus tard on a voulu nommer le réel—à l'égard des choses comme elles sont là, devant nous. Que ce soit chez Bernin [...], ou chez Poussin le désir de fonder sur l'intemporel de la valeur morale ou de la raison, il y a en eux tous la conviction que le suprême réel n'est nullement dans l'objet tangible: lequel n'existe donc à leurs yeux, et dans leur réflexion sur le rôle de l'apparence, que comme médiation entre l'*être*, invisible, et nous.[17]

Bonnefoy distinguishes between Hegelian dialectics for the Renaissance and Kierkegaardian intuition for the Baroque (127 n. 20). Setting Poussin within an account of the metaphysical ambition of the Baroque is not the explicit concern of Yourcenar's essay, but Bonnefoy's account permits us to see how Yourcenar's analysis of Poussin is trying to work. Bonnefoy helps to locate the way the depicted object stands between the perception of an eternal order and the spectator in the art of Poussin's period. Yourcenar's essay also formulates the relationship between the objects represented and the artist's vision, but for her, as opposed to Bonnefoy, the tangible quality which she detects in Poussin is achieved by his realism.

Other contexts may be applied here. Considered in the context of the art criticism of the pre-war period, the definition of painting as 'l'idiome des formes et des couleurs' in the first sentence and the reference to the 'paysage presque cubique' (Friedländer's phrase, translated literally by Yourcenar) situates the essay in the wake of Roger Fry's advocation of the formal analysis of art, notably in *Vision and Design* (1920). In another work of the same period, Fry discussed the plasticity and formal construction of Poussin.[18] The critics André Lhote and Pierre Courthion also concentrated on compositional elements and the organization of colour; Yourcenar owned books by both these critics, as well as books by Fry. They did not pay much attention to the way in which the artist, in the context of classical art, was telling a given story. In 'La peinture moderne et le secret mal gardé', Jean Paulhan would declare the approach of André Lhote excessively theoretical and dependent on seeing cylinders and cones, while Friedländer's account of 1940 points to the major development in Poussin studies, led by Blunt and himself, emphasizing Poussin's methods and the study of textual and iconographical sources for the interpretation of the allegorical aspects of the paintings. But Yourcenar read Friedländer's account through the eyes of Lhote and Courthion, so it is not surprising that she is not concerned with the question of the depiction of the narrative in *La Sainte Famille à la Baignoire*. At the same time, her emphasis on the observation from real life and the truth of the family and village also characterizes her own distinctive approach. Yourcenar's reading of Poussin's sense of form helps to explain why she locates the eternity of 'le réel' in the plasticity of the paintings.

Nevertheless, for the interpreter since Anthony Blunt's 1967 monograph, there must be reservations with the idea that Poussin worked from the life and some concern as to how Yourcenar arrives at her detection of Poussin's sense of the eternal. The bold formulation of Poussin's method passes freely from the 'real' family in *La Sainte Famille à la Baignoire* to the general theme which she sees represented, but we may feel that we do not learn exactly how Poussin is able to achieve this effect, other than by his art. Since the time of Yourcenar's essay, Howard Hibbard's study of the Washington *Sainte Famille à l'escalier* shows how Poussin carefully constructs his picture according to literary and pictorial tradition, illustrating a very different, and in this case richer, methodological approach, even if Hibbard is not infallible.[19]

By contrast with Yourcenar, in his essay Gide does refer to Poussin's use of High Renaissance methods.[20] His essay also engages with the debate about Poussin, but in addition suggests a transition from our discussion of the *ut pictura poesis* tradition and the theories of 'le réel' to the context of Yourcenar's use of Poussin for the purpose of a meditation on the state of the world in 1940–5. Concerning the elusive 'réel' in Poussin, Gide is determined to stress his anti-realism. He refers to the tradition of pictorial technique in which Poussin was working, mentioning his debt to Raphael. However, Gide's real agenda in his essay, comparable to Marcel Arland's approach in

'Promenade au Louvre',[21] is to dismiss contemporary art on account of its lack of spirituality and its bombastic claims to originality. Instead he praises the elevated pagan mysticism in Poussin's mythological paintings: 'Mais non, ne nous y trompons pas: Poussin est un peintre anti-réaliste; il n'en est pas de plus spiritualiste ou idéaliste que lui. Il n'en est pas qui transporte l'humanité plus résolument, et plus spontanément à la fois, au-dessus d'elle-même' ('L'enseignement de Poussin', s.p.). Yet, writing in March 1945, Gide is also searching for a way to articulate hope for spiritual regeneration after the war. His concluding gesture of submission to Poussin may well read as little more than his wishful attempt to enlist the painter for this cause. Gide adopts the tools and discourse of art history to celebrate Poussin's genius at the expense of his twentieth-century successors. Despite the complexities involved in the notion of realism in Poussin, Yourcenar's engagement with him is more moving and more persuasive. From the opening reference to the collapse of the Tower of Babel to the figure of menacing night that closes the essay, 'Une exposition Poussin à New York' voices her anxiety about the political climate and her exile from Europe. In the war years Yourcenar returned to mythology in the form of plays and essays; the essay on Poussin is the first example of this series of journeys.

The distinctive feature of the theme of exile in this essay is the realization of banishment from the 'pays de Toujours', a phrase taken from Barrès, as Yourcenar acknowledges, but with a capital letter applied to 'toujours' ('Le Testament d'Eugène Delacroix', 111). The writer engages with the paintings, but remains uncertainly positioned in semi-exile from the eternal visions of Poussin. Yourcenar's essay voices the anguish of a writer distanced from the Arcadia of high culture, coming to terms with the ways in which that Arcadia has in fact already represented the threat of expulsion and death: in the *Crucifixion* and the *Déluge*.

The specific contribution from Yourcenar to writing on Poussin is her negotiation with his representations of calamity. In Poussin's *Crucifixion*, she finds a few lingering indications of life set against the dark background of destruction and night: 'Dans ce paysage fuligineux, brun et gris, teinté ça et là d'un rouge sourd de braises, quelques pans d'écarlate, quelques manteaux de soldats, quelques robes de pleureuses, font l'effet de flammes subsistant encore au milieu des braises' (472). The red patches on a dark background are sufficient to

Fig. 2. Poussin, *La Crucifixion* (1645–6)
Oil on canvas, 148·5×218·5 cm
.Wadsworth Atheneum, Hartford

Fig. 3. Poussin, *Le Déluge* (1660–4)
Oil on canvas, 118×160 cm
Paris, Musée du Louvre

represent the absorption of the scene into a mysterious and threatening landscape. Here the writing has gone beyond the usual parallel with Corneille and French classicism to engage with the startling vision of Poussin's painting. Looking at the *Déluge*, meanwhile, is an encounter and engagement which threatens to effect the engulfment that it represents: 'On se souvient que dans *Le Déluge* du Louvre, l'eau épaisse et noire, la nappe étale recouvrant la terre était bien le miroir par excellence du désespoir humain' (471). In the cases of *La Crucifixion*, *Le Déluge*, *L'Education de Bacchus* and *Echo et Narcisse* (figs. 2–5), Yourcenar considers the situation in 1940 relevant for looking at Poussin and in the encounter with the paintings explores the experience of being viscerally disturbed by the visual.[22]

The first example given of this engagement with the world-picture of Poussin is the discussion of the function of metal objects and 'metallic faces'.[23] Yourcenar explicitly addresses the representation of the values that she finds in the classical outlook. Her use of 'mystique' connects with the intuitive approach already mentioned: 'Poussin retrouvait dans le bronze, dans l'or, ces qualités que le classicisme élève à un rang presque mystique, la stabilité, la fermeté, la durée paisible, que seul le marbre pourrait aussi revendiquer. Mais le marbre, comme nous le verrons dans Claude Lorrain, fait déjà partie de l'atmosphère et du paysage, tandis que le métal extrait, façonné de main d'homme, garde une dure valeur de signe humaine' (74). Here the junction of 'durée' and 'dure' can be read in reference to Valéry's 'dur–durer' reflection in a marginal note to *Introduction à la méthode de Léonard de Vinci*: '*Durée* provient de *dur*. Ce qui revient, d'autre part, à donner à certaines images visuelles, tactiles, motrices, ou à leurs combinaisons, des *valeurs* doubles' (18). If we adopt Valéry's remark to suggest that the visual sign in Poussin is also a sight of duration, then Yourcenar's gloss on Friedländer acts as a way into the paintings that comprehends the terms of Poussin's art of representation. The craft of the image and of the object is, for Yourcenar, allied in the site of man-made armour that signifies endurance and longevity.

There is, then, intuition at work here, but this differs from the intuition discussed above, in the context of realism, by being more closely linked to the physicality of the pictorial representation of values, which helps Yourcenar to become emancipated from potentially limiting symbolic interpretations. She notes the recurrence of calm and contained water, but stresses the unusual and disruptive water in, respectively, *L'Education de Bacchus* and *Le Déluge*. The lakes

Fig. 4. Poussin, *L'Education de Bacchus* (1657)
Oil on canvas, 123×179 cm
Fogg Art Museum, Harvard University

and other stretches of water in Poussin have been interpreted in terms
of Heraclitan flux, Christian symbolism and neo-Platonist mirrors.
But by interpreting them as the site *par excellence* of the seventeenth-
century theory of representation, Louis Marin moves away from a
symbolic reading.[24] Non-symbolic readings of water may also be
produced by adopting Georges Didi-Huberman's theorization of the
visual operation contained in the Narcissus myth:

Ainsi, le mythe de Narcisse ne devrait pas être seulement pensé à travers les
catégories du reflet, du miroir: car c'est aussi dans les simples miroitements
(brillances partielles et évanescentes) de l'eau, que l'œil s'absorbe, se noie,
s'abîme. Les miroitements ne sont que des effets de surface, reflets
extrêmement partiels, insensés pour cela, éclats, instants de brillances et de
disparitions. Mais où, dans la pure scansion de ris de l'eau, s'indique une
profondeur. Tout est là. [...] Car c'est bien cette aquatique profondeur qui,
dans le miroitement, nous trouble, nous appelle dangereusement. D'une
certaine façon, la peau suscite une dialectique analogue, dans les scansions de
sa pâleur, de sa brillance, de ses passages incarnats.[25]

Shifting and enigmatic, light seems to make water physical and mortal;
the idea of danger in this spectacle helps us to see the direction of
Yourcenar's essay, moving away from intuitive generalization, and also
helps us to elaborate on her suggestive analysis of the visual process in
the mysterious reflections and aquatic density within the pictures: 'Les
nus de Poussin ont une qualité métallique, sauf ceux de son vieux âge,
dans *L'Education de Bacchus* par exemple, où les corps plus fluides se
confondent presque avec leur image reflétée. [...] Et les figures de
Poussin, ces figures souvent un peu lourdes, fortement charpentées,
n'ont-elles pas cette densité que prennent les visages reflétés dans une
eau sombre?' (470, 471). By exploring the elements within Poussin's
paintings, Yourcenar has enabled her response to be free from
predetermined accounts of the pictures and therefore does not impose
a reading. The pictures invite and enact an incorporation of the body
of the spectator. For Yourcenar in America, Poussin paradoxically
provides an arena for the experience of cataclysm, displacement and
death. The 'pays de Toujours' is not a site of Arcadian escapism but in
fact the dangerous and wild Arcadia outlined by Panofsky in his 1955
essay on Poussin's two versions of the *Bergers d'Arcadie*.[26] Thus,
focusing on the sites where Yourcenar's essay departs from received
views of 1940 allows us to watch her inquiry enter into an act of
engagement with the painting.

Water: this is a good opportunity to discuss the question of Yourcenar and Bachelard. As will be seen, there are certain similarities between them, as is often argued in Yourcenar criticism, but the differences are arguably greater and, what matters more, instructive for reading both writers. Parallels between the passages in the essay on Poussin concerning the representation of water and ruminations in Bachelard's *L'Eau et les Rêves* could certainly be drawn, for example with the latter's comments on the mortal symbolism of water: 'L'eau rend la mort élémentaire. L'eau meurt avec la mort dans sa substance. L'eau est alors un *néant substantiel*. On ne peut pas aller plus loin dans le désespoir. Pour certaines âmes, *l'eau est la matière du désespoir.*'[27] Bachelard's study was first published in 1940, the year of Yourcenar's essay. However, the particular and occasionally opaque logic of Bachelard, whose work is in any case very diverse and full of insights, means that parallels need to be weighed up carefully.

There are cases where the two aesthetics simply depart from each other. When, later on in *L'Eau et les Rêves*, Bachelard discusses what he calls the desire for deformation, it is noticeable that he adopts a different position from Yourcenar's concerning Dalí's paintings. First Yourcenar, from the 'Carnets 1942–1948' (*EM*, 526–34): 'Et qu'ai-je à faire des squelettes du roman noir et des montres flasques de Dalí, moi qui, comme tout le monde, porte en moi mon squelette et mon horloge?' (527–8). Second Bachelard, with his account of how the operation of intuition disrupts order:

L'œil lui-même, la vision pure, se fatigue de solides. Il veut rêver la déformation. Si la vue accepte vraiment la liberté du rêve, tout s'écoule dans une intuition vivante. Les 'montres molles' de Salvador Dali s'étirent, s'égouttent au coin d'une table. Elles vivent dans un espace-temps gluant. [...] Qu'on médite *la conquête de l'irrationnel*, et l'on comprendra que cet héraclitéisme pictural est sous la dépendance d'une rêverie d'une étonnante sincérité. De si profondes déformations ont besoin d'inscrire la déformation dans la substance. (144)

Yourcenar's departure from a concentration on intuition, as mentioned above in connection with Poussin, metal and time, may also be seen in the difference of perspective here. Yourcenar's writing on the visual engages with the corporeal impact and the exchange of affect before and in the seen object, while Bachelard imagines the transformation of substance as a process of poetic intuition, passing via intuition to the object, involving less difficulty. The sincerity in Bachelard's poetics in fact operates a strange restriction on the observer, while the encounter with the visual is more internalized in Yourcenar's writing; 'rêve' and 'rêverie' are not elided in her outlook, although elsewhere Bachelard does differentiate sharply between them. Yourcenar was suspicious of artificial reconstructions of the visible world, however unsettling 'le réel' might seem. Hence she spoke sympathetically of Roger Caillois's split from the Surrealists: 'Mais la *rigueur obstinée* qui le distingua toujours lui a vite fait sentir la différence entre le fantastique d'ordre littéraire, toujours si proche du factice et du fabriqué, et l'étrange ou l'inexpliqué véritables' ('L'homme qui aimait les pierres', *EM*, 538).

None the less, 'Une exposition Poussin à New York' offers ways of bypassing the literal but problematic parallels drawn between Bachelardian intuition and Yourcenarian poetics. Bachelardian intuition has water in a dynamic relationship with the human: '... le lecteur comprendra enfin que l'eau est aussi un *type de destin*, non plus seulement le vain destin des images fuyantes, le vain destin d'un rêve qui ne s'achève pas, mais un destin essentiel qui métamorphose sans cesse la substance de l'être' (*L'Eau et les Rêves*, 8). Just as the relation between spectator and picture developed in Yourcenar's essay is one of potential metamorphosis, Bachelard's remarks here offer an alternative approach to the intuition *impasse* by suggesting a study of what it is that is transformed during the act of looking.

The metamorphosis observed at work in Poussin therefore illustrates the uncertainty and pessimism of the dark times of 1940. The sense of arrested change and muted catastrophe in Poussin represents, for Yourcenar, the poignant last moments before the cataclysm. She reinscribes the human disaster by switching her attention at the end of the essay to a painting where the human and the elemental are fixed at the point of metamorphosis: *Echo et Narcisse*. The human narrative stands at the edge of the unknown, at the fall of darkness and the end of vision. There is also a reference to the threat to her own work that can be read in the essay's conclusion. In 1940, her Hadrian project had not progressed much beyond her early work on a life of Hadrian's lover Antinoüs, followed by the switch of focus to Hadrian and a draft of part of the first chapter of the eventual text.[28] The allusion to Antinoüs as model for Narcissus indicates the degree of personal investment here: her hopes for the book may well be drowned in the deluge of the times: 'Ce jeune corps si proche de celui d'une statue d'Antinoüs, autre noyé, dont nous savons que Poussin avait soigneusement pris les mesures, ne semble pas

Fig. 5. Poussin, *Echo et Narcisse* (1627–30)
Oil on canvas, 74×100 cm
Paris, Musée du Louvre

complètement au repos' (473). Yet there is still life in the unsatisfied desire in the figure of Narcissus, just as there remained life in the project.[29] In the context of Yourcenar's work, in retrospect this passage represented the symbolic death of Antinoüs, whose voice, as we will see in the next chapter, only survives in Hadrien's record of him in *Mémoires d'Hadrien*. Here the visual exchange that we have read into Yourcenar's account includes the fate of her work, so that the dilemma over the question of narcissistic encounters in museums, invoked at the end of the essay 'L'improvisation à Innsbruck', now seems thoroughly exorcized and surpassed, with a new awareness of the literary challenges ahead. However, Yourcenar's interrogation of the values of humanism in the essay and her engagement with so many issues of interpretation shows that she is able to elude the sterility of self-promotion.

Yourcenar's other essay from 1940 voiced hope in the revival of fortunes for the West, with reference to its eventual regeneration long after the fall of Rome to the Huns ('Forces du passé et force de l'avenir', *EM*, 460–4). The three essays entitled 'Mythologie' are particularly relevant for the combination of private crisis and general despair in the essay on Poussin. 'Mythologie. III', published in January 1945, voices Yourcenar's sense of exile and her desire to speculate about a return to Europe to face the consequences of the dangers represented in the pictures. While the conclusion to the Poussin essay had situated her at the beginning of a calamity of unknown proportions, this essay sets out to imagine ways of proceeding after the war through a discussion of how a contemporary version of Sophocles' *Electra* might arrange the outcome of the lives of the three murderers at the end of the play, Orestes, Pylades and Electra. Yourcenar continues her triangle of passion based on her own relationship with André Fraigneau and André Embiricos.[30] More interestingly, as a writer, she also tries to imagine some connection between those who have been in exile and those who have suffered the tribulations of war in Europe, between Iphigenia in exile and Electra in the thick of the action:

La seule résolution possible se trouverait dans ces régions hyperboréennes de la pensée grecque où Goethe installe son *Iphigénie* et Gide son *Philoctète*; elle sortirait d'une possibilité de confrontation, encore inexploitée, entre Iphigénie et Electre, entre l'exilée et les fugitifs, entre ceux qui ont subi leur destin ou lutté contre lui dans les souterrains de Mycènes, et celle qu'en ont désespérément séparée les puissances de l'océan, de l'hiver et de l'exil. Impossible, à l'époque où nous sommes, de prédire quelle amertume ou quelle joie nouvelle, quelle sagesse ou quelle folie plus profonde naîtrait d'une telle rencontre: l'heure des réunions n'est pas encore venue ni celle de la résolution de l'accord. ('Mythologie. III', 45)

The emergence of such a personal investment in the permutations of the mythical story leads us to read 'Mythologie. III' in the light of the possibilities Yourcenar believed were available to the French writer and reader to explore after the Liberation. In her discussion of the 'Mythologie' essays, Loredana Primozich notes that Yourcenar combines the search for identity and the desire to re-explore old ideas; she suggests that at the time Yourcenar hesitated between taking the example of Alcestis, Electra, Ariadne or Phaedra.[31] More specifically, in the context of the present discussion, the conjunction of winter, exile and the ocean in the figure of Iphigenia relates closely to Yourcenar's position and reminds us that in the Poussin essay the *Déluge* threatened to flood over all her projects. The reference to those who submitted to the occupying forces and those who rebelled looks to dramatizations of mythological stories for possible resolution.

'Une exposition Poussin à New York' is a remarkable essay because it takes on many different personal and interpretative issues. By reading it in a way which addresses the engagement made with so many issues and trying to put forward some responses, we see that Yourcenar ends up negotiating a challenge to her method. For her, Poussin is the representative of an artistic tradition that she can retrieve and explore in exile from her projects and from Europe. Thus, approaching this essay as a crucial example of Yourcenar's writing on the visual has led to reading into and supplementing her remarks, plotting her movement from intuition to an independent and courageous confrontation with painting. Both personal engagement and the challenge to old perspectives have continued to operate since the time of the pieces on Innsbruck and Ravenna.

### 'Dreams and waking thoughts':[32] on Dürer and Ruisdael

Yourcenar moves fast in 'Sur un rêve de Dürer' (*EM*, 317–20). She includes a warning to her readers about entering the realm of visions unprepared and unushered. The various contexts that were separated in the previous section interact during the following discussion of this brief essay. This section will look at the journal for which the essay was written; at the way in which Yourcenar argues that the text and image of the dream recorded by Dürer form a unique part of his

work, despite art-historical reservations; and at the text and image
together as one work (fig. 6). The short essay on Ruisdael provides a
further example of Yourcenar's defiant art writing.

Hamsa was a Paris-based journal specializing in the esoteric. Two
special editions were dedicated to 'L'esotérisme d'Albrecht Dürer' in
1977. The foreword to the issue in which 'Sur un rêve de Dürer'
appeared gives a clear indication of the approach taken to Dürer by
the editors. Their declared aim is to use this coverage of Dürer as a
vehicle for the promotion of awareness in astrology, the occult and
mysticism. Objecting to what they believe to be the lack of
imagination and faith in the ideas of modern science, they state their
aim to be the unity of the sacred and profane sciences: 'C'est
pourquoi, au-delà des «sciences» profanes actuelles, ont toujours existé
des sciences sacrées; et c'est pourquoi les grands esprits de la Tradition
excellèrent à la fois dans les deux. Car ils visaient à une connaissance
de l'Unité' (i). While Yourcenar would not have supported some of
the sweeping criticisms of modern science in the foreword and
editorial, their programme offered a space for her to confront an
outlook with apparent similarities to her own. Hamsa, which means
'swan' in Sanskrit, a symbol of the mind, aimed to revive interest in
arcana and to explain their meanings to readers who might otherwise
miss the deeper significances which the journal believed to exist in the
world. The sign of the swan is used elsewhere in Yourcenar's work: in
Souvenirs pieux, when Octave is thinking about his relationship with
his friend José de Coppin: 'Au blason de son ami figurent les deux
plus purs symboles qui soient au monde, une croix et un cygne' (EM,
836); and in Un homme obscur, for the insignia on Madeleine's sleigh
(OR, 964).

In her opening paragraph, Yourcenar approaches Dürer's work
from the perspective of dream accounts in the Renaissance. She does
not start with reflections on Dürer as an artist but instead introduces
him as 'un homme du XVIe siècle', arguing that the visions of
Leonardo, Dante and Cardano are different and are best understood in
the context of more established genres of recording visions. In
Yourcenar's view, Dürer's dream is an authentic version in wash and in
words of his experience, whereas the trio mentioned write when fully
awake or as a result of meditation: in Le Tour de la prison, she distinguishes visio intellectualis from 'la vision où jusqu'à un certain point
les yeux participent', and both these from 'vision totale'.[33] This
distinguishes her approach from her co-contributor Claude Mettra,

Fig. 6. Dürer, *Traumgesicht* (1525)
Watercolour and ink on paper, 30×43 cm
Kunsthistorisches Museum, Vienna

who calls his essay 'La dernière vision du Maître de Nuremberg'.[34]
Unlike Mettra, Yourcenar has opted to translate 'im Schlaf hab ich
dies Gesicht gesehen' as 'je vis en rêve ce que représente ce croquis',
specifically avoiding the word 'vision' so as to distinguish this
experience from other accounts. At the same time, it should be noted
that Yourcenar's French translation of the description of the impact of
the first downpour is vague. For 'mit einer sölchen Grausamkeit mit
einem uber grossem Rauschen und Zersprützen und entränket das
ganz Land' (literally 'with such ferocity with colossal thundering and
splatter and drowned the whole land') Yourcenar's text reads, 'la
secousse et le bruit furent terrifiants, et toute la région fut inondée'.
This translation shifts attention from the concern of the text to
capture the extent of the confusion, even though the commentary
provided by Yourcenar does focus on the new and disruptive
confrontation witnessed in this text and image.

The essay avoids placing Dürer's dream within the interpretative
circle that sees everything Dürer did in terms of his experimentations
and his eagerness to write about his experiences. This is how
Panofsky sees the dream, commenting on Dürer's calculation of his
distance from the downpour and the speed of the fall.[35] In his
catalogue entry, Panofsky refers to the widespread fear in 1525 that the
bloodshed caused by the Peasants' War signalled the imminent end of
the world (*Dürer*, ii. cat. no. 1410, 135). Yourcenar also refers to the
calculations, but is sceptical about the contemporary allusion. She
does not wish a predetermined view of Dürer to control her
interpretation. There is an example of Panofsky revealing this
tendency when he remarks on Dürer's character: 'He could be
facetious and, on occasion, magnificently coarse; but he was never
given to subtle irony and sly insinuations' (*Dürer*, i. 76). How can
Panofsky be so sure? In view of Panofsky's sovereign position in Dürer
studies in 1977, Yourcenar's essay has to be read as an alternative view
to his interpretation of Dürer's *Journal* entry.[36]

Yourcenar's first point is to avoid a symbolic reading of water in this
work. She reminds us of well-known representations of the subject of
the Flood (for instance by Michelangelo or Poussin) and notes the
absence of human terror and drama in Dürer's account of the dream.
By contrast, she considers Dürer's *Apocalypse* series to chart different
territory, since its want of cosmic reference indicates its restriction to
human tragedy. In her radical view, the dream offers a unique

representation of cataclysm, removed from the traditions and rhetoric of symbolic imagery in Dürer's work, although the watered-down translation of Dürer's text hides the rhetorical flourishes in his original German.

Mettra looks closely at the wash and the text, but he prefers to see the water as being deeply significant in the context of Dürer's thinking and Renaissance cosmology: the unstable presence of water, one of the four constituent elements for the world-view of the sixteenth century, means that an imbalance is represented in the dream. He concentrates on how Dürer would have concluded that the vision formed part of the alchemical *œuvre* he was experiencing and suggests that in the final phrase Dürer is referring to his hopes and fears for the future. In Yourcenar's view, the point is that this experience cannot be so readily inscribed within the language of a Northern humanist or alchemical world-view. So despite her awareness of Dürer's interest in recording in word and image his observations and encounters, she wants to ensure that this work is not glossed over by a deterministic historical interpretation or by a general and marshalled view of the artist's work. She is fascinated by the disruptive and unique aspect of the image: 'l'effet est d'un désastre naturel perçu sans référence à aucun concept humain, tel qu'il aurait pu se réfracter dans un bloc de cristal en l'absence d'un œil d'homme. L'épouvante qui secoue le dormeur est, certes, une réaction humaine, mais un animal l'eût aussi bien éprouvée, et ce désarroi physique reste tout proche de celui de la terre qui tremble' (319). In Yourcenar's view, this image does represent an alchemical experience, but 'sans les lettres', without the accompanying alchemical signs, and definitely with the power and totality of the hermetic experiments in *L'Œuvre au noir*. The difference lies in this view of a cataclysm of more terrifying power for the alchemist than an induced test of endurance. However, it is hard to accept Yourcenar's insistence that Dürer's account is devoid of any human concept whatsoever: his written version includes a consecutive narrative, measurement of distance, distinction between speeds and reference to a specific date and religious festival, and demonstrates the desire to record a dream. Differentiating her approach from Panofsky's is liberating, but it has led here to exaggeration. At the same time, Yourcenar can stress that Dürer concentrates on a physical and elemental encounter with the disaster affecting the earth.

The account of the wash/watercolour is less problematic. It is usually the text that receives the critic's attention, so it is refreshing to

have a response to the image. As Yourcenar notes, the earth and water
are already mixing, with the water operating this process of
metamorphosis. The land is on the point of being washed away; the
calamity will effect a return to origins: 'Le paysage semble écrasé
d'avance sous les coulées bleu sale qui tombent verticalement du ciel;
la terre et l'eau déjà déversée se mélangent en un brun boueux et un
glauque trouble; [...]. Très loin, rapetissées par la distance, à peine
visibles au premier regard, quelques bâtisses brunâtres se pressent au
bord d'un golfe, prêtes, à ce qu'il semble, à retourner à l'argile' (319,
319–20). Blue, brown and green figure the dissolution of the land by
the water. Water and colour pigment in the watercolour are the
substances now undergoing dissolution. The deposition of man-made
constructions into the earth is a recurrent motif that allows Yourcenar
to set up a view of Time in which the human inquiry covers the
world, prior to realizing the ultimate insignificance of all inquiry. This
assigns a new position to the human witness to the order of the world,
now faced with disappearance by drowning. Yourcenar's outright
dismissal of a psychoanalytical reading of the dream is unnecessarily
defensive, since her interpretation could draw on the visual impact or
eruption of the dream for Dürer and for the reader-spectator as a
symptom of its effect of rupture and calamity.

To propose looking at the image and text of the dream as one work
is not necessarily inventive, but Yourcenar's account of the cataclysm
can be developed if we do so. The upper half of the sheet represents
the vertical fall of the water onto the land on the point of disappearance. The writing is placed on a second vertical drop, this time
beneath the land area, as if underground and already submerged. The
writing occurs after the deluge has begun, but before the destruction.
The signature makes us realize that the writing stands in an ambiguous
spatial relationship to the wash: both on an underground wall and on
the surface of the sheet; in both cases about to receive the impact of
the water. Perhaps this approach to Dürer's work makes the function
and position of the signature more challenging than the final phrase
of Dürer's text on which Yourcenar concludes her study: 'Gott wende
alle Ding zum besten': 'Dieu tourne pour le mieux toutes choses'.

Girolamo Cardano defended his mystical interpretation of dreams
by stating that we need to recognize God's hand and not forget his
workings: 'They are rather gifts of a bountiful God, who is in debt to
no one, much less to me'.[37] Yourcenar acknowledges this Christian
reading of the final phrase, but she does not see it as the only reading

possible. She also invites the reader to avoid a sceptical interpretation, even if we do not follow the Christian safety clause. The desire to dissolve the contradictions involved in interpreting the dream is informed by Buddhism, where such a procedure is an integral part of its way of thinking.[38] Yourcenar's strategy is to respond to such a statement speculatively, which results in close attention being given to the last words written by Dürer; in the case of the last phrase, spoken as well.

The swashbuckling Yourcenar has taken on a heavy tradition of interpretation in this essay. As in the case of the essays on Innsbruck, Ravenna and especially Poussin, her approach encourages us to test her assertions by seeing how she has arrived at her positions and by examining where they lead. Her polemic covers up some of the evidence, but her account can be read for its distinctive voice: Dürer's dream is an unusual work and needs to be considered as such, with the possibility that it may not fit into established views of the artist's work and outlook.

In contrast to her essay on Dürer, where she argued for the difference of the work in question from the rest of the artist's output, in her discussion of Ruisdael's *The Jewish Cemetery* (the Dresden version; fig. 7), Yourcenar implicitly argues that the reasons given for seeing the painting as unique do not have to be accepted without testing them first ('L'homme qui signait avec un ruisseau', *EM*, 564–6). Usually writers who dwell on the two celebrated paintings of the Jewish cemetery do so because of their alleged uniqueness in his work.[39] Yourcenar aims to offer her own response to these visions, avoiding symbolic and predetermined readings of the picture.

In his essay on Ruisdael, Goethe noted the way nature's creations endure longer than man's, though they too decay. He saw in Ruisdael's paintings evidence of the way the past is the present, focusing on how *The Jewish Cemetery* is devoted to the human and mineral past: 'The tombs in their ruinous condition even point to something more than the past: they are tombstones to themselves.'[40] John Gage argues that Goethe was drawn to the combination of natural and supernatural elements in Ruisdael. As the catalogue for the 1981 Harvard-Mauritshuis Ruisdael exhibition notes, Goethe refused to follow the standard Romantic view and perceive a definite sense of melancholy in the painting.[41] This was the response that Fromentin too would expound in *Les Maîtres d'autrefois*. Yourcenar, who

Fig. 7. Ruisdael, *The Jewish Cemetery* (*c.*1653)
Oil on canvas, 84×95 cm
Gemäldegalerie Alte Meister, Staatliche Kunstsammlungen Dresden

possessed a copy of the Harvard-Mauritshuis catalogue, feels likewise that it is not possible to specify the atmosphere in such a way, whereas many Romantics had been inclined to do so. One hundred and fifty years later, a prefatory note to her essay recognized that Yourcenar was continuing a tradition of commentary started by Goethe: 'Notre musée égoïste s'enrichit d'un chef-d'œuvre du peintre hollandais Jacob van Ruysdael auquel répondent le commentaire électif et la rêverie sereine de l'auteur de *L'Œuvre au noir*.'[42] The reference here to Goethe's *Elective Affinities* neatly frames the tradition of written responses to the painting.

However, in his enthralling study of Ruisdael, E. John Walford is suspicious of any commentator who focuses on *The Jewish Cemetery*. He aims to show that this is not an extraordinary work when looked at in the context of the Ruisdael corpus: 'He emphasized the same aspects of nature, a fact that is overlooked by those who treat *The Jewish Cemetery* paintings as unique exceptions that have no bearing on our understanding of the rest of his works' (*Ruisdael*, 102). Walford discusses the view of Ruisdael presented in the 1981 exhibition. In his judgement, taking the complete corpus of Ruisdael's works into account, the exhibition paid less attention to the dark woodlands and waterfalls, offering a selection that emphasized the views of Haarlem and open fields. *The Jewish Cemetery* does stand out amongst these paintings, even if there are several other dark ones, winter scenes and seascapes, and Walford rightly suggests that the emphasis is on the brighter landscapes (*Ruisdael*, 200–1). Although Yourcenar does not see *The Jewish Cemetery* as an exception, she suggests that it is more mysterious than any other work, and Walford's clarification of the historical context does not deny that there is something dark and strange about the painting. Yourcenar acknowledges that the painting shows the outward manifestations of religion and the world to be transitory, whether in a Christian or a Jewish framework, but she retains her sense of the 'songe' and, as she demonstrated at the end of 'Sur un rêve de Dürer', does not limit herself to the perspective of one religion.

Walford argues that enough is known about Ruisdael and his patrons to understand how his paintings would have been interpreted in his lifetime. It is also known which artists influenced Ruisdael, and he stands out much less radically than Yourcenar suggests. Ruisdael's patrons expected his paintings to offer aesthetic delight and a subject for the contemplation of the beauty of the world. The meditative tone of Ruisdael's landscapes echoes an understanding of nature common to his generation: God's design is represented in these paintings, as well as the corrupt matter of nature. In the fiercely Calvinist society of Amsterdam, writers and preachers were enjoining people to read the book of nature: 'For these and many other writers the beauty and transiency of the visible world is seen as opening windows for the beholder on the invisible, and sunlight, storm and harvest are perceived as revealing the providence of God' (*Ruisdael*, 21). In 1657 Ruisdael was received into the Calvinist Reformed Church. Ruisdael considered carefully where to position human figures in a landscape and how to represent the mutability of life, in other words on how to show his Calvinist public where they fitted into the picture.

Perhaps, in view of the problem Calvinists had with visual representations of the world, the painting lends itself to the Yourcenarian reading in terms of the 'songe' experienced by Ruisdael. In other words, a declamatory painting of the Counter-Reformation would not permit such doubts, while a Dutch landscape offers a vision or panorama that may more readily be interpreted outside the framework of the prevailing ideology of the day. In Yourcenar's response to *The Jewish Cemetery* and Ruisdael's work in general, the reader's attention is drawn to the physical mass and spatial range of the pictures and to the way in which this weight provides access to an uncanny pictorial world. The landscape is devoid of human life and yet resembles it through another form: 'la prédilection de Ruysdael pour les arbres étêtés ou ébranchés et les restes d'édifices en ruine (la tour du château d'Egmont, qu'il a souvent peinte, ressemble à un tronc d'arbre mort resté tout droit) fait penser à celle de Rembrandt pour les vieillards endurants et graves' (565). The air of defeat in the life of the painting and the appearance in others of villages that seem brutally enclosed by the winter articulate what it is that Yourcenar finds strange in the painting, mysteries that elude symbolic readings: 'On a parlé du symbolisme: assurément, tout paysage symbolise, ne fût-ce, comme on l'a dit, qu'un état d'âme' (565). The visual is not simply symbolic. As Yourcenar wrote in a letter of 1962, discussing the interpretation of 'enigmatic' works of art: 'le mystère se reforme derrière l'explication et demeure intact' (*Lettres*, 161).

Choosing to write about *The Jewish Cemetery* allowed Yourcenar to participate in the interest shown by Goethe and Fromentin, but the reason for choosing this painting for her contribution to *Le Nouvel Observateur* can be read as her desire to respond to rumours that surfaced at the time of her election to the Académie française about anti-semitism in her work.[43] This is why she nuances her final point about the resonance of this painting in our century. Noting the picture's role as a symbol for the catastrophes that have afflicted the Jews in modern times, Yourcenar points out that the Portuguese Jewish community refused to bury Spinoza in its cemetery; the phrasing of her commiseration for that community's lack of descendants (not due to the Holocaust) suggests that she does not share their dismay at the outcome. Yourcenar asserts her ability to discriminate between remembering atrocity and noting intolerance, although the manner of expressing her perspective is perhaps insensitive. In her desire to grasp the opportunity to put her critics right she uses the term 'symbole', avoided elsewhere, for the impact of the painting. An essay on painting has again provided Yourcenar with the opportunity to integrate a personal concern into her writing.

Reading these two short essays on Dürer and Ruisdael implicates several contexts. The essays are also invitations to make independent responses to the visual arts, reactions not pre-judged according to the imposing weight of art-historical interpretation. Art history is adopted in so far as it provides a way into the spectacle on offer. However, the subsequent response of the spectator can never be transferred back to the period of the work's creation. The departure from an aesthetics working through a process of intuition, a shift already detected in the discussion of the essay on Poussin above, is categorical in these essays, which seek to go beyond symbolism to find verbal responses to the visual strangeness or courage of the chosen images. Yourcenar endorses Valéry's approach to the cultural significance and survival of a work of art:

> L'œuvre dure en tant qu'elle est capable de paraître tout autre que son auteur l'avait faite.
>
> Elle dure pour s'être transformée, et pour autant qu'elle était capable de milles transformations et interprétations.
>
> Ou bien c'est qu'elle comporte une qualité indépendante de son auteur, non créée par lui, mais par son époque ou sa nation, et qui prend valeur par le changement d'époque ou de nation.[44]

Whether or not Yourcenar would have liked the idea of transformations being effected on her own work, her proximity to Valéry here may lead the reader to compare the outlooks of the two writers. In a letter of 20 November 1973 to Emile Noulet, Yourcenar states that her philosophical outlook often differs so radically from Valéry's that she finds herself only thinking about the differences when she reads him, but she acknowledges that she returns to him for 'méthode' (*Lettres*, 416–17). Connections between their writing, of course, are not dependent on Yourcenar's agreement with Valéry's thinking on every issue. With qualifications specific to each essay, Yourcenar has illustrated the uncontrollable power of images to speak and increased the capacity of the reader-spectator to respond.

## Chenonceaux's Mistresses and the Portrait of Henri III

By way of a transition from looking at Yourcenar's essays on the visual arts in the context of written responses in a certain tradition to looking at processes of visualization in her fiction, this concluding section will examine the essay on the château of Chenonceaux, with reference to the essay on D'Aubigné (*EM*, 37–74 and 22–36). The purpose here is to see how reading 'Ah, mon beau château' allows us to engage with questions of the visual that pursue the historical, literary and private concerns of the preceding sections, while at the same time focusing more on the representation of historical figures and the visualization of them as subjects. This re-orientation of analysis will serve as an introduction to the concerns of the remaining chapters, where Yourcenar's essays on Piranesi and Rembrandt are incorporated into studies of the fiction.

The presence of Michelet in Yourcenar's work has been noted by many critics.[45] One comparison between the two writers may be made by placing the portraits of Diane de Poitiers and Henri III in Yourcenar's essays on Chenonceaux and D'Aubigné alongside Michelet's portraits of the same figures in his *Renaissance et Réforme*. The basis for Yourcenar's portrait of the most celebrated mistress of Chenonceaux, Diane de Poitiers, is drawn directly from Michelet's account; the only reason that Yourcenar does not mention him could be that his dislike of the royal mistress is so well known. Along with other historians, Yourcenar follows Michelet and interprets Goujon's statue of Diane de Poitiers as the huntress-goddess Diana as an extremely fanciful piece of mythologization in view of Diane's coldness, calculation and egotism. As the historian Philippe Erlanger wrote at the time of Yourcenar's essay: 'Acquérir, consolider, garantir: ce triple souci ne l'abandonnait jamais'.[46] Yourcenar is not alone in debunking a woman celebrated for her amorous successes and stratagems.

Diane is not permitted the 'relativist' excuse that she had to be so shrewd in order to survive as a woman in the sixteenth century: the gap between the art of Goujon and the meanness of the historical figure could not, in Yourcenar's view, be wider. The other mistress of Chenonceaux who receives much attention in the essay is Louise de Lorraine, especially for the twelve-year period when she mourned for Henri III, who was murdered in 1589. The funereal chambers and decorations at the château are interpreted as genuine expressions of grief for the departed Henri and serve as a reminder of the ever-present figure of death in the sixteenth century:

A décrire ces années d'absorption dans le souvenir d'un mort comme un romantique et stérile cauchemar, on risque d'oublier la pieuse confiance de la reine en l'efficacité de la prière, son constant effort pour secourir Henri dans l'autre monde et pour le consoler. [...] Ce n'était pas à un poétique fantôme que Louise consacrait sa vie, mais à une âme. (59)

Yourcenar's essay retrieves Louise de Lorraine from semi-oblivion and makes her far more sympathetic than Diane de Poitiers. Louise did not encourage a fantasmatic myth about herself that intentionally distorted the reality of her circumstances. Her remembrance for Henri III is structured simply and poignantly; Yourcenar notes that they are now closer than they ever were during his life, when Louise found it so difficult to attract his gaze:

En un sens, la modeste épouse d'autrefois s'affirmait à Chenonceaux dans son rôle d'amante; elle y prenait pleine possession de ce mari que tant de diversions voluptueuses ou tragiques lui avaient sans cesse enlevé. (59)

Henri III deceased leaves a series of stable if intangible images for Louise to contemplate and adorn in her memory. While Diane de Poitiers set up narcissistic versions of herself, Louise strove to find the soul of her husband.

'Ah, mon beau château' announces itself as an essay about the series of widows who lived at Chenonceaux. However, what emerges from reading this essay, and bearing in mind the essay on D'Aubigné, is Yourcenar's fascination with Henri III; she joins Louise in trying to recreate his image. He features as the hedonistic instigator of the May 1577 celebrations at the château, as a king adopting a fairly skilful approach to the political world of the time and as a man subject to endless illnesses and neuroses. Yourcenar's interest in Henri III attempts to restore the image tarnished during and after his reign:

'Puis un énervé, Henri III, et l'avilissement de la France', was Michelet's verdict.[47] In the essay on *Les Tragiques*, she discusses D'Aubigné's portrait of Henri III. Her sympathetic portrait does not idolize him, but it does honour his complexity. Imagining Louise's modest daily life, Yourcenar makes an intriguing reference to a sonnet by Philippe Desportes: 'Ou bien, d'une main incertaine, Louise feuilletait un recueil de vers de Desportes, qui avait été le poète de cour de Henri III, et relisait l'étrange sonnet où il est question de fantômes désespérés rôdant autour de la tombe où une mort violente les a couchés' (60–1).

The sonnet in question, from 'Les Amours d'Hippolyte', makes us wonder whether Yourcenar may also be one of these spirits attracted to Henri III alive or dead. It is a curious allusion that suggests much about Yourcenar's investment in the project of 'Ah, mon beau château':

> Autour des corps, qu'une mort avancee
> Par violence a privez du beau jour,
> Les Ombres vont, et font maint et maint tour,
> Aimans encor leur despouille laissée.
>     Au lieu cruel où j'eu l'ame blessee
> Et fu meurtri par les fleches d'Amour,
> J'erre, je tourne et retourne à l'entour,
> Ombre maudite, errante et dechassee.
>     Legers esprits plus que moy fortunez,
> Comme il vous plaist vous allez et venez
> Au lieu qui clost vostre despouille aimee.
>     Vous la voyez, vous la pouvez toucher,
> Où las! je crains seulement d'approcher
> L'endroit qui tient ma richesse enfermee.

We note that the living unrequited lover is in a worse position than the shadows hovering at the tomb. The poem's account of neglected passion in the second stanza would make Louise think of her situation when Henri was alive and wish that she had been able to get as close to his effigy as the shadows can at his death. Some consolation is found in imagining her devotions as if she were a shadow accompanying the dead Henri. Yourcenar's essay stresses the humility, sensuality and desire in the acts of remembrance by Louise de Lorraine. If we consider the essay's engagement with these dead monarchs, then we can imagine Yourcenar, if personally unlike the timid and restricted Louise, as a wandering, free and light-footed spirit in the company of the quick and the dead, performing her own fantasmatic and elliptical communion, but at times feeling scorned or ignored by her historical subjects.

The affinity with Henri III is voiced in her enthusiasm for his sense of metamorphosis and his view of the impermanence and instability of the present and the past. Yourcenar considers these aspects to be distinctive of his epoch and finds them epitomized at the Fête of May 1577. Yourcenar here resumes discussion of the sexual ambivalence of the period which she had begun in the first version of the essay on Oscar Wilde.[48] Henri III is presented as an elusive and subversive figure: 'Au cours de cette fête imprudente, peu politique en tout cas, le jeune roi n'innovait guère: il réalisait au contraire les secrètes aspirations de la Renaissance prête à finir, son goût de l'équivoque, son sens voluptueux de la métamorphose et du travesti' (82). Yourcenar follows with a reference to Shakespeare's comedies. In the two versions of the essay on Wilde, referring to the affair between Wilde and Lord Alfred Douglas, she alternates quotations from the *Sonnets* and *De Profundis* and addresses the themes of transience and metamorphosis in the former, where the desire to avoid being fixed in the memory of the beloved motivates the search for an idiom of metamorphosis.[49] As Yourcenar notes in 'Ah, mon beau château', Henri III eludes the attempts of Louise to occupy him in death, but she is also closest to him then.

The ellipsis in the reference to Desportes is not the only example of disruptive representation. Louise's memories also lead to Yourcenar's metaphorical use of anamorphosis for the treatment of violence. The essays on Chenonceaux and D'Aubigné abound in allusions to the violent times of the French Wars of Religion, but these are always handled with brevity or careful analysis so as to avoid disinfection by historical relativism. Perhaps, as Yourcenar herself suggests, an outstanding act of violence occurs when Henri III awakes from a disturbing dream and orders the lions of the Louvre to be slaughtered. The passage comes in the middle of a list of the images of Henri III that Louise may have held in her memory after his death, from her first sight of him to his anguished face one morning after this dream: 'ou encore l'homme hagard, en proie à d'inguérissables angoisses, comme ce matin où, épouvanté par un rêve au cours duquel il s'était vu déchiré par des fauves, il avait fait sauvagement tuer à coups d'arquebuse les lions des fossés du Louvre, crime assurément plus atroce que la nécessaire liquidation des Guises' (100). The destruction is mentioned as a sort of anecdotal aside which functions anamorphically through the disruption it causes in the narrative of the paragraph once the incident is read from its own perspective of wanton cruelty and slow slaughter. The decision to place the incident here in this manner after the death of Henri III is mainly dictated by the perspective of Louise, but the power of the image is all the more startling.

Thus, a refusal to relativize and to anaesthetize the past colours Yourcenar's perspective. It encourages a reading of her essays which tries to show how they open up the picture of the past, as in the use of ellipsis and anamorphosis in the two examples just discussed, to indicate the ways in which the essays can respond to such a reading and to exploit the freedom acquired by the reader to pursue the suggestions made by her work. Following the search for her voice in the essays—hesitant but ambitious in her pieces on Innsbruck and Ravenna; hindered by certain issues but independently engaged with the challenging dynamics of Poussin's paintings; arguing against predetermined and simplistically symbolic accounts of Dürer and Ruisdael, while engaging also with questions of instability and dissolution; drawing out the violence and erotics of ritual and remembrance at Chenonceaux—shows that the meeting of intellectual preoccupations with the visual is a productive and creative approach.

Reading her essays on the visual arts and other historical subjects prepares us for the study of the nature and function of the visual, including its staging as visualization, in the longer works, as seen in their treatment of topics, themes and motifs such as the Other, memory, disappearance and endurance. In the following chapters, which focus on *Mémoires d'Hadrien*, *L'Œuvre au noir* and *Un homme obscur*, aspects of the twofold method of contextualization and analysis applied in this chapter will be adapted to investigate these ideas and, for this, the continued discussion of ideas traced in the essays will be necessary, especially in the case of Piranesi and Rembrandt.

## Notes to Chapter 1

1. Jeffrey Chipps Smith, *German Sculpture of the Later Renaissance c.1520–1580: Art in an Age of Uncertainty* (Princeton: Princeton University Press, 1994).
2. See Colette Gaudin, *Marguerite Yourcenar: A la surface du temps* (Amsterdam and Atlanta: Rodopi, 1994), 108–9, and Nicole Maroger, 'Le Changeur d'or: un essai d'histoire économique?', *Bulletin de la SIEY* 10 (1992), 23–4.

3. Paul Valéry, *Introduction à la méthode de Léonard de Vinci* (Paris: Gallimard, 1992), 28.
4. For reproductions of the mosaics, see Antonio Paolucci, *Ravenna*, trans. Simon Dally (London: Constable, 1978), 39–51.
5. Kandinsky also detects a decline of spirituality in the mosaics at Ravenna: *Du spirituel dans l'art, et dans la peinture en particulier* (1911; Paris: Denoël, 1989), 64–8 (and ill. no. 1). For Yourcenar's aesthetic of disappearance, see below, Ch. 4, p. 171.
6. Quoted in Richard Verdi, 'Poussin's Critical Fortunes' (Ph.D. thesis, University of London, 1976), 377, which cites many other examples. Like Verdi, though with a different project in mind, my approach to Poussin initially owes very much to Anthony Blunt's *The Paintings of Nicolas Poussin*, 3 vols. (London: Phaidon, 1966–7). Colour reproductions of most of the paintings discussed in this section can be found in the catalogues of the Paris and London exhibitions of 1994–5: Pierre Rosenberg, *Nicolas Poussin 1594–1665* (Paris: Réunion des musées nationaux, 1994) and R. Verdi, *Nicolas Poussin 1594–1665* (London: Royal Academy of Arts, 1995). For references, two catalogue numbers will be given, with Rosenberg first and Verdi second. For full details about the illustrations, see above, p. xv–xvi. To locate the other paintings by Poussin mentioned by Yourcenar in her essay but not discussed in this chapter, Christopher Wright's *Poussin, Paintings, a Catalogue Raisonné* (London: Jupiter, 1984) may also be consulted. Where either Rosenberg or Verdi (or both) do not include the painting, a reference to Wright's plate number will be given: *Vénus et Adonis*, Wright 116 (see below, p. 168, fig. 18); *Le Triomphe de Bacchus*, Rosenberg 55a/Wright 38; *Achille et les filles de Lycomède*, 209/fig. 7; *Paysage romantique* (or *Paysage avec Orion aveugle cherchant le soleil*), 234/84; *Paysage avec Nymphes et Satyres*, Wright 122; *Diane et Endymion*, 37/19; *L'Enterrement de Phocion*, 168/67; *Saint Paul*, 192/65, fig. 148; and *Adam et Eve*, 238/88. The *Bacchanales* briefly mentioned in the essay (p. 470) concern the set of mythological paintings commissioned by Richelieu in the 1630s: Wright, cat. nos. 80–3, groups them together.
7. Gérard Genette, *Palimpsestes: la littérature au second degré* (Paris: Seuil, 1982), 10.
8. Maria van Rysselberghe, *Les Cahiers de la Petite Dame 3*, Cahiers André Gide 6 (Paris: Gallimard, 1975), 330, 348–9.
9. Walter Friedländer, 'America's first Poussin show at Durlacher brothers', *Art News* 38/1 (Mar. 1940), 6–14.
10. They are referring to the version of *Le Veau d'Or* at the M. H. de Young Memorial Museum, San Francisco, now thought to be a copy of a lost painting: see Wright, cat. L5, and the reproduction in Rosenberg, 113.
11. Friedländer, 12; Yourcenar, 469. *La Sainte Famille Whitcomb* is now known simply as *La Sainte Famille*; cat. nos. 101/48.
12. Friedländer, 9; Yourcenar, 469–70. Such comparisons were commonplace, as Verdi demonstrates. Yourcenar also draws on the influential study by Paul Desjardins, *La Méthode des classiques français: Corneille, Poussin, Pascal* (Paris: Armand Colin, 1904).
13. Louis Marin, 'A l'éveil des métamorphoses: Poussin (1625–1635)', in his *Sublime Poussin* (Paris: Seuil, 1995).

14. Alexandre Terneuil has interestingly argued that an autobiographical reading may be applied here to Yourcenar's choice of characters from Corneille and Racine: A. Terneuil, 'Le thème de l'exil dans quelques essais de Yourcenar', in *Marguerite Yourcenar: Ecritures de l'exil*, ed. B. Deprez and A. de Medeiros (Louvain-la-Neuve: Academie Bruylant, 1998). It is also possible that Yourcenar remembers seeing Pierre-Paul Prud'hon's illustrations for Racine's plays: see, e.g., *Scène de famille, étude pour Andromaque* in *Prud'hon ou le rêve du bonheur*. Prud'hon is included in some suggestive notes Yourcenar made on further parallels between Classical and Romantic artists: 'Notes de lecture: la littérature française (pour aider l'imagination)', *Sources II*, 207.

15. Marc Fumaroli, 'Introduction', in his *'L'Inspiration du poète' de Poussin* (Paris: Réunion des musées nationaux, 1989), 23.

16. Cat. nos. 194/Wright 190.

17. Yves Bonnefoy, *Rome 1630: l'horizon du premier baroque* (Paris: Flammarion, 1970), 127.

18. Roger Fry, 'Some Questions in Esthetics', in *Transformations* (London: Hogarth Press, 1926), 18–20.

19. Howard Hibbard, *Poussin: 'The Holy Family on the Steps'* (New York and London: Allen Lane, 1974). See Rosenberg, 173a (Verdi does not include it, but see cat. no. 60, p. 265). Rosenberg explains that the painting is now thought to be a copy, by a follower of Poussin, of the Cleveland Museum of Art's version of the same subject, reminding us that Hibbard's method is of value only as far as it can go.

20. André Gide, 'L'Enseignement de Poussin', in *Poussin* (Paris: Au Divan, 1945), s.p.

21. Marcel Arland, 'Promenade au Louvre', in *Le Promeneur* (Paris: Pavois, 1944).

22. Cat. nos. 146/57; 241/91; 228/83; 38/15. Rosenberg's title for *L'Education de Bacchus* is *La Naissance de Bacchus*, but to match the passage quoted here and below (p. 30) the title used by Yourcenar is retained here.

23. Friedländer detects 'an almost metallic quality in the texture of the flesh' in the *Vénus et Adonis* (10).

24. For the first two interpretations, see Blunt, *Poussin: Text*, 348–50 and 184; for the third, Oscar Bätschmann, *Nicolas Poussin, Dialectics of Painting*, trans. Marko Daniel (London: Reaktion, 1990), 104–8; and for the last, Marin, 'Déposition du temps dans la représentation peinte', in *De la représentation*, 291–300.

25. Georges Didi-Huberman, *La Peinture incarnée* (Paris: Minuit, 1985), 85–6.

26. Cat. nos. 11/13, 93/38; Yourcenar mentions the later version during the final paragraph of her essay. See Erwin Panofsky, *'Et in Arcadia Ego*: Poussin and the Elegiac Tradition', in his *Meaning in the Visual Arts* (London: Peregrine, 1970). Panofsky differentiates between Greek and Virgilian views of Arcadia. On Panofsky's essay, see L. Marin, 'Panofsky et Poussin en Arcadie', in *Sublime Poussin*, and D. Carrier, 'Poussin's Self-Portraits', *Word & Image* 7/2 (1991), 127–48.

27. Gaston Bachelard, *L'Eau et les Rêves* (new edn. Paris: José Corti, 1956), 125.

28. Henriette Levillain discusses the story of the genesis of *Mémoires d'Hadrien* in *«Mémoires d'Hadrien» de Marguerite Yourcenar* (Paris: Gallimard, 1992), 19–45; see *OR*, 519–21.

29. On the energy and bodily transmutation in the painting, as well as its resistance

to metamorphosis as defeat, see Stephen Bann, *The True Vine: On Visual Representation and the Western Tradition* (Cambridge: Cambridge University Press, 1989), 140–7 and 150–6.

30. For the full story of this literary triangle, see Michèle Sarde, *Vous, Marguerite Yourcenar* (Paris: Laffont, 1995), and Fabrice Rozié, 'Reflets de l'entre-deux-guerres dans le paratexte de Marguerite Yourcenar', in *Marguerite Yourcenar. Aux frontières du texte, Roman 20–50* (Lille: Université de Lille III, 1995), 113–21.

31. Loredana Primozich, 'L'empire de l'esprit: sources et variantes dans l'œuvre de Marguerite Yourcenar', *Bulletin de la SIEY* 13 (1994), 25–37.

32. Adapted from a William Beckford title, *Dreams, Waking Thoughts and Incidents*.

33. 'L'Italienne à Alger', *EM*, 613–14. This passage is discussed further in Ch. 3, p. 121.

34. Claude Mettra, 'La dernière vision du Maître de Nuremberg', in *L'Esotérisme d'Albrecht Dürer II, Hamsa* (1977), 46–51.

35. E. Panofsky, *Albrecht Dürer*, 2 vols. (Princeton: Princeton University Press, 1945).

36. See also Stephen Greenblatt, 'Murdering Peasants: Status, Genre, and the Representation of Rebellion', in *Learning to Curse: Essays in Early Modern Culture* (New York and London: Routledge, Chapman and Hall, 1990).

37. Girolamo Cardano, *The Book of my Life*, trans. Jean Stoner (London: J. M. Dent & Son, 1931), 161.

38. Frits Staal, *Exploring Mysticism* (Harmondsworth: Penguin, 1975), 16.

39. E. John Walford, *Jacob van Ruisdael and the Perception of Landscape* (New Haven and London: Yale University Press, 1991), 102.

40. John Gage (ed. and trans.), *Goethe on Art* (London: Scolar Press, 1980), 210.

41. S. Slive and H. R. Hoetink (eds.), *Jacob van Ruisdael* (New York: Abbeville Press, 1981), 68.

42. 'Note d'éditeur', *Le Nouvel Observateur*, 16–22 Dec. 1983, 14.

43. See Josyane Savigneau, *Marguerite Yourcenar: L'invention d'une vie* (Paris: Gallimard, 1990), 401–4.

44. Paul Valéry, 'Littérature', *Tel Quel*, in *Œuvres II*, ed. J. Hytier (Paris: Gallimard/Pléiade, 1960), 561–2.

45. For example: Jacques Keryell, 'Variations sur Marguerite Yourcenar'; Anne-Yvonne Julien, *«L'Œuvre au noir» de Marguerite Yourcenar*, 156–7; and Patrick de Rosbo, *Entretiens radiophoniques avec Marguerite Yourcenar*, 55.

46. Philippe Erlanger, *Diane de Poitiers: déesse de la Renaissance* (Paris: Perrin, 1976), 180.

47. Jules Michelet, *Renaissance et Réforme: Histoire de France au XVIe siècle* (Paris: Robert Laffont, 1982), 441. For an account of the propaganda against Henri III during his reign, see Keith Cameron, *Henri III: A Maligned or Malignant King? (Aspects of Satirical Iconography of Henri de Valois)* (Exeter: University of Exeter Press, 1978).

48. 'Abraham Fraunce traducteur de Virgile: Oscar Wilde' (1929). The story of sexual ambivalence, prominent in this early essay, is reduced in the second and much altered version of 1982 ('Wilde rue des Beaux-Arts', *EM*, 499–509), since in the meantime Yourcenar had adapted some of her material for the Chenonceaux essay.

49. 'Abraham Fraunce', 626–7; 'Wilde rue des Beaux-Arts', 133–5.

CHAPTER 2

❖

# Looking with Hadrien: Memories of Antinoüs

This chapter concentrates on the principal act of visual reconstruction that occurs in *Mémoires d'Hadrien*: Hadrien's account of the life, death and cult of Antinoüs. First, Yourcenar's reading of the principal source for the period, the *Histoire Auguste*, is analysed in terms of the nature of its historical perspective, focusing on the use of a persistent visual metaphor for historiography and thus illustrating certain preoccupations in her portrait of the emperor Hadrian. In the second part of this chapter various aspects of the presence of Antinoüs are discussed: the account of the relationship between Hadrien and Antinoüs given in 'Sæculum aureum'; the decline of Hadrien into depressive remembrance; and the passage of Hadrien into partial equanimity at his Villa in Tivoli. Finally, the discussion of the presence of Antinoüs leads us to Piranesi's etchings of certain sites at Hadrian's Villa.

At the same time, the concern of this chapter is to investigate how reading the text through questions of the visual can lead to fresh perspectives about the text's preoccupations and organization. Discussion of the visual arts is at the service of an exploration into how issues concerning visualization and the visual are worked out in the text. This takes us away from what would risk being a limited discussion of Yourcenar's manifest aesthetic interests and focuses on the problems posed by the encounter with the visual in the text. In Chapter 1, we saw that this twofold approach can be fertile, since there the emphasis on the articulation of the visual took us partly away from a discussion of the artists in question, concentrating instead on issues arising from the textual expression of the impact of the visual. In the analysis of *Mémoires d'Hadrien* proposed here, these questions take us with Hadrien down to the underworld, although we must keep in mind and test out the bold last words of the emperor: 'Tâchons d'entrer dans la mort les yeux ouverts...' (515).

## Writing Roman History

The text 'Carnets de notes de *Mémoires d'Hadrien*' forms an appendix to the novel. The reader is given selected indications concerning Yourcenar's methods in her preparatory work on the novel and during its composition. Preparations were dominated by the continual search for the way to get as close as possible to Hadrian: 'Comme un peintre établi devant un horizon, et qui sans cesse déplace son chevalet à droite, puis à gauche, j'avais enfin trouvé le point de vue du livre' (520). Yourcenar is keen to emphasize how we need to acknowledge our distance from the emperor. She seeks to resolve this problem by making Hadrien recount his life in memoir form: 'Faire en sorte qu'il se trouve devant sa propre vie dans la même position que nous' (520). With so much attention given to orientating the book around Hadrien, the 'appendix' acknowledges that the presentation of the other figures has to be mediated via his viewpoint: 'Un certain nombre d'êtres dont on voudrait développer le portrait: Plotine, Sabine, Arrien, Suétone. Mais Hadrien ne pouvait les voir que de biais. Antinoüs lui-même ne peut être aperçu que par réfraction, à travers les souvenirs de l'empereur, c'est-à-dire avec une minutie passionnée, et quelques erreurs' (531). The passage invites the reader to recognize how the way Hadrien remembers has shaped the portraits of the other figures. The perspective applied to recounting the life of Antinoüs is endorsed and reference is made to possible errors of memory, while on the basis of the text and a later passage in the 'Carnets' (534–5), we can accept that Yourcenar is attracted by the historian Arrian.

Yet, despite the very engaging portrait of Trajan's wife, the possibility of portraying Plotina directly had been dismissed a few pages before: 'Qu'une femme se raconte, et le premier reproche qu'on lui fera est de n'être plus femme' (526). This defensive use of a jaundiced view of women as narrators is one of many curious assertions in the 'Carnets' and it is hard to see how Yourcenar would have elaborated on the portrait of Sabina. As for Suetonius, it is difficult to imagine Yourcenar detaching herself from Hadrien's reservations in *Mémoires d'Hadrien* (383, 433 and 483) if we read her remarks in the essay 'Les visages de l'Histoire dans l'*Histoire Auguste*': 'La même tendance à offrir comme caractéristique du personnage ce qui n'est souvent qu'une action isolée au cours de sa vie, le même mélange d'informations politiques sérieuses et d'anecdotes trop intimes pour n'être pas souvent fabriquées se trouvent aussi chez Suétone' (*EM*, 16). The explanations Yourcenar gives in the 'Carnets' concerning her methods demand scrutiny. Yet, in view of Yourcenar's guarded approach to clarifications about her methods, the 'Carnets' prove none the less to be surprisingly revealing.

This extract from the 'Carnets' largely concerns Antinoüs. It cannot be an accident that no mention is made in the 'Carnets' of Yourcenar's early project to write a life of Antinoüs. Antinoüs is now to be subsumed within the memory of Hadrien, whose wisdom and intelligence are praised, having eluded Yourcenar for many years; her account of the triumph in retrieving Hadrien contains, justifiably perhaps, no little self-congratulation. At the same time, we are reminded that we have read Hadrien's memories of Antinoüs. This chapter examines the 'minutie passionnée' of Hadrien's account in order to grasp what is meant by a figure being seen refractively.

The reference to mistakes in Hadrien's account suggests that his account might have been free of error; we may wonder, however, what sort of error-free version could have been possible. Earlier in the 'Carnets', we were reminded that History cannot give a definitive version of a life: 'Prendre une vie connue, achevée, fixée (autant qu'elles peuvent jamais l'être) par l'Histoire, de façon à embrasser d'un seul coup la courbe tout entière' (520). This recognition of History's limited powers does not preclude the idea that some essential truth can be ascertained by the writer. By a careful arrangement of the evidence to cover up the lacunae in the sources, the success of the historical novelist's project is within reach:

S'arranger pour que les lacunes de nos textes, en ce qui concerne la vie d'Hadrien, coïncident avec ce qu'eussent été ses propres oublis.

★

Ce qui ne signifie pas, comme on le dit trop, que la vérité historique soit toujours et en tout insaisissable. Il en va de cette vérité comme de toutes les autres: on se trompe *plus ou moins*. (528)

Elsewhere, as we saw in Chapter 1, Yourcenar dismisses adherents of historical relativism for their implicit assent to historical tragedies and for their neglect of the role of individuals in the course of history. However, her emphasis on the proximity of human biography to near-truth promotes a view that risks ascribing excessively privileged knowledge to that perspective. Also, as Paul Veyne argues in *Comment on écrit l'histoire*, the notion of historical truth can be refuted without lapsing into total relativism.[1] The coincidence of a lack of historical evidence and the weaknesses of human memory also risks veiling the

nature of the historical perspective that establishes the frames of reference in which Hadrien forgets.

No doubt, as the 'Carnets' suggest, contradictory sources can
combine to offer a convincing account of events in the Roman
Empire under Hadrian (117–38 CE). As has been shown by Rémy
Poignault, notably in his article 'Alchimie verbale dans *Mémoires
d'Hadrien* de Marguerite Yourcenar', Yourcenar's re-creation of
Hadrian's library (524) and reworking of the sources has produced a
text built upon a precise construction of remarkable organization.[2] Yet
the insight that has been acquired by performing 'les *Exercices* d'Ignace
de Loyola ou la méthode de l'ascète hindou qui s'épuise' (528) is
considered a guarantee of access to convincing complexity. Here the
nature of the interpretation of the historical sources involved is
bypassed, since the texts are read for their contribution to a picture of
human complexity rather than as products of political and social
complexity themselves. The detached third-person account of 'les
règles du jeu' (528) adds to the mystique.

Nevertheless, it is true that the 'Carnets' argue for a cautious
approach to the evidence of the intervening period: 'Travailler à lire
un texte du IIe siècle avec des yeux, une âme, des sens du IIe siècle;
le laisser baigner dans cette eau-mère que sont les faits contemporains;
écarter s'il se peut toutes les idées, tous les sentiments accumulés par
couches successives entre ces gens et nous' (528). With ambition akin
to Freud's, as examined by Malcolm Bowie in *Freud, Proust and
Lacan*,[3] Yourcenar sees herself adopting the archaeologist's methods in
her search for Hadrian: 'Refaire du dedans ce que les archéologues du
XIXe siècle ont fait du dehors' (524). While we should not be
pedantic about single statements of ambitious intention, when they
combine to form an ambiguous picture they can be problematic. The
reference to reading with the 'soul' of a second-century reader is
taken up in the long last sentence of this entry: 'S'interdire les ombres
portées; ne pas permettre que la buée d'une haleine s'étale sur le tain
du miroir; prendre seulement ce qu'il y a de plus durable, de plus
essentiel en nous, dans les émotions des sens et dans les opérations de
l'esprit' (528–9). The essentialism here can be a fertile form of
empathy, in the manner outlined in the rest of the sentence, but it also
leads us to be wary of how such an approach might veil issues of
interpretation. Later Yourcenar refers to the band of Hadrian
enthusiasts: 'de participer à cette relève de la garde impériale que
montent les humanistes et les poètes se relayant autour d'un grand

souvenir' (538). The two visual metaphors of the cast shadows and the mirror may turn out to be controversial, since the first may be apt for Yourcenar's approach, while the second may literally be obscured. The idea of a mirror makes us consider Hadrien's presentation of his own image and speculate on the author's confrontation with her own. The interdiction placed on 'ombres portées' places the reader directly in the context of Yourcenar's essay on one of the two principal sources for *Mémoires d'Hadrien*, the *Histoire Auguste*, which will now be discussed since it establishes the basic historiographical model of visualization involved in Yourcenar's creativity.

In 'Les visages de l'Histoire dans l'*Histoire Auguste*', Yourcenar discusses the inadequacies of this historical work as a source for an understanding of its period, from Hadrian to the period of the accession of Diocletian (284–5 CE). Starting from a position that reads the work as if it might offer an account of the Roman emperors after the fashion of Suetonius, Yourcenar is disappointed by the undeniable ignorance, flippancy and credulity of the source. She provides convincing arguments to show how these weaknesses indicate conformism and misunderstanding, although we need to bear in mind that this depends upon a reading of the text that expects it to provide a greater awareness of the historical process. For Yourcenar, the *Histoire Auguste* reflects a world completely detached from Hadrian's period and sunk in decline: 'Le monde avait changé au contraire au point de rendre le mode de vie et de pensée des grands Antonins à peu près impénétrables à des biographes déjà sur la route qui mène au Bas-Empire. [...] Spartien, et bien plus encore ses cinq confrères, appartiennent au contraire à une époque où s'éclipse cette tradition des vertus civiques et jusqu'au souvenir d'une morale d'homme libre' (9, 17). The term 'Bas-Empire' derives from Lebeau's *Histoire du Bas-Empire* of 1759; earlier Voltaire in his *Essai sur les mœurs* had characterized the period as decadent: 'Rome languissante, sous des empereurs cruels, efféminés et dévots'.[4] Although Yourcenar is critical of this view of 'Décadence', the term colours the perspective from the outset. While early in the essay Yourcenar acknowledged that the date of the text is uncertain, fixed 'au gré des érudits et des spécialistes' (6), and that the text may be the work of several hands, this recognition turns out to be partial, since she uses what was at the time of the essay an unresolved debate in order to dissolve these issues in her general analysis of decadence. André Chastagnol's comprehensive critical introduction to the text contains a survey of interpretations of the

*Histoire Auguste*, showing that even in 1958 most historians were becoming convinced of a date at the end of the fourth century and of multiple authorship. In Yourcenar's reading of the *Histoire Auguste*, the historical writing reveals the characters of the authors, who in turn reveal the decadence of the period. The perspective adopted in this interpretation deserves some attention when we are looking at the historical perspectives of *Mémoires d'Hadrien*.

The essay on the *Histoire Auguste* draws the reader's attention to the surprising and moving details that lie within the helter-skelter of repeated exclamation, eccentricity and turgidity in the text. In a sense, however, Yourcenar has to explain away these striking moments: 'Une effroyable odeur d'humanité monte de ce livre: le fait même qu'aucune puissante personnalité d'écrivain ne l'a marquée de son empreinte nous laisse face à face avec la vie elle-même, avec ce chaos d'épisodes informes et violents d'où émanent, il est vrai, quelques lois générales, mais des lois qui précisément demeurent presque toujours invisibles aux acteurs et aux témoins' (12). Again, the *Histoire Auguste* does read in ways Yourcenar suggests, especially in the case of the chaotic string of usurpations. Nevertheless, these writers are distinguished from the Antonines because they do not demonstrate an awareness of the preoccupation with decadence and decline shared by Plutarch, Marcus Aurelius and 'ces libres sages du monde antique' (*OR*, 530). The passage uses the question of authorship to suggest that this may explain weaknesses in consistency, but it becomes clear that the real weakness is the absence of a strong author believing in inevitable decline. This preoccupation explains why the humour of the *Histoire Auguste* is not caught in Yourcenar's reading. There is certainly no room for the author-trickster described by Ronald Syme in his books and articles on the text.[5]

Hadrien's obsession with decadence (his fixation on the topic is more than the anxiety of an ageing emperor) is a direct echo of Yourcenar's perspective; the nature of his memoirs has to be considered in the context of this authorial preoccupation and the pessimistic account of the authors of the source. The idea of decline recurs in Hadrien's thinking about his achievements in *Mémoires d'Hadrien* and in Yourcenar's accounts of the Roman Empire in that text, in the 'Carnets', in certain essays and in *La Couronne et La Lyre*.[6] In the essay on 'Oppien ou les chasses' (*EM*, 391–5), Yourcenar distinguishes between Hadrian's period and Oppian's a century later: 'Un souffle déjà barbare passe sur cette fin d'empire' (393). In 'Forces du passé', Yourcenar finds signs of regeneration in Rome and the West after the departure of the Huns, but her perspective is based on the fate of the city of Rome and, as mentioned in Chapter 1, this hopeful account of revival was written in 1940.

By the time of the appearance of *Mémoires d'Hadrien* in 1951, Yourcenar has witnessed, if mainly from far away, 'l'heure des réunions' at the end of the Second World War. The sections of the text devoted to Hadrien's plans for political, economic and social reform inscribe Yourcenar's concerns about the post-war world order. This partly explains Hadrien's obsession about stability and peace. Yourcenar is also fully aware that the Antonines were preoccupied with stability and legacy, both concerned to impose their cities and civic structures and anxious about the endurance of them; the text of *Mémoires d'Hadrien* resounds with this concentration on building projects: 'Elever des fortifications était en somme la même chose que construire des digues: c'était trouver la ligne sur laquelle une berge ou un empire peut être défendu, le point où l'assaut des vagues ou celui des barbares sera contenu, arrêté, brisé' (141).[7] Richard Sennett, writing on Hadrian's Rome in *Flesh and Stone*, stresses the fears about the longevity of the realm of stone and the need to make the authority and legitimacy of the emperor's power visible to all Rome's citizens; Sennett sees the Pantheon as the clearest expression of this rule by architecture. To convey the desire for permanence Yourcenar has Hadrien compulsively repeat his fears for a period of decline ahead.

However, as Paul Veyne argues in his preface to the French translation of Peter Brown's *The Making of Late Antiquity*, what is really going on in such accounts of decadence is retrospective projection: 'Il s'agit de changement, non de décadence. La fameuse décadence de l'Empire romain est une illusion rétrospective, une projection d'idéologies modernes ou contemporaines et une explication causale inutile. [...] l'explication causale n'est pas la seule forme d'intelligibilité.'[8] In *Comment on écrit l'histoire*, Veyne dismisses the relevance of the commonplace of decline and uses the categories 'hasard', 'matière' and 'liberté' to account for the 'intrigues' of history (p. 57 n. 4). In the text cited above, Veyne also calls the fall of Rome 'thème de la délectation morose'. Yourcenar, we noted above, forbade herself to cast retrospective shadows ('ombres portées') on her view of Hadrian and his age. Her essay on the *Histoire Auguste* suggests that she has not quite succeeded in this admittedly demanding task: 'ces historiens ne semblent pas avoir vu approcher ce grand événement, dont l'ombre

portée couvre pourtant toute l'*Histoire Auguste*: la mort de Rome. [...]
Ce n'est pas à nous [...] de nous étonner que des Romains du IIIe
siècle ou du IVe siècle se soient contentés jusqu'au bout de vagues
méditations sur les hauts et les bas de la fortune, au lieu d'interpréter
plus clairement les signes de la fin de leur monde' (12, 19). In the essay
on the *Histoire Auguste*, Yourcenar applies the idea of decline and fall
to history since Hadrian. In 'Images de l'empereur Hadrien d'après
l'*Histoire Auguste*, relue par Marguerite Yourcenar', Rémy Poignault
argues that Yourcenar's turn towards melancholy occurs after *Mémoires
d'Hadrien*, at the time of the *Histoire Auguste* essay in 1958. However,
there is enough evidence in *Mémoires d'Hadrien* and other texts to read
such a preoccupation in Yourcenar's work before 1958. In his introduction to *Genèse de l'antiquité tardive* (p. 7), Peter Brown regrets the
huge influence of Ferdinand Lot's 1926 study *La Fin du monde antique*.

Earlier, in Yourcenar's essay on the mosaics at San Vitale in
Ravenna, the tone is dominated by the theme of the 'nadir'.
Yourcenar argues that the figures in the paintings have turned away
from the world unnaturally (hence the connection with *A rebours* by
Huysmans at the beginning of the essay): 'Des fous, ces personnages
du Bas-Empire ont la manie écrivassière, le ressassement stérile, les
arguties sans fin, l'indifférence à tout ce qui n'est pas leur délire,
l'incapacité de créer' (488). By contrast with Yourcenar's position,
André Suarès, trumpeting the sensual passion of the mosaics, does not
see evidence of decay and death. In his essay on Marcus Aurelius, he
is suspicious of those harping on about decline and fall; he notes that
architecture in the time of Marcus Aurelius was limited to sewers,
aqueducts and bridges, such was the veneration for the Parthenon:

De là, pour ma part, que j'ai tant admiré à Ravenne un art brûlant, dans sa
fraîcheur, plein de sens, d'ardeur secrète, riche de ces neuves merveilles, la
musique et la couleur; et que j'y ai vu, le premier, un printemps de l'âme
humaine, contrairement à l'opinion des docteurs et de Taine, qui n'y a
rencontré que l'agonie, la pourriture et la mort. Mais Taine pense toujours
en stoïque et en décadent: il est de ceux que flatte la perfection de Marc-
Aurèle, et qui se flattent en elle.[9]

The robustness of Suarès's critique of Marcus Aurelius offers an
alternative view of that emperor, his writing and his period. We will
return to the difference, as seen by Yourcenar, between Hadrien and
Marc-Aurèle, but on the obsession with decline, Suarès deftly urges
us to be sceptical about accusations of decadence.

The motives behind the casting of an 'ombre portée' therefore need to be considered. It is precisely the motif of the shadow which dominates the 'Carnets' and recurs in the text. This motif needs to be contextualized before it can be recuperated in the course of Hadrien's mourning for Antinoüs. One example of the interpretation given to shadows and history is the account of the remains of the Aurelian Wall around Rome. Yourcenar cannot avoid seeing melancholic decline, but also dismisses the contemporary significance of the construction, using phrases such as 'les mieux temporaires', 'produit hâtif', 'immédiatement utiles et finalement futiles' (15, 16). In his scintillating and balanced study of the question of decline, *Décadence romaine ou antiquité tardive?*, Henri-Irénée Marrou reminds us that we must beware of overlooking the historical context of the wall:

en ce sens, les puissantes murailles dont Aurélien, dans les années 270, ceinture Rome, jusque-là ville ouverte—près de 19 kilomètres de long, 18 portes, 382 tours…—, sont bien symboliques de cette volonté de préservation, de conservation, de continuité.

Sous des formes et avec des modalités dont la nouveauté est certes frappante, c'est bien en effet la même civilisation qui se prolonge, s'épanouit, nullement 'décadente', mais avec une vitalité retrouvée et comme renouvelée.[10]

In the 'Carnets', Yourcenar refers to shadows cast by walls when writing about the floating and ineffable nature of our memories: 'Ce ne sont jamais que murs écroulés, pans d'ombre' (527–8). Remembering Hadrien, and thereby retrieving Antinoüs, involves searching amongst the shadows, but fortunately in *Mémoires d'Hadrien* they are not all signs of morose regret. In distinction to Marcus Aurelius' *Meditations*, where 'the art of living is more like wrestling than dancing' (VII, 61), Hadrien dances in un-Roman fashion (343) and unites metaphors of the body and the mind in his description of the harmony attainable by the Roman Empire, where both philosophers and dancers would have their place (390–1). In Hadrien's frequent celebrations in dance the reader perhaps finds him able to escape from Yourcenar's shadow and revel in his own.

Thus Yourcenar's attitude to her sources for the project of writing Hadrian's fictitious memoirs, as exemplified by her reading of the *Histoire Auguste*, allows us to contextualize certain statements from the 'Carnets de notes de *Mémoires d'Hadrien*'. This in turn suggests that her construction of Hadrien involves her own strategies of presenting his period; instead of distancing Yourcenar from Hadrien, the signs are that Hadrien's memoirs operate procedures very close to hers. They both involve a vigorous commitment to the possibility of retrieving a coherent view of the past, an obsession with transience, and an attitude to sources and to the other historical figures which slips into essentialism. This reading of the *Histoire Auguste* makes a vital contribution to our reading of the *Mémoires*, preparing us for the memories of Antinoüs recorded by Hadrien.

## Looking for Antinoüs

The aspect of Hadrien's visualization of Antinoüs that is central to this discussion is the way his melancholic outlook shapes his account both before and after the death of Antinoüs. Hadrien's view of his life posits a necessary framework of recollection and desire. This section studies the following aspects of Hadrien's presentation of his story: his persona as emperor; his use of mythological stories; his account of the encounter with Antinoüs; the role of death in his understanding of the departed lover; how to fix the lover in memory and to respond to his gaze; the colour of melancholy and the cult of remembrance.

First, let us look at how the emperor's persona helps us in our discussion of visualization. Among the many examples of his search for plenitude, we have, happily, Hadrien's dancing, as already mentioned, and his critique of stoical strictures on pleasure. Michel Tournier concludes his essay 'Gustave et Marguerite' with the themes of harmony and plenitude: 'Hadrien se présente à nous comme un cosmos harmonieux où ses chasses, ses expéditions et ses amours occupent chacune leur juste place. D'autres—des saints, des cyniques, des anchorètes—peuvent atteindre un équilibre comparable, mais c'est à force de détachement, de renoncement. La sagesse se veut plénitude. Le sage se doit de ne renoncer à rien'.[11] Otherwise the coldness of the final entry in 'Carnets' might cast its pessimistic gloom over the text: 'Notre commerce avec autrui n'a qu'un temps; il cesse une fois la satisfaction obtenue, la leçon sue, le service rendu, l'œuvre accompli. Ce que j'étais capable de dire a été dit; ce que je pouvais apprendre a été appris. Occupons-nous pour un temps d'autres travaux' (541). Hadrien, of course, reappears in Yourcenar's writings.[12] He also observes early on: 'je n'ai jamais compris qu'on se rassasiât d'un être' (297). His recollections of Antinoüs enable us to test this assertion in the face of other remarks which verge on a coldness and detachment comparable to the 'Carnets' entry quoted above, for example his remark on ideal courage: 'Celui qu'il me plairait de posséder toujours serait glacé, indifférent, pur de toute excitation physique, impassible comme l'équanimité d'un dieu. Je ne me flatte pas d'y avoir jamais atteint' (327). In the opening section 'Animula vagula blandula' he warns himself against an impersonal account of his life, since the latter would then be 'aussi glacée que les théories que je puis élaborer sur les nombres' (304). As Linda Klieger Stillman argues in 'Marguerite Yourcenar and the Phallacy of Indifference', the risk of indifference signals the complexity of the question of the enunciation of desire in Yourcenar's work.[13]

The next issue is Hadrien's self-presentation. The pages where he describes how he developed a method for negotiating a path through the conflicting requirements on his life are subtle and persuasive: he is required to proceed with the skill of an actor and the poise of an acrobat: 'Ma versatilité m'était nécessaire; j'étais multiple par calcul, ondoyant par jeu. Je marchais sur la corde raide. Ce n'était pas seulement d'un acteur, mais d'un acrobate, qu'il m'aurait fallu les leçons' (332). In a lecture in March 1994, Paul Veyne described the figure the Roman emperor was expected to cut as 'cette image abracadabrante'. Reading Hadrien's memoirs, we are drawn into feeling that perhaps his mental and political acrobatics would benefit from being brought down to earth, that perhaps the dancer needs to be tripped up. As he gets closer to power he has to have a façade for constant display and assessment by others: 'j'en voulais à leur affection de s'inquiéter pour moi plus que moi-même, de ne jamais voir, sous les agitations extérieures, l'être plus tranquille à qui rien n'importe tout à fait, et qui par conséquent peut survivre à tout. [...] Ma personne s'effaçait, précisément parce que mon point de vue commençait à compter' (340). 'Sæculum aureum' will afford a timeless holiday from this obligatory indifference, but it will depend on Hadrien how this is remembered.

In the engaging and skilful opening 'essay' on illness, sensuality, sleep, memory and self-presentation, 'Animula vagula blandula', whose composition is memorably described in the 'Carnets' (526), Hadrien expresses his sense of directionless, roadless helplessness when trying to recollect his own life: 'Je m'efforce de reparcourir ma vie pour y trouver un plan, y suivre une veine de plomb ou d'or, ou l'écoulement d'une rivière souterraine, mais ce plan tout factice n'est qu'un trompe-l'œil du souvenir. De temps en temps, dans une

rencontre, un présage, une suite définie d'événements, je crois reconnaître une fatalité, mais trop de routes ne mènent nulle part, trop de
sommes ne s'additionnent pas' (305). Despite being a Roman
emperor, Hadrien will come to accept that some roads have to lead
nowhere. Looking for himself in the river of memory, he experiences
the ambiguous 'freedom' of the unfixed image: 'ses traits se brouillent
comme une image reflétée sur l'eau' (305). Unlike Narcissus, Hadrien
does not see a clear reflection, either of himself or of the desired
other.[14] At this point in the memoirs, which, chronologically, must be
set just before Arrien's letter arrives at the start of the final section
'Patientia', Hadrien's inability to remember helps him, albeit un-
wittingly, to emerge from the narcissism risked in peering into the
sources of his desires. However, his memoirs will have to embrace
some fixed images in order to plot a recognizable story.

Hadrien is challenged by the power of images of the self and others
to fix memory's gaze. In Yourcenar's *Feux* (1936), the mythological
figures all encounter the distressing confusion and fixating power of
images of themselves and each other in their respective quests for love.
Many of them do not succeed in surpassing these images, which
confront them in each other's eyes, in mirrors and in their delusions.
They act out the game identified with regret by Yourcenar in her
lucid preface of 1962:

Ce qui semble évident, c'est que cette notion de l'amour fou, scandaleux
parfois, mais imbu néanmoins d'une sorte de vertu mystique, ne peut guère
subsister qu'associée à une forme quelconque de foi en la transcendance, ne
fût-ce qu'au sein de la personne humaine, et qu'une fois privé du support de
valeurs métaphysiques et morales aujourd'hui dédaignées, peut-être parce
que nos prédécesseurs ont abusé d'elles, l'amour fou cesse vite d'être autre
chose qu'un vain jeu de miroirs ou qu'une manie triste. (1053)

Very soon after Antinoüs' first 'live' appearance in the text, in
'Sæculum aureum', Hadrien embarks on a process of mythologization
which runs the risk of being just such a game. We will see that this
ambivalent account mainly rests on visual elements: it involves seeing
Antinoüs as an Ovidian hunter, as a (silent) sculpture and as a version
of Hadrien's own image before he loses faith in this 'golden age'.

Hadrien's reconstruction of the halcyonic days with Antinoüs has
been studied in detail, demonstrating a combination of a skilful use of
the sources by Yourcenar within a credible retrospective arrangement
by the emperor.[15] Rémy Poignault has also examined the functions of

the various myths employed by Hadrien.[16] Elsewhere in the text, Hadrien admits that he lacks originality as a writer (455); it is true that we have a very standard evocation of the time with Antinoüs. The latter is cast as a youthful hunter: 'Il y eut la mer d'arbres: les forêts de chênes-lièges et les pinèdes de la Bithynie; le pavillon de chasse aux galeries à claire-voie où le jeune garçon, repris par la nonchalance de son pays natal, éparpillant au hasard ses flèches, sa dague, sa ceinture d'or, roulait avec les chiens sur les divans de cuir' (407). Hadrien sets the scene in the mysterious forests of Asia Minor, with phallic stress on the strong, thick oaks and slimmer pine trees: Hadrien the mature emperor and Antinoüs the adolescent. The youthful hunter has conquered the emperor with the arms of the goddess of Love. Antinoüs can be seen here as both male beloved and female vanquisher, as ideal image and object of desire. This dual role assigned to Antinoüs is repeated in further mythological associations.

Hadrien is preoccupied by the rebirth and exploits of Antinoüs. At the culmination of the first series of visits to mythological sites, the sanctuary dedicated to Neptune is placed in the womb of a new temple. Hadrien thereby returns the god of the sea to his origins and, adopting the role as symbolic mother, thanks Neptune for the 'birth' of his beloved. A column is erected to commemorate Epaminondas and a young companion; Hadrien's parallel draws on his own experience of recalling a mythologized past of idealized male love: 'une colonne, où un poème fut gravé, s'éleva pour commémorer ce souvenir d'un temps où tout, vu à distance, semble avoir été noble et simple, la tendresse, la gloire, la mort' (408). In the 'Carnets' (530–1), Yourcenar refers to Plutarch's mention of Epaminondas' two companions. It is not difficult to see why Yourcenar has Hadrien reduce them to one; her text also draws on Epaminondas' sacred friendship with Pelopidas, whose life he saved in battle (as Hadrien saves Antinoüs during the lion-hunt), and on his renown as an elegant dancer and skilful musician.

In 'Sæculum aureum', Hadrien conflates the passage of time with the passing of passion; the previous reference to the hare as harbinger of tragedy—'Un lièvre, que mon jeune chasseur avait apprivoisé à grand-peine, fut déchiré par les chiens: ce fut le seul malheur de ces journées sans ombre' (408)—is now explicitly linked to commemoration. One of the first descriptions of Antinoüs involves a homo-nymically similar animal: 'Ce beau lévrier avide de caresses et d'ordres se coucha sur ma vie' (405). As in Ovid, and in Poussin's representations of his stories, hounds play with their master and *putti* trap a hare in reference to the forthcoming tragedy.[17] Hadrien's obsession with transience interrupts his evocation of his halcyonic days because his view of his time with Antinoüs is inseparable from his melancholic pessimism. The passage concerning Neptune and Epaminondas, therefore, discloses the force of desire motivating Hadrien's adoption of mythology. Hadrien takes us to a place where the mythical narratives reflect back the problems involved in his search for a picture of Antinoüs, difficulties that are not simply memory's obscurities. In 'Une exposition Poussin à New York', Yourcenar, as we saw, concludes with the Louvre *Narcisse*, calling it 'ce chef d'œuvre crépusculaire' (473), and identifies Antinoüs with Narcissus. The prism through which Hadrien sees Antinoüs at this stage is visualized: here we have to look in our search for Antinoüs. This site is Narcissus' spring: 'Des chasses nous entraînèrent dans la vallée de l'Hélicon dorée par les dernières rousseurs de l'automne; nous fîmes halte au bord de la source de Narcisse, près du sanctuaire de l'Amour: la dépouille d'une jeune ourse, trophée suspendu par des clous d'or à la paroi du temple, fut offerte à ce dieu, le plus sage de tous' (408). The picture of love constructed by Hadrien involves various elaborations upon the Narcissus story. The time of year is late autumn, the crepuscular season before the darkness of winter; the story of Echo and Narcissus in Ovid's *Metamorphoses* stresses the secrecy of the pool and, possibly referring to Apollo's desiring gaze, the absent sun: 'Around it was a grassy sward, kept ever green by nearby waters; encircling woods sheltered the spot from the fierce sun, and made it always cool.' Looking back to sources for his story, as in the evocation of Epaminondas, leads him to a direct reflection of the workings of desire and distress in his memory, functioning as mirror images on the surface of myth.

The god of love here is the male Cupid, whose arrows previously replaced the arrows of war. In 'Animula vagula blandula', Hadrien saw himself without regret crucified on the body of his lover: 'Cloué au corps aimé comme un crucifié à sa croix, j'ai appris sur la vie quelques secrets qui déjà s'émoussent dans mon souvenir' (296). The sacrificial bear is the female victim offered up to Amor: the sacrifice in love, which Hadrien argued for uncynically in 'Animula vagula blandula', is transferred onto the ritual of sacrifice. The mythical narrative recognizes the violence that prevails later in 'Sæculum aureum'. When Hadrien confronts himself in the spring of Narcissus, he sees his love as an idealized projection of himself and a feminized object of desire. In her study of Alberti's adoption of the Narcissus story, Cristelle Baskins argues that the surface image is read by Alberti as feminine, while the substance of the image is masculine: 'Whereas the mutual gazing initially posits male to male attraction, the feminine coding of the reflection qualifies the staging of homoerotic desire' ('Echoing Narcissus', 29). The frustration and underlying melancholy split the idealized Other into two. It seems likely that Winckelmann's writings on Antinoüs statues act as an organizing intertext here, since his interpretations involve an idealized ego, mythic manhood, narcissism and desexualized, draped statues, all of which relate to Hadrien's remembrance of Antinoüs.[18] In *Mémoires d'Hadrien*, we read how this visualized love can be seen as a stage and not necessarily fixating, and that memory can recuperate the Other from this process of projection and division.

Antinoüs' voice, meanwhile, is never heard when he is alive. In distinction to Echo, his is an embodied silence figuring in Hadrien's personal world of mythology. Hadrien is the master and Antinoüs the silent companion: 'Je n'ai été maître absolu qu'une seule fois, et que d'un seul être' (405–6); 'Sa présence était extraordinairement silencieuse: il m'a suivi comme un animal ou comme un génie familier' (405). Again Hadrien finds it difficult to retrieve a picture of the whole of Antinoüs, but he does manage a profusion of details: 'Mais les figures que nous cherchons désespérément nous échappent: ce n'est jamais qu'un moment' (406). His observation of the changes in Antinoüs leads him to consider that he has caused the transformation: 'La moue boudeuse des lèvres s'est chargée d'une amertume ardente, d'une satiété triste. En vérité, ce visage changeait comme si nuit et jour je l'avais sculpté' (406). Hadrien comes to fetishize a number of the parts of Antinoüs' body that he mentions in his portrait, particularly 'les jambes dansantes' (412; see also 406). Hadrien asserts that the 'truth' of their time together was that Antinoüs embodied the ideal form of beauty; this is another example of Hadrien confronting the problem of fixing an image of his lover. It is his memory, which has to rely on recollections of parts of the body, that releases Antinoüs from being a sculpted essence.

The idea of the 'sculpture' of lovers was explored by Yourcenar in her prose poem 'Sixtine' of 1931 (*EM*, 281–8). Many of her early ideas about love, beauty and time can be detected in the monologues of Michelangelo and his models: male homoerotic love is inseparable from solitude and loss, and only exists because of the inability of men to remain alone; women in general are weaker, faithless creatures who can only be improved by sculpture, but even then they are still not men; the fragmentary is closer to essential beauty; and ordinary heterosexual happiness is an impoverished delusion. It is in 'Sixtine' that we might look for echoes of the voice of Antinoüs 'silenced' in *Mémoires d'Hadrien*. Tommai dei Cavalieri, one of the young noble-men loved by Michelangelo, is given a brief monologue in which he ponders the differences between himself and the way Michelangelo has represented him in the Sistine Chapel and in sculpture: 'Le Maître, qui m'aime, m'a peint, dessiné, ou sculpté dans toutes les attitudes que nous imprime la vie, mais je me suis sculpté avant qu'il me sculptât' (284). Tommai asserts his independence from the forms that Michelangelo imposes upon him for posterity. Antinoüs also eludes his master when he tries to recall a whole re-membered form in 'Sæculum aureum'.

Tommai differentiates himself from the master and struggles to find a way to translate this perfection into action. It becomes clear that Tommai has substituted one fixed form for another and the only exit he proposes is death; the reader has been deceived if it seemed that the pupil would be permitted to escape from the artist:

Le maître, qui a plus que moi son génie, n'est en ma présence qu'un pauvre homme qui ne se possède plus, et Michel-Ange changerait son ardeur contre ma sérénité. Que faire? [...] Le morcellement de l'action me désabuse d'agir, et chaque victoire n'est qu'un miroir brisé, où je ne me vois pas tout entier. [...] Me possédant, quel enrichissement m'apporterait l'univers,—et le bonheur ne me vaut pas. [...] O vie, vertigineuse imminence: celui à qui tout est possible n'a plus besoin de rien tenter. (284, 285)

By relating Tommai's monologue to the relationship between Antinoüs and Hadrien, we have heard the voice of a young male object of desire (desired by lover-artist) expressing serenity, unfulfilled difference, stasis and the 'trompe l'œil-du-lecteur' of a flight into elusive mystery. It is difficult to agree with Camillo Faverzani when in an article comparing Michelangelo's poems and Yourcenar's 'Sixtine', he argues that the tone of the reflections on love in the latter is quite indulgent ('... *non sendo*').[19] 'Sixtine' is dominated by the voice of the master, Michelangelo, and is therefore very relevant for our discussion here. We have caught an earlier voicing of the pupil's view of his master 'par réfraction'.

In 'Sæculum aureum', meanwhile, Hadrien's thirst for plenitude allows him some satisfying criticisms of the timidity and sourness of stoical and cynical attitudes to love.[20] In pointed contrast to Zénon's meditations in the chapter in *L'Œuvre au noir* entitled 'L'abîme' concerning his short-lived physical relationships, Hadrien declares that he is unable to do justice to his happiness at the time and that it is therefore impossible for him to deny its cause retrospectively: 'Et je m'étonne que ces joies si précaires, si rarement parfaites au cours d'une vie humaine, sous quelque aspect d'ailleurs que nous les ayons cherchées ou reçues, soient considérées avec tant de méfiance par de prétendus sages, qu'ils en redoutent l'accoutumance et l'excès au lieu d'en redouter le manque et la perte, qu'ils passent à tyranniser leur sens un temps mieux employé à régler ou à embellir leur âme' (413). This remark is also addressed specifically at his young reader, Marc (Marcus Aurelius), who from an early age is a follower of the Stoics.

Part of Hadrien's struggle is to rework the commonplaces of classical literature: 'Mais là comme ailleurs les lieux communs nous encagent' (455). He succeeds in adopting the timelessness of the maxim, but his temperament is more suited to elaborations upon maxims than to the moulding of new ones for Marcus Aurelius. Montesquieu considered the role of maxims in the decline of the Roman Empire:

Voici, en un mot, l'histoire des Romains. Ils vainquirent tous les peuples par leurs maximes: mais, lorsqu'ils y furent parvenus, leur république ne put subsister; il fallut changer de gouvernement: et des maximes contraires aux premières, employées dans ce gouvernement nouveau, firent tomber leur grandeur.[21]

The notion of the commonplace, so important for Yourcenar, as for Antiquity, comes from the employment in classical rhetoric of visual props as 'aide-mémoires', as Frances Yates explains in *The Art of Memory*.[22] Hadrien's architectural projects expand upon existing buildings or 'common places', rather than inventing new structures or ways of thinking. Hadrien's concern for permanence leads him to attempt to articulate his outlook as clearly as possible and he therefore avoids dependence on the maxim for his thinking. In his controlled but elaborate essayistic style, he explores the labyrinth of the senses during the festivals and sacrifices leading up to the death of Antinoüs, whose impending suicide heightens the physical excitement and adventure for Hadrien.

It is when Hadrien starts to narrate the events leading up to

Antinoüs' suicide that he considers how his interpretation of events controls the access the reader has to the thoughts ascribed to Antinoüs in the text. Again the language concerns master, sculpture and masterpiece:

Mes remords même sont devenus peu à peu une forme amère de possession, une manière de m'assurer que j'ai été jusqu'au bout le triste maître de son destin. Mais je n'ignore pas qu'il faut compter avec les décisions de ce bel étranger que reste malgré tout chaque être qu'on aime. En prenant sur moi toute la faute, je réduis cette jeune figure aux proportions d'une statuette de cire que j'aurais pétrie, puis écrasée entre mes mains. Je n'ai pas le droit de déprécier le singulier chef-d'œuvre que fut son départ; je dois laisser à cet enfant le mérite de sa propre mort. (420)

Two forms of manipulation occur: Hadrien's fear of losing his happiness, coupled with his investment in familiarity with the mythical figure he has made of Antinoüs, leads him to protect himself by turning sadistically on Antinoüs; and the arrangement in his narrative of the series of hunts, religious rituals and sacrifices functions as an inexorable drive towards the death of Antinoüs

The first process is veiled in Hadrien's sculptural metaphor. A passage from *Feux* ('Patrocle ou le Destin') also deals with silence and the lover-beloved visualization: 'La haine inavouée qui dort au fond de l'amour prédisposait Achille à la tâche du sculpteur: il enviait Hector d'avoir achevé ce chef-d'œuvre; lui seul aurait dû arracher les derniers voiles que la pensée, le geste, le fait même d'être en vie interposaient entre eux, pour découvrir Patrocle dans sa sublime nudité de mort' (1074). Sculpture is evoked by Achilles and Hadrien to demonstrate their desire to fix the form of Patroclus and Antinoüs respectively. It is only possible to see the Other completely after death, therefore in retrospect. All the while, Hadrien is proclaimed more and more divine, with the continual thoughts of transience that accompany many of his zeniths: 'Ce fut alors qu'une mélancolie d'un instant me serra le cœur: je songeai que les mots d'achèvement, de perfection, contiennent en eux le mot de fin: peut-être n'avais-je fait qu'offrir une proie de plus au Temps dévorateur' (422–3). Although there is a passage where Hadrien asserts an exception to this habitual preoccupation (418–19), we are seeing that Hadrien's melancholy is the primary power at work in the process of refracting the passage of Antinoüs through the text of the emperor's memoirs.

Freud's paper 'Mourning and Melancholia' helps to clarify the problems being negotiated by Hadrien and connects these to our discussion above of Hadrien's narcissism:

If the love for the object—a love which cannot be given up though the object itself is given up—takes refuge in narcissistic identification, then the hate comes into operation on this substitutive object, abusing it, debasing it, making it suffer and deriving sadistic satisfaction from its suffering. The self-tormenting in melancholia, which is without doubt enjoyable, signifies, just like the corresponding phenomenon in obsessional neurosis, a satisfaction of trends of sadism and hate which relate to an object, and which have been turned upon the subject's own self in ways which we have been discussing.[23]

As we have shown, the course of memory's melancholia outlined here has started for Hadrien before his account of the death of Antinoüs. This is not simply due to the fact that Antinoüs is dead at the beginning of the text. Looking back over his life with Antinoüs, Hadrien can be seen to adopt myths which betray manipulation and division and to apply his knowledge of the conclusion to the story by retrospectively punishing Antinoüs for abandoning him. In turning Antinoüs into an art object, Hadrien reduces him to an impoverished image and is therefore acting in the sadistic way discussed by Sartre in *L'Imaginaire*.[24] Hadrien's abandonment of beliefs and of tranquillity voices his melancholic state.

First, Hadrien's loss of faith in myth. Although Hadrien espoused the Arcadian atmosphere of Greek legend in his own writing earlier in the text, where a succession of evocations proceeded from mythical place to mythical story in commendation and commemoration, Hadrien now understandably distrusts the evocation of literary predecessors: 'Je ne sus pas reconnaître dans le jeune faon qui m'accompagnait l'émule du camarade d'Achille: je tournai en dérision ces fidélités passionnées qui fleurissent surtout dans les livres; le bel être insulté rougit jusqu'au sang' (424). Later he will rediscover the relevance of the myth, but at this point he is succumbing, as he admits, to the Roman disgust for passion, considered as 'une manie honteuse'. He now considers love in the negative manner mentioned above concerning the quotation from Yourcenar's preface to *Feux*: 'l'amour fou cesse vite d'être autre chose qu'un vain jeu de miroirs ou qu'une manie triste' (1053).

In a passage reminiscent of the sexual politics of the Achilles and Patroclus stories in *Feux*, brilliantly analysed by Katherine Cullen King,[25] Hadrien focuses on Antinoüs' forehead and eyes in a passage of fixating gazes and sadistic punishment: 'Des caprices dangereux, des colères agitant sur ce front têtu les anneaux de Méduse, alternaient avec une mélancolie qui ressemblait à la stupeur, avec une douceur de plus en plus brisée. Il m'est arrivé de le frapper: je me souviendrai toujours de ces yeux épouvantés. Mais l'idole restait l'idole, et les sacrifices expiatoires commençaient' (424). The stylized motifs of whim, anger, melancholy and tenderness cannot hide the trouble experienced by Hadrien in sustaining the look of and from Antinoüs. Following one of the versions of the story of Medusa, Antinoüs' locks of hair have become serpent's coils, signifying the transformation that has occurred after the violation of the sacred aura of their love when Hadrien mocks Antinoüs' identification with the myth of Patroclus. The sight of Antinoüs has Medusan power and Hadrien can only break that stare through violence. Symbolic decapitation for both Hadrien and Antinoüs is to follow during the ceremony of self-emasculation in honour of 'la déesse Syrienne' (425).

Hadrien's path has diverged from that of Antinoüs by the time of the second ascent of Mount Cassius. Hadrien by then is concerned with his own investigations and Antinoüs is preparing for his suicide. In our search with Hadrien for memories of Antinoüs, we have so far looked at recollections in the text of Antinoüs alive, as companion to the emperor. Hadrien's adoption of mythical scenarios, or visualized dramas, structures his narrative and he very carefully sculpts the figure of Antinoüs in his attention to details and his attempts to control Antinoüs' thoughts. Before the tone changes, we recognize within the myths and the sculpting certain conflicts of self-representation and desire which escape Hadrien's careful arrangement of his memoirs. We have seen enough signs of obsessions about transience, loss and death to find it hard to accept Hadrien's assertion, near the end of Antinoüs' life, that the light remained constantly bright and shadow-free during his 'Sæculum aureum': 'Aucune ombre ne se profilait sur mes jours, ni la mort, ni la défaite, ni cette déroute plus subtile qu'on s'inflige à soi-même, ni l'âge qui pourtant finirait par venir. Et cependant je me hâtais, comme si chacune de ces heures était à la fois la plus belle et la dernière' (426). The reference to self-imposed chaos demonstrates too much control on Hadrien's part. In this passage he reminds us despite himself that 'ombres portées' are as much his obsession as Yourcenar's in the 'Carnets'.

It has become clear that those who are castigated in the 'Carnets' for saying to Yourcenar, 'Hadrien, c'est vous' (536), were pointing to a way to do justice to the arrangement of voices in the text of *Mémoires d'Hadrien*. Yourcenar's 'Carnets de notes de *L'Œuvre au noir*' also put forward her depersonalized ideal: 'Se désincarner pour se réincarner en autrui. Et utiliser pour le faire ses os, sa chair et son sang, et les milliers d'images enregistrées par une matière grise' (53). Linda Klieger Stillman suggests that this depersonalized ideal indicates a desire to hide corporeal affiliation, due to Yourcenar's disturbed narcissistic development.[26] Yourcenar's view of Hadrien as a father-figure supports the idea that the look at a source-spring acts as a displaced repetition of unfulfilled desire. Hadrien feels comfort in sources: 'Nos rivières sont brèves; on ne s'y sent jamais loin des sources' (321). The purity and mystique of the spring resurfaces in *Quoi? L'Eternité*: '*Le Trésor des humbles* et *La Sagesse et la Destinée* de Maeterlinck dont le mysticisme et le moralisme s'écoulent mélodieusement goutte à goutte, filet dérivé d'antiques sources qu'on sent à la fois abondantes et pures' (1243). Having looked at memories of Antinoüs alive, we now turn to remembrance of Antinoüs deceased.

### The Melancholic Cult of Repetition

Hadrien's memoirs, composed at the end of his life, are shot through with melancholic reminiscences of Antinoüs. We have seen how it proved impossible for Hadrien to loosen himself entirely from this perspective in his account of his halcyonic days with Antinoüs. There are stages in the process of mourning, since there are acts of remembrance for a dead lover as well as recollections of a life. It is just prior to Antinoüs' suicide and during the mourning of his loss up until the account of the Second Jewish War in the latter part of 'Disciplina augusta' that Hadrien's melancholia prolongs and shapes the process of mourning. For all Yourcenar's pronounced distrust of what she called Freudian psychology, Freud's analysis, as we have seen, is well suited to the case of Hadrien.[27] Yourcenar's text can also be seen to operate a cure.

   The principal feature of Hadrien's reaction to the death of Antinoüs is to displace his grief onto other people. As emperor, he is able to achieve this displacement by imposing a very visible cult of Antinoüs across the Roman Empire. Unlike his reflections elsewhere, Hadrien has no sense of excess when it comes to leaving traces of the beloved's face, which (as in Achilles' sense in *Feux* cited earlier), is easier to encounter now that he is dead: 'Sitôt qu'il compta dans ma vie, l'art cessa d'être un luxe, devint une ressource, une forme de secours. J'ai imposé au monde cette image: il existe aujourd'hui plus de portraits de cet enfant que de n'importe quel homme illustre, de n'importe quelle reine' (389). Hadrien's pride in the profusion of statues is self-regarding; he is naïve to believe that such multiplication of images means that they will necessarily be respected after his death. In the first sentence of the passage above he refers to a 're(s)source', repeating the act of searching for the image in the spring; as a form of 'se-cours', the use of art images sees Hadrien hastening to help himself. Hadrien then turns his attention to the place and function of these images within the myths and the cult he elaborates around Antinoüs.

Although the organization of a cult has to be simple and grandiose in order to have any chance of finding a place among the many cults of the Roman Empire, the cult of Antinoüs as presented by Hadrien is over-determined. Hadrien plans exactly how Greece, Asia and Egypt will worship: 'L'Egypte, qui avait assisté à l'agonie, aurait elle aussi sa part dans l'apothéose. Ce serait la plus sombre, la plus secrète, la plus dure: ce pays jouerait auprès de lui un rôle éternel d'embaumeur' (441). This form of prescribed mystery and secrecy can only lead to sterility. Hadrien's careful strictures enact his desire to lay down every detail of ritual. The mythical associations with which he smothers the memory of Antinoüs cover the main gods in the catalogue: 'Ce visage unique, je le retrouvais partout: j'amalgamais les personnes divines, les sexes et les attributs éternels, la dure Diane des forêts au Bacchus mélancolique, l'Hermès vigoureux des palestres au dieu double qui dort, la tête contre le bras, dans un désordre de fleur' (389). Hadrien is attempting to create differences within his eclectic picture of Antinoüs, but the danger of repeating doubles of an amalgamated image is present here in the image of a flower for the sleeping Hermaphroditus.

The idea of the metamorphosis from statue to flower means that the memory of Antinoüs in human form risks being supplanted by statuary and by literary versions of transformation suffering from the rigidity of doctrine. The metamorphosis resulting from a statue is spelt out more explicitly in comments on the marble piece by Papias d'Aphrodisie: 'Il y a ce marbre où Papias d'Aphrodisie a tracé un corps plus que nu, désarmé, d'une fraîcheur fragile de narcisse' (390). The use of the name Aphrodisia, both a town and an island where Venus was worshipped, works well in the text, while the narcissus flower figures Hadrien's preoccupation and, perhaps, his literary limitations as well. Narcissus does not leave Hadrien's thoughts for long. As in the formulation from 'Patrocle ou le Destin' cited above, the dead, naked figure is considered less distant, since in this form Antinoüs is easier to grasp. Nevertheless, the position of the departed lover remains precarious.

The main site of public remembrance is to be the new city Antinoé. In contrast to Alexander's bloody commemoration of Hephaestion, Hadrien redirects his passion for building cities to establish enduring monuments to Antinoüs. The city is later laid out with many references to people close to Hadrien throughout his life, but his first thoughts constitute a sentimental fantasy: 'Je trouvais plus beau d'offrir au préféré une ville où son culte serait à jamais mêlé au va-et-vient sur la place publique, où son nom reviendrait dans les causeries du soir, où les jeunes hommes se jetteraient des couronnes à l'heure des banquets' (441–2). Choosing this incident, we also need to remember that one of the impressive features of *Mémoires d'Hadrien* is the structure of the narrative which combines historical fact, conjecture and memory. One mention of a myth or reflection has its counterpart or several variations elsewhere in the text; the danger of a fetishization of 'significant' details by the reader needs to be remembered here. However, in the cases discussed in this chapter and in that of the city of Antinoé, these problematic and interesting passages are not isolated parts of the text. In the other mentions of Antinoé, there is further evidence of the melancholy and fixation on Hadrien's part which has been translated into all these cults (387, 441–2, 455–6, 509).

The two discussions of Antinoé referred to so far are similar in content. In the first, Hadrien mentions his general plans for the city and refers to the organization of the streets and the incorporation of his private memories. In the second, as mentioned above, figures from Hadrien's past are honoured. Thinking of Antinoé is as much a tour around an imaginary city as an exploration of his past and his body: 'J'ai choisi les noms de ses blocs urbains et de ses dèmes, symboles apparents et secrets, catalogue très complet de mes souvenirs' (387). As we have seen, the association of sites with images of the self is treated by Yourcenar in the early essay 'L'improvisation sur Innsbruck', where she expresses her unease at the way our knowledge of the past is fragmentary while figures from the past seem to have known so much more about their own lives. The signs offered of life's choices are too restrictive and final for the essayist, who declares herself lost in self-exploration: 'Que ne nous est-il donné de gâcher plusieurs vies! [...]

à force de traîner, comme un touriste qui voyage par ennui, dans ce musée catalogué qu'est nous-mêmes, nous finissons par nous déplaire dans ces lieux de féeries immobiles, galeries, ruines, bibliothèques, eaux gelées, miroirs mallarméens, sources où, lentement, s'est pétrifié Narcisse' (454). The temples and palaces of knowledge are sources for the writer and also surfaces for disappointing and alarming reflections of private preoccupations.

In the cult of Antinoüs respected in private at the Villa, Hadrien is for extended periods unable to escape from the unsettling vision of repeated doubles and elusive essences. As Rémy Poignault has noted in 'Antinoüs: un destin de pierre', the statues at Hadrian's Villa were cold simulacra, repetitive images, ghostly white figures;[28] in *Mémoires d'Hadrien* the emperor reports that the sibyll in Britain foresees 'un spectre blanc qui n'était peut-être qu'une statue' (394). Hadrien has been entranced by the images in his search for Antinoüs and he struggles to control them: 'j'avais envoûté des pierres qui à leur tour m'avaient envoûté; je n'échapperais plus à ce silence, à cette froideur plus proche de moi désormais que la chaleur et la voix des vivants' (464). Unsatisfied, he orders another statue that is a better likeness. As it was in the sculpted life of Antinoüs, so it is in the statues commemorating him. Jean-Pol Madou argues that Hadrien's memoir includes a course of initiation: 'Dans *Mémoires d'Hadrien*, le discours de l'aveu (confession/confidence) inscrit dans sa trame une quête initiatique dont la Mort détient le secret'.[29] In search of the essential form of Antinoüs, Hadrien is again comparable to Michelangelo in 'Sixtine'. On this occasion the latter ponders his statue of a dead friend: 'Sa beauté, que tant de gestes, de pensées, avaient morcelée vivante en expressions ou en mouvements, redevenait intacte, absolue, éternelle: on eût dit qu'avant de le quitter il avait composé son corps' (*EM*, 287). In another example of the conjunction of death and tangible form, this fixed form allows the master to possess his friend. In 'Sixtine' Gherardo Perini records his master's voice: '"On ne possède éternellement que les amis qu'on a quittés"' (*EM*, 284). In the practice of his private cult of worship for Antinoüs, Hadrien is caught by the cold gaze from the repetitive simulacra.

Lacan's analysis of repetition in *The Four Fundamental Concepts of Psycho-Analysis*[30] offers an interpretation of this use of repetition which connects Hadrien's form of mourning with the detached and split engagement with Antinoüs discussed above in the second part of this chapter. Hadrien's attempts to conjure up the ghost of Antinoüs in

statues can be seen as a search for a lost Other that was only ever
essentialized: 'That is why, in the misunderstood concept of repetition,
I stress the importance of the ever avoided encounter, of the missed
opportunity. The function of missing lies at the centre of analytic
repetition. The appointment is always missed—this is what constitutes,
in comparison with *tuché*, the vanity of repetition, its constitutive
occultation'.[31] The discussion of Piranesi later in this chapter will offer
further examples of occultation. As Lacan later remarks in the work
just cited, with the endless vacillation of the subject, no mastery is
available: 'The function of the exercise with this object [the 'objet petit
a'] refers to an alienation, and not to some supposed mastery, which is
difficult to imagine being increased in an endless repetition, whereas
the endless repetition that is in question reveals the radical vacillation
of the subject'.[32] Despite his interest in the occult, Hadrien's attempt
to control images of Antinoüs leads him to miss the private memory
sought when this is the result of such over-determination.

This can be seen to contrast with his construction of public
buildings, which would usually be considered to involve this question
of controlling interpretation by creating monumental and powerful
architecture. Hadrien provides another instance of his desire to order
and master objects in his field of vision, when he comments on the
colossal Egyptian statues at Memnon: 'J'étais excédé par ces figures
colossales de rois tous pareils, assis côte à côte, appuyant devant eux
leurs pieds longs et plats, par ces blocs inertes où rien n'est présent de
ce qui pour nous constitue la vie, ni la douleur, ni la volupté, ni le
mouvement qui libère les membres, ni la réflexion qui organise le
monde autour d'une tête penchée' (444). The enormous Egyptian
statues are unfamiliar to Hadrien who, presented with an endless line
of colossal figures, does not see the parallel with his own memorials
to Antinoüs. This is also the case when he endeavours to translate his
visions of Antinoüs in his dreams into appropriately huge monuments
to him: 'Les effigies colossales semblaient un moyen d'exprimer ces
vraies proportions que l'amour donne aux êtres; ces images, je les
voulais énormes comme une figure vue de tout près, hautes et
solennelles comme les visions et les apparitions du cauchemar,
pesantes comme l'est resté ce souvenir' (389). The problem with these
acts of visualization lies in the adjectives 'hautes', 'solennelles' and
'pesantes': they are too literal and again too formulaic. Hadrien's
encounter with these figures might be placed in the context of Freud's
paper 'The Uncanny', especially in Georges Didi-Huberman's analysis

in *Ce que nous voyons, ce qui nous regarde* of the visual processes
discussed by Freud. Repeated alienating statues will be beyond the
spectator's control: 'Le double, c'est-à-dire l'objet originairement
inventé "contre la disparition du moi", mais qui en vient à signifier
cette disparition même—notre mort—lorsqu'il nous apparaît et nous
«regarde»'.[33] The life-size statues of Antinoüs at the Villa will be a
hindrance to Hadrien until their independence or alterity beyond
mastery is acknowledged.

In the next section, we will see how the experience of mourning
brings about a less fixed translation of these dreams and visions:
'J'acceptais de me livrer à cette nostalgie qui est la mélancolie du
désir', Hadrien remarks on his return to the Villa after the Jewish War
(483). In the aspects of his cult of Antinoüs discussed in this section,
we have seen how in both its public and its private expressions
Hadrien has been unable to release himself from his desire to fix an
image of Antinoüs in the context of a set of myths, a set of rituals and
civic memories and a series of unsatisfying statues. In '«Portrait d'une
voix»', Pierre Brunel reminds us of the relevance of Flaubert's
celebrated description of the period between the decline of the Gods
and the beginning of Christianity, or from Cicero to Marcus Aurelius,
as one when 'l'homme seul a été', cited by Yourcenar at the beginning
of the 'Carnets': Hadrien is such a man alone and so to revive the
sacred he has to create his own religion.[34] We have been looking at
the curious prism in which Antinoüs is caught, remembered by a
melancholic lover for the period when they were alive and then by a
mournful emperor endeavouring to escape from his melancholy,
partly by displacement of his grief onto his subjects. We have seen that
again we need to read Hadrien's memoirs against his wishes in order
to catch the recollections of Antinoüs in the text.

## A Palimpsest of Shadows

Different features of the private and public acts of remembrance for
Antinoüs see Hadrien recover to a less determined and sterile state of
mourning towards the end of the text. Again, the wider context of
Hadrian's architectural projects helps to illustrate the visualization that
occurs in *Mémoires d'Hadrien*. This section argues that it is possible to
recuperate the problematic role of shadows cast across the view in the
text of the Roman Empire in the second century and the
representation of the emperor. By looking at Piranesi's etchings of sites

at Hadrian's Villa, through and alongside Yourcenar's comments on them, we are assisted in examining Hadrien's explanations of his self-restoration and remembrance.

After the inauspicious sacrifice at the top of Mount Cassius, Antinoüs refuses to allow the amateur chiromancer Polémon to read his palm, 'cette paume où m'effrayait moi-même une étonnante chute d'étoiles' (429). This passage is recalled later when the Egyptian priests responsible for Antinoüs' burial rites assure Hadrien that Antinoüs has obeyed a divine decree. Hadrien is sceptical and senses the void of death: 'Je revoyais en pensée cette paume lissée par la mort, telle que je l'avais regardée pour la dernière fois le matin de l'embaumement; les lignes qui m'avaient inquiété jadis ne s'y trouvaient plus; il en était d'elle comme de ces tablettes de cire desquelles on efface un ordre accompli. Mais ces hautes affirmations éclairent sans réchauffer, comme la lumière des étoiles, et la nuit alentour est encore plus sombre' (456). The text that replaces the signs of the stars on Antinoüs' palm is the main text of *Mémoires d'Hadrien*, Hadrien's letter to Marc; this is Hadrien's response to the effacement of Antinoüs caused by his death. This text placed next on the palimpsest also plots traces of Antinoüs' passage. At this point in the text, the form of this tracing is divined, but Hadrien does not yet see its nature: the combination of light and dark in the stars at night establishes the visual motif that will figure the restoration of Antinoüs for Hadrien at the end of his life.

A maxim from the philosopher and mystic Saint-Martin is included in Yourcenar's personal anthology, *La Voix des choses*: 'Il y a des êtres à travers qui Dieu m'a aimé' (70). Mystical value is ascribed to the vision of light passing through a confined space in Yourcenar's writing from the early 'Essai de généalogie du Saint' (1934; *EM*, 1678–88) to the essay on Dürer (1977) and *La Voix des choses* (1987). In the essay on Saints, Yourcenar takes the commonplace motif of crystals from the writings of the Christian Church:

Sa sainteté est un état d'intellect autant qu'un état d'âme: le phénomène est pareil à celui que nous offre, dans la nature, parmi l'opacité des corps, la claire épaisseur du cristal. (1679)

Nous voyons le saint se mouvoir dans un univers logique, translucide, mais fermé, et cohérent parce qu'il est fermé, pareil à ces sphères de cristal, qui, du dedans, peuvent sembler infinies parce qu'elles sont transparentes. (1687)

The crystal acts as physical substance and perfect conveyor of light; the world of the saint is seen as hermetically sealed but apparently infinite. The role of the visual in divine communion is given its central role, although for Yourcenar, in the essay cited above, it remains enclosed and does not surpass the verbal.

In the preface to her 1937 translation of Virginia Woolf's *The Waves*, Yourcenar's opening paragraph stands out in an otherwise derivative account of Woolf's writing (*EM*, 490–8). Yourcenar quotes Beatrice from Shakespeare's *Much Ado About Nothing* ('But then there was a star danced, and under that was I born', II. i. 313–14) to preface her interest in the vision that orientates Woolf's work: 'Si l'on s'arrête à considérer la profondeur scintillante de l'œuvre de Mrs. Woolf, sa légèreté rivée à on ne sait quel ciel abstrait, les pulsations glacées d'un style qui fait penser tour à tour à ce qui traverse et à ce qui est traversé, à la lumière et au cristal, on en vient à se dire que cette femme si singulièrement subtile naquit peut-être à la minute précise où une étoile se prenait à penser' (490). The rays of light from the stars at night connect the cosmos with the quotidian in the manner experienced by Hadrien at the Villa. A comparable passage in 'Sur un rêve de Dürer' posits the possibility that Dürer's dream gets close to representing a vision unmediated by the human eye, as we saw in Chapter 1: 'tel qu'il aurait pu se réfracter dans un bloc de cristal en l'absence d'un œil d'homme' (*EM*, 319). Moving from the source of the light to the spectacle of its passage through the text of his memories is a process brought about in Hadrien's inner sanctuary and in the chapels dedicated to Antinoüs at the Villa, a process that is unprepared and undetermined: 'Je pensai aussi aux chapelles égyptiennes que j'avais, par caprice, fait bâtir à la Villa, et qui s'avéraient soudain tragiquement utiles' (442).

In these chapels and temples, Hadrien provides a modest space in which to allow his mourning to occur. There is no pre-established cult for others to worship, nor a manipulation of myth. Memory and stone now combine differently in these places of visitation and meditation: 'Les chapelles d'Antinoüs, et ses temples, chambres magiques, monuments d'un mystérieux passage entre la vie et la mort, oratoires d'une douleur et d'un bonheur étouffants, étaient le lieu de la prière et de la réapparition: je m'y livrais à mon deuil. [...] Chaque pierre était l'étrange concrétion d'une volonté, d'une mémoire, parfois d'un défi. Chaque édifice était le plan d'un songe' (385–6). Silence faces Hadrien, as it does Michelangelo, but in *Mémoires d'Hadrien* light provides access to communion. We are seeing that

Hadrien's dialogue with Antinoüs is one conducted within: 'je pouvais désormais retourner à Tibur [...] reprendre en paix mon dialogue interrompu avec un fantôme' (497–8). Hadrien's equation of Antinoüs with the gods of the passage between this world and the next fuses his thoughts for Antinoüs with his own impending death. The passage of light through the heavens to his Villa also traces his own imminent departure. Thus, although he relies on repeating the invocation several times over and on the knowledge that the worship is also being conducted elsewhere, the association with Hermes and Bacchus is personalized in the context of how Hadrien now remembers Antinoüs: 'A Delphes, l'enfant est devenu l'Hermès gardien du seuil, maître des passages obscurs qui mènent chez les ombres. Eleusis [...] en fait le jeune Bacchus des Mystères, prince des régions limitrophes entre les sens et l'âme' (508). The place of the utterance of the oracle's ambiguous predictions is used to position Antinoüs at the threshold of this message, at the gateway from and to the world beyond. The palimpsest is therefore both a site of passage and the bearer of new signs in Hadrien's text of remembrance.

The Canopus is one of the chapels at the Villa where Antinoüs is celebrated. In the 'Carnets', Yourcenar relates how she came across Piranesi's etching of the Canopus (fig. 8). She applauds its insights into the emperor's mind: 'Le génie presque médiumnique de Piranèse a flairé là l'hallucination, les longues routines du souvenir, l'architecture tragique d'un monde intérieur' (523). Piranesi's wide view of the chapel opens up the dome to the spectator, allowing us to look, from a distance and inside, at the private world of Hadrian. The massive vaults of stone supporting what remains of the ceiling describe bold curves and cast deep shadows. Two massive 'jawbones' lead to this inner world. Yourcenar has the dome as an enormous skull: 'Structure ronde, éclatée comme un crâne, d'où de vagues broussailles pendent comme des mèches de cheveux' (522–3). The hall in the centre of the chapel leads the eye back through areas of light and shade to an elusive back wall.

The reading of the *Canopus* as inner world draws on the same passage from inner to outer described by Hadrien in the context of his completion of the Pantheon: 'J'avais voulu que ce sanctuaire de Tous les Dieux reproduisît la forme du globe terrestre et de la sphère stellaire, du globe où se renferment les semences du feu éternel, de la sphère creuse qui contient tout. [...] Ce temple ouvert et secret était conçu comme un cadran solaire' (416). The cosmic and global are

Fig. 8. Piranesi, *Hadrian's Villa, Tivoli: Canopus (Exterior)*
Late 1760s, from *Vedute di Roma*

represented here in the Pantheon, the combination of exposure and inner secrecy within one building. In the Canopus, the shadows cast are more secretive and figure the passageway to the next world and the visitation of Antinoüs. In 'Sixtine', Michelangelo sees a split between his work and nature's: 'C'est en quoi, peut-être, toute mon œuvre est contre nature. Le marbre, où nous croyons fixer une forme de la vie périssable, reprend à tout instant sa place dans la nature, par l'érosion, la patine, et les jeux de la lumière et de l'ombre sur des plans qui se crurent abstraits, mais ne sont cependant que la surface d'une pierre' (286). The split is healed for the architect-emperor when he is no longer anxious about the nature of the form he has created. Hadrien has built the structure but it is nature's work ('les jeux de la lumière et de l'ombre') that produces the return of Antinoüs.

He reads in Arrien's letter of the island of Achilles. Stories abound about Achilles appearing in sailors' dreams; Patroclus is also seen: 'Et l'ombre de Patrocle apparaît aux côtés d'Achille' (500). Now the myth, previously treated disparagingly, offers Hadrien a way to see beyond his own infirmity, since even the private sanctuary is not a sufficient cure for his melancholy (500–1). When he thinks of the island, however, he finds calm and catches glimpses of Patroclus ('j'aperçois Patrocle', 501). The emperor, recumbent in the sanctuary, is a complicated convergence of fears and desires: 'la lueur des astres se faufilait par les fentes ménagées dans la muraille, mettait çà et là des miroitements, d'inquiétants feux pâles. [...] Parfois, à de longs intervalles, j'ai cru sentir l'effleurement d'une approche, un attouchement léger comme le contact des cils, tiède comme l'intérieur d'une paume' (510). The palm of the hand is the palimpsest named again. Hadrien is alarmed by the apparent elusiveness of this imagined palimpsest, even if it seems close to some mystery. In his dreams of desire and recollection, discussed by Hadrien in 'Animula vagula blandula', Hadrien encounters a world akin to the floating movement of the domain of memory: 'Et pourtant, si enchevêtrés, si profonds sont ces mystères d'absence et de partiel oubli, que nous sentons bien confluer quelque part la source blanche et la source sombre' (301). Hadrien is again at the spring, where he finds the pale reflections of the stars in the previous passage. The spring acts as source and destination, and as the persistent sight of the visual encounter with Antinoüs. There is such a spring at the very back of the inner hall of the Canopus.

Fig. 9. Piranesi, *Hadrian's Villa, Tivoli: Canopus (Interior)*
1775–8, from *Vedute di Roma*

We find this spring if we look at the second etching of the Canopus made by Piranesi, this time done inside the skull, looking down the hall (fig. 9). A detail of this etching is included with the 'Carnets' in the illustrated edition of *Mémoires d'Hadrien* (328); here we may speculate on its particular function. Piranesi's key to the etching reads: 'A. Siti dov'erano anticame delle Fontane' (site of the old fountain room). The fountain-spring is set in half-light, behind the bold play of light and shadow. Narcissus remains at the back of his mind: 'une image, un reflet, un faible écho surnagera au moins pendant quelques siècles' (509). Antinoüs is at last assigned his role as Echo, but the projection is no longer harmful.

In this etching of the interior, the shadows are even bolder, emphasizing the passage of light inside from the sky above, making the interior as much an exterior. For Yourcenar, the space filled by the light exterior has the voluminous presence of water and she imagines her dialogue with the past as a connecting series of vases:

le grand rythme brisé des aqueducs et des colonnades, les temples et les basiliques ouverts et comme retournés par les dépradations du temps et par celles des hommes, de sorte que le dedans est devenu à son tour une sorte d'extérieur, envahi de toutes parts par l'espace comme un bâtiment par l'eau. Un équilibre de *vases communicants* s'établit chez Piranèse entre ce qui est encore pour lui le moderne et ce qui est déjà, pour lui comme pour nous, l'antique, entre le monument solidement établi dans un temps qui est encore le sien, et le monument touchant déjà à l'extrémité de sa trajectoire de siècles. (82; my italics)

In *Les Vases communicants*, André Breton adopts the chemical term to support his view that the worlds of reality and dreams are in fact in constant exchange and inseparable; his interest in science reflects his desire to investigate and uncover what is usually kept hidden and secret. However, Breton does not develop the chemical metaphor and he switches to the term 'fil conducteur' to convey the same proposition.[35] Yourcenar, meanwhile, is more interested in the idea of an experiment in which space and stone interconnect and interact in Piranesi's vision of this transhistorical chain. This use of water as an element with alchemical powers is repeated in a less grand manner in *L'Œuvre au noir*, as we will see in the next chapter; and we saw in Chapter 1, in Yourcenar's analysis of Poussin's *Le Déluge*, that the power of water is not imaginary. Yourcenar's visualization of dialogue with Hadrien is underscored in the last phrase by the return of the idea of decline, but the emphasis on *seeing* the passage of time is the striking feature.

Awaiting his own passage to the next world at Baïes on the coast to the south of Rome, Hadrien orchestrates the complicated set of visual practices and mythical narratives discussed in this chapter. The palimpsest of shadows has created a means of seeing where Antinoüs has a place in his impending journey. This figure has also enabled us to show how the text of *Mémoires d'Hadrien* recuperates itself from seeming fixated with the shadow of transience, a problem discussed in the first part of this chapter. It has been necessary to be sceptical about accepting his assertions earlier in the text about how he managed to resolve all contradictions in his over-worked amalgamation of personal and common mythology at the city of Antinoé: 'Ce lieu triste devenait le site idéal des réunions et des souvenirs, les Champs Elysées d'une vie, l'endroit où toutes les contradictions se résolvent, où tout, à son rang, est également sacré' (456). The real site of Hadrien's personal associations is the Villa ('la tombe des voyages, le dernier campement du nomade', 385). It is from there that an outlook motivated by the desire for plenitude (as Michel Tournier has observed) and by narcissistic anxiety is projected over his life and his empire.

We have seen how the concentration on fixed images of Antinoüs led to a fragmented picture of him for the mourning emperor. Under the influence of melancholia, Hadrien is unable to advance beyond the need to manipulate myths in his remembrance of Antinoüs, involving a process of projection and division. This chapter has proposed that it is possible to plot a course for the emperor out of his melancholy. This operates through the acceptance of the power of the visual in the form of unconstrained memory, offering a passage beyond the prison of narcissism and the unresolved condition of alterity. At the same time, in looking for a site of equilibrium, it would be naïve to accept what Hadrien says about his city projects without looking at the context of the myths he is trying to impose on the population in question. Hadrien was susceptible to naïvety, but the text allows us to see through his more simplistic solutions while also elaborating upon others.

Hadrien lies at 'ce carrefour sinistre entre ce qui existe éternellement, ce qui fut, et ce qui sera' (511). Pursuing his inquiry into knowledge of the next world, Hadrien ponders the spectral form taken by Achilles in Arrien's letter. He has given up trying to specify the origin of the phantom of the Other, content to accept it as a feature of the confluence of ideas at the crossroads: 'il m'importe peu que les fantômes évoqués par moi viennent des limbes de ma mémoire ou de ceux d'un autre monde. Mon âme, si j'en possède une, est faite de la même substance que les spectres' (510). In the etching of the interior of the Canopus, the other world is represented in two ways: the sky visible above, whose light fills the chamber; and the hole in the floor of the hall, leading down to an undefined and unknown space. This strange hole explains the absent statues: the disappearance of the architect has been accompanied by the removal of the statues. It acts as a Lacanian screen in this view of the Canopus: absence engulfs Hadrien, Antinoüs and the spectator of Piranesi's etching. For readers of Yourcenar, and spectators of Piranesi's other work, this hole leads to the underworld of the *Prisons*, which will be explored in the next chapter.

The aim of this chapter was to investigate the ways in which Antinoüs is visualized in *Mémoires d'Hadrien*. Reading the text through this perspective introduced us at the beginning to problematic issues concerning the nature of the historical vision being presented. The figure of the shadow of preoccupation led to an examination of the way the memories of Antinoüs reflect the anxieties and desires of the emperor. This inquiry has placed the Yourcenarian themes of fragmentation and duration in the context of the principal feature of the text, namely the workings of Hadrien's memory. It has been necessary to challenge some of Yourcenar's comments on her hero, but since this chapter has been concerned with the text itself, this issue has not proved central to the study. Reading *Mémoires d'Hadrien* with an eye on the processes of visualization at work leads to the recognition of how the visual, in the form of thresholds, passages and spectres, provides a conclusion to Hadrien's search for the articulation of how to accept death. The method of contextualization and development, applied to Yourcenar's writings on the visual in Chapter 1, has been pursued in this chapter, with due attention to the complexities of negotiating the visual in the text. Looking at two of Piranesi's etchings at the end of this chapter enabled us to show how the visual is employed in the text to effect its bold confrontation with death.

# Notes to Chapter 2

1. Paul Veyne, *Comment on écrit l'histoire* (Paris: Seuil, 1979).
2. Rémy Poignault, 'Alchimie verbale dans *Mémoires d'Hadrien* de Marguerite Yourcenar', *Bulletin de l'Association Guillaume Budé* 3 (1984), 295–321.
3. Malcolm Bowie, *Freud, Proust and Lacan: Theory as Fiction* (Cambridge: Cambridge University Press, 1987).
4. Voltaire, *Essai sur les mœurs*, ed. René Pomeau (Paris: Garnier Frères, 1961).
5. See especially *«Historia Augusta» Papers* (Oxford: Clarendon Press, 1983). In 1984 Syme gave a lecture largely devoted to *Mémoires d'Hadrien*: 'Fictional History Old and New. Hadrian'. The lecture does not refer to Yourcenar's essay.
6. In *Essais et Mémoires*, see 'Oppien ou les chasses' (*TGS*), 'Forces du passé et forces de l'avenir' and 'Ravenne ou le péché mortel' (both *PE*). In *La Couronne et la Lyre*, see the notices for 'Les derniers oracles païens proprement dits', 421–2, and 'Palladas', 449.
7. Examples abound in *Mémoires d'Hadrien* while we follow Hadrien's positive and negative phases: *OR*, 371–2, 375, 384–6, 390–1, 475, in choosing his successor, 491–8, and his final instructions, 505–9. The historian Colin Wells quotes Yourcenar's text (386) to illustrate Hadrian's major achievement: C. Wells, *The Roman Empire*, 2nd edn. (London: Fontana, 1992), 206. On Hadrian's architectural ideas, see Mary Tannero Boatwright, *Hadrian and the City of Rome* (Princeton: Princeton University Press, 1987).
8. Paul Veyne, 'Préface', in P. Brown, *Genèse de l'antiquité tardive*, trans. Aline Rousselle (Paris: Gallimard, 1983), p. xiii.
9. André Suarès, 'De Marc-Aurèle', in his *Xénies* (Paris: Plon, 1923).
10. Henri-Irénée Marrou, *Décadence romaine ou antiquité tardive?—IIIe–VIe siècle* (1977; Paris: Seuil, 1991), 27–8.
11. Michel Tournier, 'Gustave et Marguerite', in *Marguerite Yourcenar, SUD* (Marseille) 55 (1984), 76.
12. *Souvenirs pieux*, in *EM*, 757; *Archives du Nord*, in *EM*, 1031, 1038; the essay 'Ton et Langage dans le roman historique', *EM*, 293–7; and *CL*, 401–4.
13. Linda Klieger Stillman, 'Marguerite Yourcenar and the Phallacy of Indifference', *Studies in Twentieth Century Literature* 9/2 (Spring 1985), 261–77.
14. My analysis in the following pages of the passages concerning Hadrien and the spring of Narcissus was prompted by an article by Cristelle L. Baskins: 'Echoing Narcissus in Alberti's *Della Pittura*', *Oxford Art Journal* 16/1 (1993), 25–33. For narcissism in *Alexis* and *Denier du rêve*, see G. H. Shurr, 'Narcisse: le mythe caché chez Yourcenar', in *Roman, histoire et mythe dans l'œuvre de Marguerite Yourcenar*, ed. S. and M. Delcroix (Tours: SIEY, 1995), 411–18.
15. Rémy Poignault, 'Du soleil de Lambèse aux boues du Nil', in *Voyage et connaissance dans l'œuvre de Marguerite Yourcenar*, ed. C. Biondi and C. Rosso (Pisa: Libreria Goliardica, 1988), 195–206; id., 'Chronologie historique et chronologie du récit dans *Mémoires d'Hadrien*', in *Marguerite Yourcenar*, ed. A. Nysenholc and P. Aron, *Revue de l'Université de Bruxelles* 3–4 (1988), 19–31.
16. Rémy Poignault, *L'Antiquité dans l'œuvre de Marguerite Yourcenar. Littérature, Mythe et Histoire*, 2 vols. (Brussels: Latomus, 1995).
17. See Poussin's *Venus and Adonis* (Providence, Rhode Island School of Design) below, fig. 18.

18. See Alex Potts, *Flesh and the Ideal: Winckelmann and the Origins of Art History* (New Haven and London: Yale University Press, 1994), Chh. 4 and 5.

19. Faverzani Camillo, '...*non sendo in loco bono, né io pittore* [from *Rime*, no. 5]: Quelques notes comparatives entre les *Rime* de Michel-Ange et *Sixtine* de Marguerite Yourcenar', in *Roman, histoire et mythe dans l'œuvre de Marguerite Yourcenar*, ed. S. and M. Delcroix (Tours: SIEY, 1995), 177–88.

20. On the limitations of the Stoics, see also Paul Veyne, '*Humanitas*: les Romains et les autres', in *L'Homme romain* (Paris: Seuil, 1992), 428.

21. Montesquieu, *Considérations sur les causes de la grandeur des Romains et de leur décadence*, in *Œuvres complètes* ii. (Paris: Gallimard, 1951), 173.

22. Francis Yates, *The Art of Memory* (London: Ark Paperbacks, 1984).

23. Sigmund Freud, 'Mourning and Melancholia', in *On the History of the Psycho-Analytic Movement, Papers on Metapsychology and Other Works* (London: Hogarth Press, 1957), 251.

24. Sartre, *L'Imaginaire*, 229–33.

25. Katherine Cullen King, 'Achilles on the Field of Sexual Politics: Marguerite Yourcenar's *Feux*', *Literature Interpretation Theory* 2/3 (1991), 201–20.

26. Stillman, 'Marguerite Yourcenar and the Phallacy of Indifference', 272.

27. The best study of Yourcenar's lofty and misguided remarks on Freud is Josette Pacaly, '*Les Songes et Les Sorts*. Préface et dossier', in *Marguerite Yourcenar. Aux frontières du texte, Roman 20–50* (1995), 31–42. Her critique of Yourcenar covers similar ground to the analysis of Valéry's attitude to Freud by Jacques Derrida in 'Qual Quelle: les sources de Valéry', in *Marges: de la philosophie* (Paris: Minuit, 1972), esp. 356–7.

28. Rémy Poignault, 'Antinoüs: un destin de pierre', in *Marguerite Yourcenar et l'art. L'art de Marguerite Yourcenar*, ed. J.-P. Castellani and R. Poignault (Tours: SIEY, 1990), 107–19.

29. Jean-Pol Madou, 'L'art du secret et le discours de l'aveu', in *Marguerite Yourcenar: Une écriture de la mémoire, SUD* (1990), 54.

30. Jacques Lacan, *The Four Fundamental Concepts of Psycho-Analysis*, trans. Alan Sheridan (Harmondsworth: Penguin, 1991).

31. Lacan, *Four Fundamental Concepts*, 128.

32. Lacan, *Four Fundamental Concepts*, 239.

33. Didi-Huberman, *Ce que nous voyons*, 180.

34. Pierre Brunel, 'Portrait d'une voix', in *Transparences du roman: Le romancier et ses doubles au XXe siècle* (Paris: José Corti, 1997), 185–91.

35. André Breton, *Les Vases communicants* (Paris: Gallimard, 1970), 103.

# CHAPTER 3

# Piranesi and the Trace of Zénon

Yourcenar's essay 'Le cerveau noir de Piranèse' maps out the legacy of the creator of hundreds of engravings and etchings of Rome and a celebrated set of etchings of imaginary prisons.[1] The essay also invites the reader to search for the appearances of Piranesi in Yourcenar's texts. In the previous chapter we saw ways of reading Yourcenar and Piranesi together to discuss Hadrien's approaching death. The links proposed were experimental in the context of trying to find a method for placing fiction alongside the visual arts. Looking at two etchings by Piranesi enabled us to see the importance of the visual at the end of the text; the connection proposed between Piranesi's image and Yourcenar's text follows up the suggestion in the 'Carnets de notes de *Mémoires d'Hadrien*' concerning the strangeness of the etchings of Hadrian's Villa. In the analysis proposed the link was orientated around the visual dynamics of the verbal and visual representations of the Villa and established specifically between the way the end of the text works, a passage from Yourcenar's essay on Piranesi and the use of shadow and space in the etchings.

This chapter traces the passage of Yourcenar's writing through the visions of Piranesi by looking more closely at the essay, the novels *Denier du rêve* and *L'Œuvre au noir*, and the dream-book *Les Songes et les Sorts*. *Denier du rêve* and *Les Songes et les Sorts* serve respectively as an entrance to and exit from the interaction between Piranesi's *Prisons* and the investigations of Yourcenar's Zénon. The chapter is in three parts and traces this spiral of connections: first, a discussion of Yourcenar's analysis of the *Views of Rome*; next, Zénon's experiences and experiments, mainly in the section 'L'abîme'; and, finally, the trace of Zénon within and without the abyss, ending up *in loco carceris* in Bruges (306).

## A Dialogue with Ruins: Yourcenar and Piranesi

'Le cerveau noir de Piranèse' (*EM*, 75–108) sets out to offer a survey of Piranesi's work in four principal sections, a fact which has been overlooked by commentators who concentrate on the section devoted to the *Prisons*.[2] Yourcenar starts with a discussion of Piranesi's training and predecessors, emphasizing the solitary and somewhat eccentric passions of the man. Then the *Views of Rome* and *Antiquities* are discussed in terms of their representation of time. (The *Antiquities*, which are archaeological diagrams and detailed maps of famous sites, receive less attention.) Connections are made with the *Prisons*, the work which receives the most attention. The essay concludes with Piranesi's legacy. The present discussion will also encompass Yourcenar's analysis of the *Views* with the aim of prefacing the discussion of the role of the *Prisons* in Yourcenar's work.

Her essay includes several quotations from Piranesi and his biographers, concerning his 'archaeological' methods, great ambition and interest in all sections of Roman society. In his most recent study of Piranesi, *Piranesi as Architect and Designer*, John Wilton-Ely includes a passage from one of Piranesi's prefaces which covers many aspects of the discussion here: 'These speaking ruins have filled my spirit with images that accurate drawings, even such as those of the immortal Palladio, could never have succeeded in conveying, though I always kept them before my eyes.'[3] The statement draws our attention to the different visual processes involved when considering an essay on Piranesi: the impact of the ruins on Piranesi the artist (as far as this can be gleaned); the representation of these 'speaking ruins' of ancient Rome that Piranesi studied at first hand and whose 'voices' he some-how captured; the role of the essayist and interpreter in responding to Piranesi. Piranesi's remark acts as a starting-point for our study of the impact of his etchings on Yourcenar's writing.

For Yourcenar, it is Piranesi's obsessive attention to detail and to the play of light on the ruins that is the secret of his vision. In para-doxically enlisting the movement of the eye to try to fix the figures of the ruins, Yourcenar sees Piranesi trying to dig into the monuments: 'Il est facile de se représenter, sous l'insupportable éclat de midi ou dans la nuit presque claire, cet observateur à l'affût de l'insaisissable, dans ce qui paraît immobile cherchant ce qui bouge et change, fouillant du regard la ruine pour y découvrir le secret d'un rehaut, la place d'une contre-hachure, comme d'autres l'ont fait pour y repérer des trésors ou pour y faire lever des fantômes' (79). In speaking of 'l'insaisissable', digging and secrecy, Yourcenar uses Legrand's remarks (cited in the essay just before the above passage) to point to our experience of being drawn into Piranesi's etchings. This entrance into the etchings occurs when we follow his use of light and shade and search out its gradations. The reference to the search for treasure and ghosts at ancient sites (Hadrian's Villa is mentioned earlier in the paragraph) places Piranesi's search in a romantic context of adventure. The passage also articulates his pride in the achievements of Roman architecture and Yourcenar's evocation of the two chief ghosts resident at the Villa, Hadrian and Antinoüs.

Yourcenar pursues the idea of archaeology in her analysis of the speaking ruins. The fascination with stone detected in Piranesi leads her to argue that he is concerned primarily with Rome and its buildings in themselves and does not treat Rome as a backdrop in the manner of a history painter or landscapist. This direct confrontation with the substance of Rome sidesteps the commonplace theme of Rome's decline and fall. Piranesi's access to the 'secrets' of the ruins means an audience with their 'movement and immobility': 'L'édifice se suffit; il est à la fois le drame et le décor du drame, le lieu d'un dialogue entre la volonté humaine encore inscrite dans ces maçonneries énormes, l'inerte énergie minérale, et l'irrévocable Temps' (84–5). Here Yourcenar maintains her disregard, voiced earlier in the essay, for the Piranesi–Winckelmann dispute concerning the relative merits of Roman and Greek architecture by passing over the immediate intentions expressed by Piranesi in his polemical writings on Rome's antiquities.[4] For Yourcenar, the dialogue to which we may listen has broader frames of reference, involving human achievements in a natural and transhistorical order. The spectator sees nature and culture in symbiosis on the stage of Time. The visual experience of the combination of these forces is a recurrent motif in Yourcenar's thinking.

The progress from the position attributed to Michelangelo in 'Sixtine' to the position of Hadrien at the culmination of his memoirs, discussed in the last chapter, namely the abandonment of a strict division between the work of nature and the art of culture, is resumed and developed in the essay on Piranesi and in later writings. In the essay on the story about the sparrow in Bede's *A History of the English Church and People*, Yourcenar mentions the High Priest Coifi smashing idols and considers the consequent re-emergence of the mineral form as the appearance of the sacred: 'privant ainsi les musées de l'avenir de quelques-unes de ces statues à peine ébauchées, où la pierre pour ainsi dire remonte à la surface et abolit la gauche forme humaine, comme si le dieu figuré de la sorte appartenait davantage au monde sacré du minéral qu'à l'humain' ('Sur quelques lignes de Bède le Vénérable', *EM*, 278). This chapter discusses the fullest articulation of this struggle for visual supremacy and the positions of artist and interpreter in the engagement.

The grand dialogue has been given a setting, but it is necessary to consider both the visual exchanges making up this 'conversation' and the attention given to the harmony of the whole. Yourcenar tackles the nature of the visual experience of this dialogue by describing the ruins as double images. Again Piranesi's attention has created this drama: 'Cette secrète poésie métaphysique semble parfois, chez ce compatriote d'Archimbaldo, aboutir à un rudiment de double image, moins dû à un jeu d'esprit qu'à l'intensité du regard du visionnaire' (85). Yourcenar provides an example with which we are familiar from the previous chapter: 'La coupole effondrée de *Canope* et celle du *Temple de Diane à Baïes* sont le crâne éclaté, la boîte osseuse d'où pendent des filaments d'herbe' (85). In Yourcenar's view, when looking at Piranesi's etching we see a dissolution of differences, especially when the buildings elude their original designs and adopt the forms of the natural world: 'le bâtiment prend des aspects de scorie ou d'éponge, atteint à ce degré d'indifférenciation où l'on ne sait plus si ce galet qu'on a ramassé sur la plage a été jadis travaillé de main d'homme ou façonné par le flot. L'extraordinaire *Mur de Fondation du Tombeau d'Hadrien* est une falaise battue par les siècles; le *Colisée* vide est un cratère éteint' (85). The inclusion here of Hadrian's Mausoleum, via Piranesi's engraving of the massive foundations, allows Yourcenar to include the emperor—and her revival of him in *Mémoires d'Hadrien*—within this transhistorical scheme. We will return to the Colosseum shortly.

For Yourcenar, the problem here is the turbulence of these grand perspectives. In the later etchings at Paestum she finds resolution of the unruly power of the ruins to double as natural phenomena:

Mais la violence fait place au calme; la métaphore s'y dissout en une simple affirmation de l'objet contemplé. [...] Le temple détruit n'est plus qu'une épave sur la mer des formes; lui-même est Nature: ses fûts sont l'équivalent d'un bois sacré; ses pleins et ses vides sont une mélodie sur le mode dorien; sa ruine reste un précepte, une admonition, un ordre des choses. L'œuvre de

ce poète tragique de l'architecture touche à sa fin sur cette extase de sérénité.
(85–6)

The groundswell of Piranesi's etching of the Forum Romanum also invites Yourcenar's metaphor of the sea, the metaphor which persists;[5] the transformation into the mineral realm is again seen as collectively sacred; and the doric columns are recognized for their intended significance of order and repose.[6] The visual process involved in the trajectory from the 'secrète poésie métaphysique' to 'cette extase de sérénité' has sought to negotiate the problem of visual doubles by turning to the concept of indifferentiation.

Although the essay provides explanation of Piranesi's positioning of the spectator's viewpoint, the visual encounter with Piranesi's etchings is located in Piranesi's search amongst the ruins and in the metaphysical fusions found in the *Views*. The double image discussed by Yourcenar proves more difficult to resolve in terms of final serenity when its instability is considered. We may doubt whether indifferentiation, appealingly grand as an idea, sufficiently covers the way we look at one side of the double at one moment and then the other side at another; the passage between the two may be unsettling in a visual way instead of (or as well as) signifying a cosmic tragedy of meaning. This problem has an analogy in Wittgenstein's celebrated 'duck-rabbit', where a picture represents either a duck or a rabbit, depending on whether we see the ears of a rabbit ('listening') or the open beak of a duck ('speaking'). In his discussion of this image in *Picture Theory*, W. J. T. Mitchell suggests that the visual paradox should take us away from covering the pictorial with verbal explanations. He includes the duck-rabbit in his category of the 'metapicture' because it reflects on the nature of pictures, staging the picture's self-knowledge. Mitchell then places them in the context of the issue of how pictures might talk and look back at us:

That is why the use of metapictures as instruments in the understanding of pictures seems inevitably to call into question the self-understanding of the observer. This destabilization of identity is to some extent a phenomenological issue, a transaction between pictures and observers activated by the internal structural effects of multistability: the shifting of figure and ground, the switching of aspects, the display of pictorial paradox and forms of nonsense.[7]

Mitchell touches on both the problems with Yourcenar's account of the double image mentioned above: the twofold image is not as stable as we are asked to believe; the question of the impact on the spectator needs further consideration.

A good example of the first question is provided in the various views of the Colosseum (ill. nos. 10–13). The observation 'le *Colisée* vide est un cratère éteint' refers to the etching devoted to an aerial view of the whole construction (fig. 10). The metamorphosis detected by Yourcenar can be seen occurring; the erosion seems to carry on before our eyes. Trying to pin down how this sight is achieved proves elusive, since we are reminded of our distance from the object represented the closer we try to scrutinize the image. Certainly the play of light and shade works cumulatively as the eye passes round the building. Yourcenar points to this 'baroque' feature in Piranesi: 'Il lui doit aussi ces grands jeux imprévus de l'ombre et des rayons, ces éclairages qui bougent' (83). Meanwhile, in the etching where the Colosseum is placed behind the Arch of Constantine, the building appears like a resident ghost briefly lit up by Piranesi's watchful gaze (fig. 11). If we take up Yourcenar's suggestion of bodily parallels, we are struck by the pallor of the inner wall. Less spectral and more bodily is the inside view, as if from within the rib-cage, of the Colosseum (fig. 12). Yet the 'intérieur–extérieur' transfer is above all strange and unsettling. This third image of the Colosseum is as visually irruptive as any of the fantastic palace interiors of the *Prisons*.

In the case of Hadrien and the Egyptian statues discussed in Chapter 2, the repetitive image confused Hadrien because its deceptive stability had the power to elude control of his essentializing and humanizing gaze. In the case of the essay on Piranesi, the context of looking at the etchings underlines the necessary relaxation of the controlling gaze. Georges Didi-Huberman's *Ce que nous voyons, ce qui nous regarde* is again relevant here, especially for the second question of the nature of our distance from the visual image. Didi-Huberman uses the term 'double distance' for the space between spectator and object, understood, following Merleau-Ponty, in terms of 'profondeur': 'On peut dire en effet que l'objet visuel, dans l'expérience de la profondeur, se donne à distance; mais on ne peut pas dire que cette distance elle-même soit clairement donnée.'[8] Reading Yourcenar on Piranesi's visionary views of metamorphosis between the constructions of culture and those of nature, we need to consider how she treats our distance from the etchings.

Compared with the process of visualization outlined in *Mémoires d'Hadrien*, there is a different form of visual negotiation of alterity in

Fig. 10. Piranesi, *Colosseum*
*c.*1775–8, from *Vedute di Roma*

Fig. 11. Piranesi, *Arch of Constantine (with Colosseum)*
Early 1750s, from *Vedute di Roma*

Fig. 12. Piranesi, *Colosseum, Interior*
Late 1760s, from *Vedute di Roma*

*L'Œuvre au noir.* That is partly absent from Yourcenar's discussion of Piranesi, where the artist is considered to be wholly immersed in the edifices which he is representing. Piranesi's etchings, meanwhile, can be approached via more problematic visual processes. The baroque figuration of the visual discussed by Christine Buci-Glucksmann in *La Folie du voir: de l'esthétique baroque* stresses the relevance of alterity: 'Le Regard, porté à son état d'incandescence, y est toujours puissance d'altération. Une sorte de séduction mortifère y règne, oscillant entre l'*éclat* de l'apparaître et ce regard «empierré» et «empierrant», cette mise en pièce et pierre du corps d'amour.'[9] The intensity, power and attraction found in Piranesi by Yourcenar are all here, but the question of alterity draws our attention to the unsettling wavering between spectator and etching and the disruptive instability inherent to the representation. These features are apparently glossed over in the essay. Without neglecting the potential problems in the essay's desire for resolution, it is still possible to trace a passage in Yourcenar's texts where these problems are confronted. This may be done by finding ways of reading the shift of attention from the *Views* to the *Prisons*, in the essay, in *Denier du rêve* and in *L'Œuvre au noir*. In our discussion of Zénon's investigations in the next section, we will return to Buci-Glucksmann's variation on the Medusan gaze of the Other.

In the analysis and definition given of Baroque in the essay, Yourcenar, as we noted above concerning the Colosseum, includes the unexpected effects of light. Her main exposition of Baroque features focuses on the *Views*: 'C'est au baroque qu'il doit, dans les *Vues de Rome*, ces soudaines ruptures d'équilibre, ce réajustement très volontaire des perspectives, cette analyse des masses qui a été à son heure une conquête aussi considérable que plus tard l'analyse de la lumière par les Impressionnistes' (82–3). Yourcenar does cover the intended visual effect of surprise, movement and invention caused by Piranesi's techniques. In her essay, she offers examples of these alterations and disruptions (81–3). We could add to them the dramatic close-up of the exterior of the higher side of the *Coliseum* (fig. 13), which must be the 'fastest' etching by Piranesi, where the arches race back and forth and towards the spectator. In *Baroque and Rococo*, Germaine Bazin defines the characteristics of the Baroque as, among many others, flux, open-endedness, movement and emotion.[10] Bazin also discusses the way the artists of the Baroque handled the integration of subjects in space. These qualities are combined in the Baroque aspect of the Rome of *Denier du rêve*, which Yourcenar

Fig. 13. Piranesi, *Colosseum*
c.1761, from *Vedute di Roma*

mentions in one of her letters to Léonie Siret ('Lettres à Mlle. S.', 190). Here we can see how Yourcenar's work in the 1950s reflected the scholarly introduction of baroque studies into France at the time of the ascendancy of phenomenology and existentialism. According to Yourcenar's chronology of her work, the substantial revision of this novel took place in 1958–9 (*OR*, p. xxvii), while the essay was written in 1959–61 (*EM*, 108). Looking at *Denier du rêve* enables us to put together an account of the passage from external *Views* to internal *Prisons*.

In the 1934 version of *Denier du rêve*, in his excited but cynical tirades to Marcella concerning her plan to assassinate Mussolini, Massimo invokes the ghosts of Mary Magdalen, Electra, Charlotte Corday, the Jewish heroine Deborah, the African Christian martyr St Perpetua and Nemesis (138–41). In the same conversation he uses the word 'spectre' four times to describe the houses of Rome, their inhabitants and the generality of humankind (139, 142–3). In the 1959 version, these spectres are condensed into their role as the crowd passing through the streets of Rome on its way to hear the Duce. Massimo follows Marcella, convinced that she will carry out the assassination:

mais certain seulement de cette certitude démentielle qu'on a dans les songes. Elle marchait rapidement, le distançant de plus en plus, avançant à longs pas silencieux, comme si elle adoptait déjà sa démarche d'ombre. Elle déboucha sur une grande artère; les passants se multipliaient, spectres vains, bulles sans consistance, fétus de paille humaine aspirés par l'appel d'air d'une énorme voix. Le fleuve infernal s'élargissait, s'incurvait le long des façades noires en d'imprévus méandres, roulait dans ses flots d'inertes noyés qui se croyaient des vivants. Elle marchait, comme une Grecque dans Hadès, comme une chrétienne dans Dité [...] (236)

The inclusion of the spectres in the 1959 version and the emphasis on the dream world of the crowd expand the texture of the crowd in the earlier version (149). Marcella joins the dream world of the crowd's collective unconscious. The bodily metaphor of the artery operates the 'intérieur–extérieur' movement found in Piranesi's ruins, as we saw in the passage from *Mémoires d'Hadrien* cited at the end of the previous chapter. The crowd surges like the Tiber with the baroque curves and unexpected alterations of direction detected in Piranesi's etchings of Baroque Rome. From the dream world we pass, via the transformation of the Tiber into one of the rivers of Hell, down to the underworld—Hades and Dante's city of Dis—the architecture of both the pagan classical and Christian Baroque city of Rome describing the space in the world below.[11] The Tiber doubles as the Styx, which instead of circling Nether Hell now floods through its streets.

In her study of Joyce and Piranesi, Jennifer Bloomer uncovers an altar to Dis (here as god of the underworld) in an engraving by Piranesi from his polemical series *Ichnographia*. The site lies near the Tiber, across from Hadrian's Mausoleum, and is labelled 'Terentus occulens aram Ditis et Proserpinae'. Bloomer notes that the Terentus was the site of the secular games:

The site of the [GAME]s occludes a means of access to the dark void beneath it. This forms a point of connection in 'The Eternal City' to a subterranean labyrinth of which the overlying city is an iteration. The en[CRYPT]ed underworld, the world beyond the real, with its sevenfold, labyrinthine geography, is the unknown that can be reached through the known, the city labyrinth above. Piranesi's crater is a Viconian keyhole, a Freudian screen.[12]

Bloomer is right to emphasize the occlusion since in the plate the word 'occulens' is uncannily inscribed over the ghostly, light-toned centre of the site, which is therefore highlighted, while the rest of the words are written against a dark background. The site acts as a second mundus, the traditional place of communion with the gods below.[13] Marcella in *Denier du rêve* wanders in this double world; Yourcenar's discussion of Piranesi in her essay points out the motifs in the subterranean *Prisons* that are repeated from Piranesi's etchings of the city above. The principal subterranean figure in her work is Zénon, to whose experiences in the labyrinth below we will turn in the next section.

The dialogue with ruins that Yourcenar finds in Piranesi's etchings of ancient Rome is largely a dialogue which works along two axes. For Yourcenar the principal axis is located in the structures themselves, where Piranesi represents a flow of significance passing between man, nature and Time. The secondary axis is located when Yourcenar suggests that Piranesi's searching archaeological gaze opens up the monuments, energized by his mastery of Baroque techniques of shifting line and dramatized space. We have seen that this analysis of the visual experience of both axes needs some modification, since the site of the dialogue may express a less predictable process of metamorphosis (involving more of our gaze) and the spectator's engagement with the etchings needs to be distinguished from Piranesi's. These principal issues are tackled in Yourcenar's essay, but have demanded elaboration and further theorizing. In this case, the novel *Denier du rêve* permits us to see how aligning her essay on Piranesi with her fiction traces the figures of visual instability and ghostly but corporeal alterity discussed in this section. The main challenge to the reader, as is often the case with Yourcenar's texts, is to work out how points of theory are managed within the grand positions Yourcenar adopts. The essay on Piranesi demands that we look at what is involved in the negotiation of alterity in *L'Œuvre au noir*, one of the main critical issues raised by that work.

## Zénon: Notes from the Underworld

Une sympathie l'attirait vers les reptiles calomniés par la peur ou la superstition humaine, froids, prudents, à demi souterrains, enfermant dans chacun de leur rampants anneaux une sorte de minérale sagesse. (*ON*, 584)

'Qui serait assez insensé pour mourir sans avoir fait au moins le tour de sa prison?' asks Zénon at the beginning of *L'Œuvre au noir* (564). When looking for links between the novel and Piranesi's *Prisons*, we have to remember this ambitious prelude to Zénon's investigations. The primary 'prison' in *L'Œuvre au noir* is the city of Bruges and the chapter in the text which is most concerned with investigating the world as a prison is 'L'abîme'. It is an account, in a form resembling an essay or treatise, of Zénon's reflections on himself, on the people he has encountered during his tour and on the course and results of his investigations into the physical—animal, mineral and vegetable—world. Zénon only spends one night in a real prison and the sixty days spent *in loco carceris* during the trial are paradoxically presented as the time of his escape from the prison of the world.

As for the reptiles in the prefatory quotation above, Zénon too is subject to censure and persecution from his fellow men; he employs the protective strategies of coldness, caution and subterranean secrecy; the moving rings of his investigations trace a spiral in their enclosed search for insight and wisdom. However, the idea of a spiral takes us far ahead, since this configuration is part of the achievement of Zénon's experiments. Zénon negotiates the problem exposed by Derrida in his discussion of Hegel's *Introductory Lectures on Aesthetics*: 'La philosophie de l'art est donc un cercle dans un cercle de cercles:

un "anneau", dit Hegel, dans le tout de la philosophie. Il tourne sur lui-même et s'annulant s'enchaîne à d'autres anneaux. Cette concaténation annulaire forme le cercle des cercles de l'encyclopédie philosophique'.[14] In *L'Œuvre au noir*, we will see how the spiral represents the defeat inflicted on inquiry by the inclusive circle of knowledge. This is what Zénon fears as much as censure. We will also see what it means when at the end of the text this spiral stops at the cell.

Zénon is initially surprised that his life in Bruges should become an apparently restricted and repetitive series of taciturn days at the dispensary, with occasional herboralist excursions. Thinking that he could easily leave the place with his habitual expression of freedom, Zénon is none the less disturbed: 'Sa vie sédentaire l'accablait comme une sentence d'incarcération qu'il eût par prudence prononcée sur soi-même' (684). The light of freedom seems to desert him; he is beginning to undergo the alchemical *œuvre au noir*: 'Et pourtant, son destin bougeait: un glissement s'opérait à l'insu de lui-même. Comme un homme nageant à contre-courant et par une nuit noire, les repères lui manquaient pour calculer exactement la dérive' (684). The main dark chamber investigated by Zénon is inside his body, its labyrinthine arteries or 'waterways'. Here he is free to conduct his secret search, at the deepest point underground available to him.

Zénon speculates on the autonomy of his private underworld:

Il semblait à Zénon que le dégoût des raffinés et le rire sale des ignares étaient moins dus à ce que ces objets offusquent nos sens, qu'à notre horreur devant l'inéluctable et secrète routine du corps. Descendu plus avant dans cette opaque nuit intérieure, il portait son attention sur la stable armature des os cachés sous la chair, qui dureraient plus que lui, et seraient dans quelques siècles les seuls témoins attestant qu'il avait vécu. [...] Il tentait çà et là de projeter quelques lueurs dans ces galeries noires. (691)

These dark passageways are the secret site of Zénon's deliberations. His engagement with the spectacle of his secret inner world is part of a process of releasing the control he tried to obtain over the external world. In her 1969 lecture 'André Gide Revisited', Yourcenar spoke of the occupation and crossing of this passageway by the writer: 'l'auteur a pris vis-à-vis de ses problèmes une distance assez grande pour pouvoir adopter ce ton semi-impersonnel, parfois désinvolte, pour s'installer, pour ainsi dire, dans ce glissement entre ce qu'il y a de plus secret, de plus important pour lui, et le regard quasi extérieur posé sur les problèmes' (32–3). The 'glissement' is the means of access both to the clandestine experiments of the alchemist and to the inner world of the doctor-philosopher. This spectacle has the double configuration discussed above concerning the axes which operate when we look at Piranesi's work, including, this time, the areas of uncertainty discussed earlier: the metamorphosis undergone in the body of Zénon and the encounter with the signs and markings of the world.

This method and movement is set out in another talismanic early passage. Zénon, bored by the scholastic productions of books, imagines the world as a vast text in motion, moving from left to right and from right to left. The conflicts and scientific puzzles are figured on the pages of this text: 'Des ratures qui sont la peste ou la guerre. Des rubriques tracées au sang rouge. Et partout des signes, et, çà et là, des taches plus étranges encore que des signes … Quel habit plus commode pour faire route inaperçu? … Mes pieds rôdent sur le monde comme des insectes dans l'épaisseur d'un psautier' (15). Here the problem of reading the world is presented differently from the question of Hadrien and maxims in *Mémoires d'Hadrien*: in *L'Œuvre au noir*, the text of the world is the text itself. Zénon's life of inquiry is figured as undercover, within the thick covers and the dense texture of the book world. The directions in which he can journey are infinite. The psalter can be imagined as claustrophobic, enclosed density, or as unlocked, released and open to the elements.

The topos of the secret or hidden world is relevant for the tradition of textual responses to Piranesi's *Prisons*. The classic account is the description by Coleridge in Thomas De Quincey's *Confessions of an English Opium-Eater*. Coleridge probably had plate VII (fig. 14) in mind, but as Luzius Keller has shown in his study of the influence of his comments on French writers from Musset (who first translated it) to Mallarmé, it is De Quincey's text that carried the lasting impact of Piranesi.[15] Yourcenar's essay, cited by Keller, also offers a survey of Piranesi's legacy, in much briefer form, although she does not acknowledge this textual mediation of Piranesi's images. In his discussion of Keller's study, Georges Poulet concentrates on the spatialization of the writers' quests for self-knowledge. The space occupied by the writer has the constrained form of Piranesi's etchings and the descent into the matter of the self: 'A la limite, l'immobilisation est absolue, parce qu'il n'y a plus de différence entre ce monde de la pierre où il rôde et la pierre qu'il devient en ne bougeant plus. [...] La prison parfaite est celle où il n'y a plus de prisonnier, où le prisonnier est devenu la pierre même qui le retient en prison.'[16] Zénon commences

Fig. 14. Piranesi, *Carceri VII*
Second state (1761)

his secret flight into the unknown of the labyrinth of inquiry in an attempt to break out from this threat of immobility. Yves Bonnefoy includes embedding and invisibility when he sets out some definitions of the Baroque in *Rome 1630*: 'La "dépense" baroque, c'est un profond enracinement. [...] Le baroque, c'est le passage dans l'invisible. Ce qui n'empêche pas qu'il y ait, dans les synthèses qu'il tente, des restants d'extériorité.'[17] The procedures for negotiating and passing between 'enracinement' and 'extériorité' are the subject of Zénon's investigations.

Following our discussion in the previous section of Buci-Glucksmann's analysis of Baroque alterity, where the threat of immobilization figured the confrontation with the object that is at once distant and captivating, we can read Zénon's struggle in the context of his negotiation of otherness. These efforts will be discussed in the context of his hold on the spectacle of the world; the relationship between the self and the world can be investigated through the position of Zénon as spectator in the prison, with reference to the visual process experienced by the spectator in the Piranesian prison. His hermetic existence runs the risk of floundering in stasis, but his alchemical 'operation' allows him to discover a new approach to his surroundings:

Maintenant, renonçant pour un temps à l'observation qui, du dehors, distingue et singularise, en faveur de la vision interne du philosophe hermétique, il laissait l'eau qui est dans tout envahir la chambre comme la marée du déluge. [...] il faisait siens l'immobilité temporaire du gel ou le glissement de la goutte claire obliquant inexplicablement sur la vitre, fluide défi au pari des calculateurs. Il renonçait aux sensations de tiédeur et de froid qui sont liées au corps; l'eau l'emportait cadavre aussi indifféremment qu'une jonchée d'algues. (688)

In his version of the Piranesian prison, Zénon avoids the imprisonment discussed by Poulet by surrendering any attempt to fix the relationship between the self and the world. At this stage in the alchemical process of transformation, the threshold between the seeing subject and the spectacle is subverted. For Zénon, this separation is visualized as a space to be transgressed continuously and freely; it is not a process that he controls and directs. 'L'abîme' stages the struggle of the human will to relinquish its desire for power.

Yourcenar's contribution to writing on Piranesi is twofold. First, in *L'Œuvre au noir*, as we are seeing here, Piranesi's *Prisons* provide examples with which we can assess the underground experiences of

Zénon. Writing about the *Prisons*, Yourcenar directs our attention to their mathematical sublimity and strangeness. Discussing the story that the first set of the *Prisons* was created as a result of a fever, Yourcenar recognizes that Piranesi gained access to a vaster architectural kingdom: 'Elle a surtout augmenté jusqu'à l'éréthisme, et presque jusqu'à la torture, les perceptions de l'artiste, rendant ainsi possible d'une part l'élan vertigineux, l'ivresse mathématique, et de l'autre part la crise d'agoraphobie et de claustrophobie conjuguées, l'angoisse de l'espace prisonnier dont sont à coup sûr issues les *Prisons*' (88). Vertigo and mathematical infinity are also encountered by Zénon as scientist and surgeon in the enclosed space of his time in Bruges. Yourcenar's essay points out the violence conveyed in these etchings: 'Mais ces images qui rentrent par bien des aspects dans un genre à la mode en sortent délibérément par l'intensité, l'étrangeté, la violence, par l'effet d'on ne sait quel coup de soleil noir' (88). The Kantian 'Mathematical Sublime' seems relevant here, since Kant locates the sublime in a 'relative magnitude beyond evocation by mathematics' and argues that the sublime operates via 'a subjective movement of the imagination which does violence to the internal sense'.[18]

In the variations on Piranesi orchestrated by De Quincey, Coleridge, Yourcenar, Keller and Poulet, a common theme is the power represented in the *Prisons*. Yourcenar refers to 'les *Prisons* mégalomanes' (92) and 'ces fantastiques palais' (94). In her interpretation of the visual power of these etchings, the spectator who enters the *Prisons* is confronted with sublime sights and terrible sounds:

l'ouïe alertée perçoit ici un formidable silence où le moindre pas, le moindre soupir des étranges et diminutifs personnages perdus dans ces galeries aériennes résonnerait d'un bout à l'autre de ces vastes structures de pierre. Nulle part à l'abri du bruit, on n'est nulle part à l'abri du regard dans ces donjons creux, évidés, semble-t-il, que des escaliers et des claires-voies relient à d'autres donjons invisibles, et ce sentiment d'exposition totale, d'insécurité totale, contribue peut-être plus que tout le reste à faire de ces fantastiques palais des prisons. (94)

Here we have the second axis at work, and Yourcenar's second contribution to writing on Piranesi, this time when she comments on what seems to happen within the scenes represented, as if independently of our gaze. Looking at plates VI and VIII (fig. 15–16), we can see how Yourcenar finds these qualities in the vast palatial structures, although perhaps her interest in the function of sound in

Fig. 15. Piranesi, *Carceri VI*
Second state (1761)

Fig. 16. Piranesi, *Carceri VIII*
Second state (1761)

dreams has led her to be too literal about the connection between sight and sound. Rather than couple these qualities within a system of enclosure and menace, it is possible to dwell on the potential for accumulation and multiple lines of visual flight in the etchings; this is discussed in the next section of this chapter.[19]

Yourcenar refers to Huxley, who reached a similar conclusion about the human figures in the *Carceri*, for example in plates VI and VIII, and who also uses the metaphor of the labyrinth: 'They are, quite literally, lost souls, wandering—or not even wandering, but merely standing about—in a labyrinthine emptiness.'[20] For Yourcenar, the lost eye of the spectator and Huxley's wandering souls reflect an abuse of the power of creativity achieved by the Baroque: 'Sade et le Piranèse des *Prisons* expriment tous deux cet abus qui est en quelque sorte la conclusion inévitable de la volonté de puissance baroque' (100). At issue here is how we can clarify Zénon's experiments by reference to the vast spaces and alarming perspectives which confront the spectator. As well as the representation of a clandestine inner world of investigation and experiment, which, as we have seen, may be linked to the trail outlined by Keller and Poulet, the *Prisons* can be seen to figure the potential available to the inquiries of Zénon. In an essay on the *Prisons* that shares many of Yourcenar's preoccupations, Max-Pol Fouchet writes of a 'Valéryenne victoire du trait et du dessin sur la masse'.[21] Victory over himself and the world in the form of control of his thoughts, body and the laws of physics is Zénon's ambitious project. The reference to Valéry could apply to the 1919 'Note et Digression' added to the 1894 *Introduction à la méthode de Léonard de Vinci*, where Valéry elaborates on his picture of Leonardo's capacities as a thinker and artist, already touched on in Chapter 1.[22] The 1894 essay voices Valéry's fascination with the processes of thought: 'On voit que nous touchons ici à la pratique même de la pensée' (33). Zénon too is absorbed by the mind's activity: 'Les idées glissaient elles aussi. L'acte de penser l'intéressait maintenant plus que les douteux produits de la pensée elle-même' (686). 'L'abîme' incorporates Valéry's interest in Leonardo's writings on proportion and asymmetry. However, an important difference emerges in the two conceptions of the course of mental processes. While Valéry compares the mind's activity to the movement of the dancer, the presentation of Zénon's meditations rarely escapes the density of a closely argued treatise, although the alchemical process as cited above represents release and exchange. This attempted mastery of thought and vision, set against

the power of others to disrupt this process, is the central problem
encountered by Zénon in 'L'abîme'.

Valéry's writings on the visual arts are motivated by the search for
the articulation of artistic poise, impersonality and purity, not least in
his contribution to enthusiasm for the dance amongst modern
writers.[23] Control over the self and body is, for Valéry, a prerequisite
for artistic creation. A passage in the *Cahiers* draws together the idea
of control and movement, by connecting the thinker and the dancer:
'usant de son esprit comme celui-ci de ses muscles et nerfs; qui, perce-
vant ses images et ses attentes, ses langages et ses possibles, ses écoutes,
ses indépendances, ses vagues, ses nettetés,—distingue, prévoie,
précise ou laisse, se lâche ou se refuse—circonscrive, dessine, se
possède, se perde [...] artiste non tant de la connaissance que de soi.'[24]
Precision, solitude, patience and experiment are all features of Zénon's
investigations. Perhaps the main reason for the density they show is
that Yourcenar provides much more detail of the processes of experiment and of the objects of knowledge: both 'connaissance' and 'soi'.
Contrary to John Weightman's reservation about the text,[25] it is more
a question of thoroughness than of heaviness on Yourcenar's part:
*L'Œuvre au noir* explains the meditations as they work themselves out.

There are two areas of deliberation where Zénon struggles for
mastery: over his body and over his understanding of other people.
Although, as we saw above, he is prepared to leave aside the common
superstition about anatomical research, this boldness does not allow
him to loosen his desire for control over his body. Discussing, with
reference to Rimbaud's 'Noël', the balance between 'l'âme', 'l'esprit'
et 'le corps' in Zénon, Yourcenar acknowledges the emphasis on the
mind in the portrait of Zénon, although she also suggests that an
interaction operates: 'L'esprit domine davantage chez Zénon, mais
l'esprit est en quelque sorte activé par l'élan continu et presque
furieux de l'âme, et ne se développerait pas non plus sans les
expériences et le *contrôle* du corps' ('Carnets de notes de *L'Œuvre au
noir*', 41). Initially, however, this counterbalance provided by the body
and soul is consciously challenged by Zénon. In 'L'abîme', his desire
for mastery leads him to consider an uncontrollable flood of tears as
scandalous (690). Later, thinking about the young monks burned alive
without receiving the 'coup de grâce' of strangulation, Zénon's
distress leads him to weep 'à sa honte' (794). He has a similar problem
with sexual intercourse, which in his view undermines the mysteries
of erotic love, although his main complaint is that his mastery is not

assured: 'et il doutait à part soi qu'un acte si sujet aux routines de la matière, si dépendant des outils de la génération charnelle ne fût pas pour le philosophe une de ces expériences qu'on se doit de faire pour ensuite y renoncer' (704). The reflections on sex attributed to Zénon could have been lifted directly from Valéry's 'Note et Digression' in his study of Leonardo: 'La machine érotique l'intéresse, la mécanique animale étant son domaine le préféré; mais un combat de sueurs et l'essoufflement des *opranti*, un monstre de musculatures antagonistes, une transfiguration en bêtes—cela semble n'exciter en lui que répugnance et que dédain...'[26] The real danger underlying Zénon's aversion is the threat of the loss of power over himself to another person. Zénon needs to negotiate this problem before the freedom of the Valerian dance and the potential of Piranesian space can be exploited.

In the middle of 'L'abîme' there is a six-page section in which Zénon recalls the people he has known on his travels. These pages could be considered as a short treatise on the Other. Zénon considers the way his memory teaches him to avoid exaggerating his dependency on others and in turn his significance for them, but he also distorts the degree of emotional exchange in these relationships. Zénon realizes that this distance from others can distort, but justifies his perspective because of its ability to describe the detachment that comes with age. The problem with Zénon's account is that we realize that for all the stress on his mastery of perspective, his memories do less than justice to others when he assesses their actions from his grand viewpoint: 'Mais l'effort même d'évoquer ces personnes en exagérait l'importance, et surfaisait celle de l'aventure charnelle. [...] L'amitié ou l'aversion comptaient d'ailleurs finalement aussi peu que les blandices charnelles' (697). Zénon does not explain convincingly why such an effort is required in order to remember others; it may well be because he has to overcome his aversion to them. The involvement of other people in their contact with Zénon is then reduced to undifferentiated anonymity. To claim parity of encounter between the baker in Salzburg and 'la dame de Frösö' is to cover up his fear and belittlement of prolonged sexual and emotional contact (697). After this treatise, it is no surprise to read of Zénon's pleasure in coldness: 'La chasteté, où il avait vu naguère une superstition à combattre, lui semblait maintenant un des visages de la sérénité: il goûtait cette froide connaissance qu'on a des êtres quand on ne les désire plus' (704). Valéry's Leonardo is again an antecedent: 'Rien de plus libre, c'est-à-dire, rien de moins humain, que ses jugements sur l'amour, sur la mort.'[27] The idea of serenity in later life is a commonplace, but it is the endorsement of haughty disdain that limits Zénon's thinking at this point in the text.

In 'La conversation à Innsbruck', Zénon contrasts his sexual orientation with Henri-Maximilien's. After the latter's literary pane-gyric on women, Zénon implicitly criticizes his cousin's naïvety and states that he prefers to encounter projections of himself: '—Moi, dit Zénon, je goûte par-dessus tout ce plaisir un peu plus secret qu'un autre, ce corps semblable au mien qui reflète mon délice, cette agréable absence de tout ce qu'ajoutent à la jouissance les petites mines des courtisanes et le jargon des pétrarquistes' (649). At the end of the first chapter of L'Œuvre au noir, Zénon had declared that he was setting out in search of another person, 'Hic Zeno, dit-il, Moi-même' (565). Zénon's preference for solitude and secrecy is both subversive and introspective.

The question of narcissism is addressed by Pierre-Yves Bourdil in 'Portrait de Zénon': 'Zénon préfère se dédoubler dans le miroir plutôt que dans l'enfant. C'est lui-même, son propre contentement, qu'il attend d'un corps où il se voit, et dont il a gommé toute altérité. Le sexe du sage est simplement esthétique. On le domine. Après tout, le miroir "réfléchit" aussi bien que l'entendement...'.[28] His encounters with others form a series of repeated assurances of his mastery over sexual intercourse. Bourdil is referring to Zénon's vision of a child he might have procreated with the lady of Frösö, to his encounter with the Florentine mirror at the end of 'La vie errante', the first part of the novel, and to his experiment with masturbation in 'L'abîme'. The mirror reflects the multiple images of Zénon in the novel (there are twenty mirror images for the twenty-six ways used to refer to Zénon in the text: philosophe, philosophe-médécin, médecin, médecin-chirurgien, chirurgien, chirurgien-barbier, accusé, inculpé, condamné, voyageur, sorcier, alchimiste, sodomite, clerc, étudiant, prisonnier, pèlerin, masse brunâtre, enfant, louveteau, artificier, docteur, homme de l'art, herboriste, Sébastien Théus and Zénon) and also the problem of sameness and alterity. The reference to the 'laughing philosopher', Democritus, brings a sour smile from Zénon.[29]

Another instance of the visual encounter with alterity occurs during the remarkable description by Henri-Maximilien of his exper-ience of looking at a statue of Venus. The passage recalls Hadrien's difficulties with the elusive resemblances of statues. For Henri-Maximilien the statue has the power to transform his conception of pleasure and mortality. He is obliged to face the rupture and separation that the visual threatens to inflict: 'Vous parlez de statues; je sais peu de plaisir plus exquis que celui de contempler la Vénus de marbre, celle que mon bon ami le cardinal Caraffa conserve dans sa galérie napolitaine: ses formes blanches sont si belles qu'elles nettoient le cœur de tout désir profane et donnent envie de pleurer. Mais que je m'efforce à la regarder une moitié de quart d'heure, et ni mes yeux ni mon esprit ne la voient plus' (652). First, Henri-Maximilien is transfixed by the formal perfection of the statue and is so filled by this beauty that his body responds with a physical expression of upheaval. When he tries to grasp the statue in all its detail, he sees as if his eyes have been shut. Henri-Maximilien makes sense of his experience by suggesting that his confusion is caused by the melancholic Platonism which finds the supreme Good in a different world.[30]

This passage challenges any unifying view of the visual in *L'Œuvre au noir*. Zénon does not respond to the confusion expressed by his cousin. He follows Henri-Maximilien as the latter arrives at his conclusion, but does not agree with the Platonist argument: '—*Sempiterna Temptatio*, fit Zénon' (117). In 'conversation' with Louis Aragon, Jean Cocteau discusses this question by imagining the poverty of a Platonist response to pictorial colour: 'Peut-être faut-il mettre cette concordance sur le compte d'un phénomène comparable à la sexualité. Il se produirait devant certaines œuvres, j'ose dire une érection morale, et si elle ne se produisait pas, il n'y aurait que platonisme et dilettantisme.'[31] Although it does not occur in 'L'abîme', the stakes of the conversation between Henri-Maximilien and Zénon need to be considered in the context of the visual labyrinth-abyss negotiated by Zénon in the novel. Didi-Huberman, using the visual spectacle of the dream as a paradigm in *Devant l'image*, wishes to include the combination of what is recalled after the dream with what is forgotten in order to do justice to the impact of the visual:

Autrement dit: l'événement visuel du tableau n'advient qu'à partir de cette déchirure qui sépare devant nous ce qui est représenté comme souvenu, et *tout ce qui se présente comme oubli*. Les plus belles esthétiques—les plus désespérées aussi, puisqu'elles sont en général vouées à l'échec ou à la folie— seraient donc les esthétiques qui, pour s'ouvrir tout à fait à la dimension du visuel, voudraient que l'on ferme les yeux devant l'image, afin de ne plus la voir, mais de la regarder seulement, et ne plus oublier ce que Blanchot nommait "l'*autre* nuit", la nuit d'Orphée. De telles esthétiques sont toujours singulières, se dénudent dans le non-savoir, et n'hésitent jamais à nommer *vision* ce que nul éveillé ne voit.[32]

These remarks on the pictorial image are applicable to the sculpture admired by Henri-Maximilien. In his failure to grasp the statue, he is forced to close his eyes. He has to acknowledge the limit of his capacity to know; Zénon becomes more aware of the limits of knowledge in the novel. As Didi-Huberman remarks in a footnote to the page quoted above, the 'night' of vision has a parallel in the mystical contact with the Other (God). Henri-Maximilien's encounter with the excessively beautiful statue can be understood in terms of a negative theory of aesthetics, whatever his own conclusion given in the text. Zénon himself is unwilling to attribute such significance just to a work of art, though in his philosophical, medical and alchemical investigations a negative aesthetics or mystical configuration of the visual may be detected. In the next section of this chapter we will consider ways in which Zénon's reflections on colour lead him to recognize the visual challenge of alterity.

As we have seen in our discussion of Piranesi, Yourcenar's essay and Valéry, ways of confronting the visual dilemma do not have to be framed by Zénon's arrangement of his investigations. In the chapter 'L'abîme', the dissolution of the categories of time, place and substance is an attempt to stretch the gaps in the wall surrounding the human mind (700). The wall itself loses its solidity, since objects no longer depend on their place in the order imposed by man:

Cet escabeau, mesuré sur la distance qui sépare du sol le cul d'un homme assis, cette table qui sert à écrire ou à manger, cette porte qui ouvre un cube d'air entouré de cloisons sur un cube d'air voisin, perdaient ces raisons d'être qu'un artisan leur avait données pour n'être plus que des troncs ou des branches écorchés comme des saints Barthélemy de tableaux d'église, chargés de feuilles spectrales et d'oiseaux invisibles, grinçant encore de tempêtes depuis longtemps calmées, et où le rabot avait laissé çà et là le grumeau de la sève. (700)

The tree parallel began in 'Les loisirs de l'été': 'Le clerc se sentait libre comme la bête et menacé comme elle, équilibré comme l'arbre entre le monde d'en bas et le monde d'en haut, ployé lui aussi par des pressions s'exerçant sur lui qui ne cesseraient qu'à sa mort' (584–5). The violence that Zénon notices all around him is figured by the sap/blood remaining on the surface of the wood. The reference to St Bartholomew looks ahead to the massacre of a few years later, which Yourcenar incorporates into her essays on D'Aubigné and Chenonceaux (EM, 31, 35, 54–5). St Bartholomew himself was represented in painting either carrying the knife with which he was flayed alive or as a flayed figure holding his skin, as Michelangelo represented himself in the Sistine Chapel 'Last Judgment'. Zénon stands as a flayed saint of secular learning and science and as a planed tree.[33] The Saint is also attributed an apocryphal gospel, known as the 'Gnostic Questions of Saint Bartholomew', which includes an account of Christ's descent into Hell and the summons of the Devil to judgment.[34] The allusion, therefore, works as historical, pictorial and double textual referent (to the novel and to the apocryphal gospel). As a response to the visual challenge identified above, this passage opens itself out to a reading that incorporates the visual reference in the textual interplay in process, operating 'laterally' from outside the descriptions of Zénon's attempts to gain visual mastery over himself and the world.

This section has considered the issues raised by linking Piranesi's *Prisons* with 'L'abîme' in *L'Œuvre au noir* in order to see where the Yourcenar–Piranesi intersections may best be located, with reference to the 'myth' of the Piranesian staircase. These links were located along two axes of investigation: the encounter with vertiginous sub-limity when looking at the etchings and when carrying out experi-ments as Zénon does; the internal dynamics of the images, leading to space for flight which Zénon's difficulties with other people close off at this stage. Bringing together the essay and the novel here enables us to specify Yourcenar's contribution to the tradition of French writing inspired by the *Prisons*. The comparison with Valéry on the subject of the ideal artist supplements the clues taken from the essay on Piranesi. The investigation of ideas of self-exploration, of the mastery of others and of the repetition of desire for the Other arises from this link and is here read within the context of the ongoing treatment of the visual in the portrait of Zénon. The exposition of Zénon's ideas on sexual intercourse and the rupture of alterity figured by the Caraffa *Venus* leave Zénon akin to the solitary St Bartholomew. We now move on to consider further ways of responding to Henri-Maximilien's confusion by looking at the lines of flight from the abyss to the prism of colour at the end of *L'Œuvre au noir*.

## The Prism of Colour

One potential contribution of Yourcenar's 1955 essay on Thomas Mann to our reading of *L'Œuvre au noir* is the way it clarifies how in the initiation of the alchemist the beloved acts as a threshold god, although in the cases listed by Yourcenar the role is strictly limited to that of assistant: 'Les objets aimés [...] sont tout au plus des divinités psychopompes, des Hermès du seuil; ils s'effacent dès qu'ils ont conduit le vivant ou le mourant au bord du gouffre intérieur' ('Humanisme et hermétisme dans l'œuvre de Thomas Mann', *EM*, 182). The idea of the superior alchemist using others for his experiments will be familiar from the comments on Zénon and alterity above. However, it is possible to see the roles played by Aleï and Gerhart as more substantial than the detached figures in Mann's stories. Zénon employs a term also used in alchemical language to reject his old way of thinking about Gerhart: 'Ces fréquentations de Lübeck, semblables à une sorte d'été de la Saint-Martin de sa vie errante, lui revenaient, non plus réduites à *une sèche préparation* de la mémoire, comme ces souvenirs charnels qu'il avait évoqués naguère en méditant sur soi-même, mais capiteuses comme un vin par lequel il fallait avant tout ne pas se laisser griser' (738, my italics). The adjustment made to his memory relates to the way his recollections of Aleï in conversation with Henri-Maximilien in Innsbruck were subsequently demeaned during the 'treatise' in 'L'abîme'. This contrasts to Zénon's state when we first heard of Aleï, since he then admitted, somewhat in spite of himself, that he was plunged into melancholy and inertia by the death of his valet (649–50). In the case of his memories of his nomadic days, Zénon is still on his guard.

In 'Le cerveau noir de Piranèse', Yourcenar suggests that the Coleridge–De Quincey response to the *Prisons* is true to the spirit of the etchings but in error concerning their detail. In his study of the myth of the Piranesian staircase, Luzius Keller argues that her criticisms are misguided.[35] Even without Keller's clarification, Yourcenar does seem to claim that the response she has constructed was not influenced by her own preoccupations. In fact, the conclusion to her treatment of the *Prisons* claims that they represent the mind of modern man, increasingly trapped in a space of fantastic and pernicious constructions. The asymmetrical world she detected in the *Prisons* need not be fixed in the way she circumscribes it in the essay, since *L'Œuvre au noir* offers other interpretations.

Among the forms of movement envisaged for the investigations of Zénon there are two that offer ways of finding liberty within the labyrinth or prison. When Zénon is concentrating on his memories of people as memories *per se*, he ascribes mystery to the movement of these figures across and within his memory:

Il en était des créatures abordées, puis quittées, au cours de l'existence comme de ces figures spectrales, jamais vues deux fois, mais d'une spécificité et d'un relief presque terribles, qui se détachent sous la nuit des paupières à l'heure qui précède le sommeil et le songe, et tantôt passent et fuient à la vitesse d'un météore, et tantôt au contraire se résorbent en elles-mêmes sous la fixité du regard interne. Des lois mathématiques plus complexes et plus inconnues encore que celles de l'esprit ou des sens présidaient à ce va-et-vient de fantômes. (698)

The metaphor of the meteor allows the figures of other people light, speed and freedom in the passage between memory and sleep. Later in his cell Zénon seems to fluctuate between dreaming and being awake. The second formation, that of the figures dissolving into themselves, offers a further response, during Blanchot's 'other night' cited by Didi-Huberman, to the problem of the fixed gaze and the object. Here Zénon's gaze is fixed, but the object has the freedom of mobility to disappear; his gaze becomes less fixed and less restricted to the inner world.

Another passage from 'L'abîme' resumes the mathematical trope by way of the sublime. Zénon's experiences in 'L'abîme' may be thought of as moments before the sublime, temporarily and spatially, emerging as infinite lines setting out after the sublime. Zénon is no longer a detached Kantian spectator, since in his new world the abysses are potentially everywhere. They have become part of the quest. The fascination now lies in the potentially infinite Baroque curves which the processes of thought traverse:

Comme il arrive à un homme qui gravit, ou peut-être descend, la pente d'une montagne, il s'élevait ou s'enfonçait sur place; tout au plus, à chaque lacet, le même abîme s'ouvrait tantôt à droite et tantôt à gauche. [...] Mais la notion d'ascension ou de descente était fausse: des astres brillaient en bas comme en haut; il n'était pas plus au fond du gouffre qu'il n'était au centre. L'abîme était à la fois par-delà la sphère céleste et à l'intérieur de la voûte osseuse. Tout semblait avoir lieu au fond d'une série infinie de courbes fermées. (706)

The abyss now acts as either a single example or a series of strange 'vases communicants' that convey the alchemist's thoughts along the channel from the internal to the external and back. If we link the 'vase communicant' of the abyss with the 'vision du vide', a phrase from the essay on Mishima, then we obtain the trope of the empty vase, which, for Yourcenar, is a sign of non-immobility: 'Pour le bouddhisme et pour le taoïsme et pour la théologie négative, les mystiques ont tous recouru à l'idée du vide comme représentant la non-immobilisation, la non-limitation par des idées'.[36] This emptiness, which is conversely infinite and fluid, comprises a response to the despair of Henri-Maximilien.

This vision of movement persists despite the unavoidably finite nature of the space traversed by Zénon. Using this language, Yourcenar differentiates between sight and vision in the 1991 posthumous collection of essays *Le Tour de la prison*:

Aucune *vue* qui ne prend pas possession de tout l'esprit n'est vision; aucune pensée, si valable qu'elle soit, n'est autre chose qu'un fruit ou un sous-produit passager, dénué de ce sens d'éternité dans l'instant, d'étendue à l'intérieur d'un point fixe, qu'à de très longs intervalles la vision de l'esprit parfois confère, et qu'il est quelquefois possible de ressusciter par le souvenir. De la vision qui suit, l'œil ne fut qu'un point de départ. (*EM*, 614)

The mind is subordinate to the vision. The opening of Blake's 'Auguries of Innocence', cited in *La Voix des choses*, provides the temporal scale and the counterpart to Zénon's infinite space within fixity (23). In a further articulation of a mystical sense of space and vision which seems to thrive on negation, Yourcenar provides another riposte to the Platonism of Henri-Maximilien. In the essay on Thomas Mann, Yourcenar writes of a secret space sought by his work: 'Œuvre allemande: [...] par la recherche d'une sagesse magique dont les secrets chuchotés ou sous-entendus flottent entre les lignes, destinés, semble-t-il, à rester volontairement le plus inaperçus possible' (*EM*, 165–6). Zénon always seeks invisibility and now his search is leading to a state of wisdom.

During 'La promenade sur la dune', Zénon passes by a farm that he visited fifty years before. He recalls that a young woman gave him an eggshell. The game which he used to play involves the various axes of movement and repose we have encountered so far: 'Le jeu consistait à courir dans le sens du vent sur les dunes toutes proches, en tenant sur la paume cet objet léger qui s'échappait pour voleter devant vous, puis se posait un instant, comme un oiseau, de sorte qu'il fallait perpétuellement tenter de s'en ressaisir, et que la course se compliquait d'une série de courbes interrompues et de droites brisées. Il lui semblait parfois avoir joué ce jeu toute sa vie' (755). Zénon's lines of flight are affected by the violence and censure of his times. The bird simile reminds us that in her essay on Bede, Yourcenar had compared the space traversed by a bird to the expanses of the human mind: 'On pourrait aller plus loin et faire de la salle assiégée par la neige et le vent, illuminée, pour un temps, au sein de la triste grisaille de l'hiver, un autre et également poignant symbole. Celui du cerveau, chambre éclairée, feu central, temporairement placé pour chacun de nous au milieu des choses, et sans quoi ni l'oiseau ni la tempête ne seraient ni imaginés ni perçus' (*EM*, 280). The human brain is here considered as a temporary site of existence. This formulation constitutes a shift and a relaxation of the hold of interpretation since the time of the essay on Piranesi, and indeed the essay on the *Histoire Auguste*, when Yourcenar partly used the occasion for a vigorous assault on modern society.

While Zénon is working towards a new openness to the experience of the visual, the social circumstances of his investigations are darkening. Yourcenar concludes the 'Note' that follows the text (850) with an acknowledgement of her use of Bosch's *Garden of Earthly Delights* for the rough sketch that Florian leaves out for Zénon (745–6). The 'Note' also states: 'les thèmes boschiens et breughéliens du désordre et de l'horreur du monde envahissent l'ouvrage' (838 n.). The Prieur des Cordeliers refers to King Philip II's acquisition of the Bosch: 'Il paraît aussi qu'il detenait un tableau que le duc avait ordre d'acquérir pour Sa Majesté, une de nos diableries flamandes où l'on voit des démons grotesques qui supplicient des damnés' (724). Later in the same conversation one of the Prieur's remarks anticipates Breughel's *Massacre of the Innocents*: 'si ce n'est comme un innocent sur la paille, tout pareil aux nourrissons gisant sur la neige dans nos villages de la Campine dévastés par les troupes du Roi' (728). The Prieur alludes wistfully to Raphaël's depiction of doctrinal dispute in the Vatican—the vibrant, crowded but dignified *Disputa* in the Stanza della Segnatura—contrasting it with the harsh historical reality of his country.

At the beginning and the end of the chapter concerning Philibert and Martha Ligre's residence at Forestel, this Northern–Southern contrast operates vividly, added to which there is a dichotomy between the Classical and the Biblical stories depicted in murals and tapestries at the house. At the opening of the chapter we learn that the ceilings of the grand rooms have been decorated with scenes from ancient history and mythology. The subjects represent stories of human nobility, contrasted with tales of the lust of Jupiter: 'la générosité d'Alexandre, la clémence de Titus, Danaé inondée par la pluie d'or et Ganymède montant au ciel' (805). In the course of the chapter the darkening times are signalled by the Duke of Alba's visit; Zénon's fate is sealed by Martha's timidity and Philibert's concern to protect his own interests. The historical situation surrounding the sumptuous residence invades the interior of the house and the ceiling decorations now seem a distant Arcadia. We learn that the Ganymede room is to receive a set of Aubusson tapestries to hang and be read at eye level, under the mythological scenes overhead.

The subjects are taken from the Old and New Testaments: 'L'Adoration du Veau d'or, Le Reniement de Saint-Pierre, L'Incendie de Sodome, Le Bouc émissaire, Les Hébreux jetés dans la fournaise ardente' (299). In the first two titles, Yourcenar uses common subjects; for the third, a less common one; she 'coins' subjects for the last two.[37] These subjects are chosen to apply to the narrative of L'Œuvre au noir, where folly, betrayal and violence abound: the issue of idolatry is discussed by the Prieur and Zénon; like St. Peter, Martha has not acted in defence of a prisoner; Münster is destroyed for its lawless follies; Zénon is a scapegoat in the doctrinal arguments of the Church; and the young monks have been burned. The narratives represented no longer attribute folly to the gods and nobility to men. This arrival of new narratives for the Ganymede room also signifies the form the web of the tapestry of L'Œuvre au noir has taken: Zénon has become enmeshed in its lines, as a much earlier passage, concerning his mother, had predicted: 'Ses mains restaient étendues sur la trame, et ces longs doigts frémissants sur les rinceaux inachevés faisaient penser aux entrelacs de l'avenir' (573). Enclosure and freedom operate in the spaces for flight within the historical and textual situation discovered during the chapter of evasion, 'La promenade sur la dune'.

The principal episode drawing on Bosch and Breughel occurs during the final evasion from Bruges. In 'Lecture d'un chapitre—La promenade sur la dune', Claude Soulès has demonstrated how the landscape where Zénon wanders uses specific scenes from the two artists.[38] Soulès rightly distinguishes between the pictorial and the textual: Yourcenar adopts scenes but does not attempt to fix Zénon within a 'pictorial' framework. As Soulès notes, Yourcenar represents Zénon as the Jungian Adam Cadmon: 'Il redevenait cet Adam Cadmon des philosophes hermétiques, placé au cœur des choses, en qui s'élucide et se profère ce qui partout ailleurs est infus et imprononcé'. It is necessary to make this distinction between the pictorial and the textual in order to be clear that the visual in L'Œuvre

*au noir* is mediated by language and its shadows; Zénon is not a figure
in a painting. That is why it is problematic to fuse painting and text
in the way that Geneviève Spencer-Noël does in her discussion of the
scene where Zénon's surroundings are coloured by the pale sky and
green grass, while the ground seems in perpetual flux. We have to be
wary of transferring 'details', because looking at the Breughel as
closely as Spencer-Noël's argument leads us to do raises the question
of the stability of the representation in the area of the painting she has
in mind: 'Ce tableau, on se prend à l'imaginer dans les verts de la
"viriditas" alchimique, avec des vagues minutieusement ourlées à la
Brueghel, formant des spirales à sous-entendu mystique, comme on
voit aussi sur le ciel de cette miniature indienne du pèlerin bouddhiste
Sudhana, approchant de la Cité sacrée de Krishna.'[39] One example of
the foam of waves that Spencer-Noël mentions is the foam in
Breughel's *Fall of Icarus*. As Didi-Huberman has argued, the seafoam
in that picture is semiotically unstable, since the strokes of white paint
act as the feathers of Icarus' wings, the feathers of the quill of narration and the seafroth all at once.[40] Spencer-Noël is reading Breughel
as a transparent text when she constructs her imaginary painting;
when we look at the painting or paintings she has in mind we do not
necessarily see what she asserts is represented there; and the difference
between an imaginary painting and a real one by Breughel is not
discussed. The nature of the mediation of the visual by the verbal
needs to be considered with regard to pictorial allusions in *L'Œuvre
au noir*.

Spencer-Noël and Soulès argue that 'la promenade sur la dune'
constitutes the *œuvre au blanc* of Zénon's transmutation. Patches of
colour increasingly carry the visual experiences of Zénon. In his cell
during the trial, Zénon is visited by visions of colour while he passes
from dream to reality: 'Toutefois, la vie elle-même, vue par un
homme prêt à la quitter, acquérait elle aussi l'étrange instabilité et la
bizarre ordonnance des songes. Il passait de l'un à l'autre, comme de
la salle du greffe où on l'interrogeait à sa cellule bien verrouillée et de
sa cellule au préau sous la neige' (794). The idea of passage between
the two states continues the movement experienced in 'L'abîme'.
Zénon's investigations now occur around him without his being
preoccupied by the struggle for mastery. A Valerian remark in the
'Dossier' to *Les Songes et les Sorts* underlines the exploration of the
dream: 'Le rêve comme forme rudimentaire de l'investigation' (*EM*,
1616).

However, the mental exertions of 'L'abîme' are still required, even if in these notes for *Les Songes et les Sorts* Yourcenar tries to harmonize the visual experience of the dream by locating its cause: 'Qui ne voit que ces souvenirs qui remontent presque automatiquement à la surface ont le décousu, l'incongru, l'absurde futilité, et aussi l'obsédante intensité de ceux du rêve, leur air de sortir d'un autre monde où tout est plus significatif, partant plus beau que dans le nôtre?' (1615–16). As we saw in our discussion of Henri-Maximilien's encounter with the statue of Venus, proposing a Platonist solution to the disruptive power of the visual is a matter of faith and closes off inquiry. Yourcenar's desire for a 'barrière de sérénité' (1536), stated in the context of which dreams to include in *Les Songes et les Sorts*, expresses a similar suppression of the power of the visual that is otherwise so strikingly at work. Fortunately, the author exerts less control over the role of dreams in *L'Œuvre au noir*, not simply because of the reader's liberty, but also because of the risk and dynamism required by the alchemical process. In an interview she in fact rejected traditional attempts to impose coherence on the visual-verbal: 'Dans cette transcription, fondamentale, m'apparaissait la fonction du rêve et m'intéressait toute cette zone d'ombre, ce passage informulé qui séparent ce qu'on appelle la vie réelle et la vie rêvée [...] C'est cette sollicitation du rêve qui m'amena à mettre en doute tout ce que la psychologie traditionnelle, telle qu'elle s'exprime dans le roman classique, comporte de rationalité abusive, de cohérence surimposé'.[41] Zénon now inhabits this 'passage informulé', an empty space that is the site of transgression and vision. We will see that the intriguing reference to 'cette zone d'ombre' leads us to the final example of the presence of Piranesi in Yourcenar's text.

In her writings on dreams, Yourcenar is much closer to Caillois than to Bachelard, since the latter makes clear his distrust of nocturnal dreams in *La poétique de la rêverie*.[42] Zénon does not engage in Bachelard's 'rêverie'.[43] The difference between Yourcenar and Bachelard is especially clear in *Les Songes et les Sorts*, whose 'Dossier' contains Yourcenar's reflections on colour. She stresses the chromatic domination of the visual experience of her dreams, the diverse symbolism of colour acording to cultural context, the association between colour and space and the sublimely imposing spectacle of naked colour. Yourcenar is tackling the difficulty observed by Kandinsky: '*C'est pourquoi les mots sont et resteront simplement des indications, des marques assez extérieures des couleurs*':[44] 'Les mots manquent pour dire la profondeur, la suavité, le rayonnement, l'éclat ou la sombre violence de ces grandes nappes de couleur des ciels... Couleurs qui par leur allégresse font danser de joie ou, par leur beauté, serrent le cœur. C'est à l'intensité et aux modulations de la couleur que se reconnaissent ce que, faute d'un nom plus précis, j'appelle les grands rêves' (*EM*, 1608). Kandinsky's writings on the inner joy of colour are echoed here. His theory of the inner necessity or principle in the impact of colour on the eye is adopted in the 'Dossier', while in *L'Œuvre au noir* there is emphasis on the space traversed by the rays of light.

During the chapter 'L'acte d'accusation', Zénon considers what the activity of dreaming has taught him. He realizes that he can no longer distinguish between dreams and reality because the old certainties about time and space have dissolved. He is endowed with the power of vision obtained in the 'eyeless' night world: 'Mais rêver devenait inutile. Les choses prenaient d'elles-mêmes ces couleurs qu'elles n'ont que dans les songes, et qui rappellent le vert, le pourpre et le blanc purs des nomenclatures alchimiques: une pomme d'orange qui vint un jour luxueusement orner sa table, brilla longtemps comme une boule d'or; son parfum et sa sapidité aussi furent un message' (795). Everyday objects have a strange power that marks their independence from the observer; surface colours have density and completeness, relieving the objects of dependence on physical matter and permitting them to contain and carry their own light.

The radical strangeness attributed to colour when it is associated with the transformation of alchemy makes pictorial comparison a contentious issue. Hugo von Hofmannsthal provides support for the point made earlier about the caution required when discussing Breughel's colour in the same context as alchemical viriditas. In the text entitled 'Lettres du voyageur à son retour', Hofmannsthal is interested in the fragmentary; Kandinsky's harmony is no longer relevant:

Mais que sont les couleurs, tant que la vie la plus intérieure des objets ne s'y révèle pas? Et cette vie très intérieure était là, arbre et pierre et mur et chemin creux livraient le plus profond d'eux-mêmes, me le jetaient pour ainsi dire au visage, non pas la volupté et l'harmonie de leur belle vie silencieuse, celle que jadis déversait parfois sur moi, dans les tableaux anciens, son atmosphère envoûtante: non, le poids de leur existence, le miracle furieux, fixé d'yeux incrédules, de leur existence, m'assaillit.[45]

Zénon is experiencing this inner life of everyday objects, while they both display their depth and seem to throw themselves at the spectator. Of course, it is possible to suggest examples of pictorial colour which carry the weight of existence sensed by Hofmannsthal. He has in mind modern painting, specifically Van Gogh, about whose use of yellow he writes elsewhere (pp. 151–5). The visual impact of the material world is under consideration, an encounter which Hofmannsthal's Lord Chandos, for his part, does not find represented in Old Masters. Zénon shares the sense of ferocious wonder at the visual field.

The infinity of space, the lines of flight, the gaps in the interstices and the strangeness of the visual are present at the end of *L'Œuvre au noir*. After he has cut his wrist and ankle, Zénon's awareness of space is compared to the multiplicity of thoughts and feelings experienced since being left alone by Campanus: 'l'espace de quelques coudées qui séparaient le lit de la table s'était dilaté à l'égal de celui qui s'approportionne entre les sphères: le goblelet d'étain flottait comme au fond d'un autre monde' (831). Zénon, placed in the 'zone d'ombre', has the experience of infinity within a fixed point. In this state, darkness and light (colour) exist together. During the period of the trial, Zénon experienced sound as if in a dream, as if the sound arrived from a point within the space of his mind: 'A plusieurs reprises, il crut entendre une musique solennelle qui ressemblait à celle des orgues, si celle des orgues pouvait s'épandre en silence; l'esprit plutôt que l'ouïe recevait des sons' (796). A discursive passage reflecting on this characteristic of dreams interrupts one of the dream accounts in *Les Songes et les Sorts*:

Il parle, en paroles entrecoupées, et il en est des mots qu'il prononce comme de presque tous ceux qui résonnent dans les rêves: ils ne viennent pas du dehors frapper nos oreilles, mais vibrent au-dedans de nous-mêmes, car les dormeurs entendent avec leurs artères, avec leurs entrailles, et non avec les organes de l'ouïe qui servent à l'état de veille et décèlent les bruits étrangers; et de même qu'il y a une voix blanche, une décoloration de la voix par la douleur ou l'angoisse, il semble aussi qu'il y ait une oreille blanche, une décoloration de l'ouïe par le rêve, où l'on ne reçoit plus que des spectres de son. (*EM*, 1566)

The interior is the space of the labyrinth of the body which carries the sound and sight. Hearing is represented as a vessel for the passage of ghosts: colour and words as previously understood have to be transmuted and in this process they pass through a state of spectral whiteness or blankness.

This passage through blankness conveys the arrangements of sight and sound in Piranesi's *Prisons* better than the idea of terrifying exposure put forward in 'Le cerveau noir de Piranèse'. The spaces marked out by the etchings offer passages within and without. Paradoxically, the transformation in the novel from the *œuvre au blanc* to the *œuvre au rouge* prompts the reader-spectator to consider the colour of Piranesi's etchings. In Zénon's eyes, the series of etchings would merge into each other one after the other:

La nuit aussi bougeait: les ténèbres s'écartaient pour faire place à d'autres, abîme sur abîme, épaisseur sombre sur épaisseur sombre. Mais ce noir différent de celui qu'on voit par les yeux frémissait de couleurs issues pour ainsi dire de ce qui était leur absence: le noir tournait au vert livide, puis au blanc pur; le blanc pâle se transmutait en or rouge sans que cessât pourtant l'originelle noirceur, tout comme les feux des astres et l'aurore boréale tressaillent dans ce qui est quand même la nuit noire. (832–3)

Looking at the Piranesi etchings used in this book, not just the *Prisons*, we see the black and white stages of the alchemical process; the other colours which implode describe the variations available within the monochrome.

Zénon's attempts to gain mastery over his surroundings belong to a different 'sphere of narration', to adopt Maurice Blanchot's phrase relating to Thomas Mann.[46] At the encounter with the magnifying glass in *L'Œuvre au noir* the function of the eye was interpreted by Zénon as a guarantee of human will: 'En un sens l'œil contrebalançait l'abîme' (705). Then the eye is 'reminded' how it is only a point of departure. Now the eye is subsumed within the inner space of an angel, as described by Rilke and quoted by Leishman and Spender in their introduction to the *Duino Elegies*: 'Everywhere appearance and vision came, as it were, together in the object, in every one of them a whole inner world was exhibited, as though an angel, in whom space was included, were blind and looking into himself. This world, regarded no longer from any human point of view, but as it is within the angel, is perhaps my real task, one, at any rate, in which all my previous attempts would converge.'[47] For Rilke in this passage, the revelation of the secret world inside the object seems to happen independently of the human gaze. As we saw in our discussion of the internal dynamics of the etchings, it is possible to see how Zénon strives to gain access to this secret world. If, following Coleridge, Yourcenar and Didi-Huberman, we look at the *Prisons* of Piranesi as memories of dreams, then the absence of colour may be read metaphorically as an invisible sign of what is forgotten, of the vision of the encounter with otherness.

The finale to *L'Œuvre au noir* has the delirium of the dream admired by the Romantics, Caillois and Yourcenar. The violent spectacle of the Troubles of the 1560s in the Low Countries increases the necessity for Zénon's inner experiments. While the paintings and tapestries incorporated into the text frame and enclose the narrative of his persecution, Zénon's vision faces the perils of the alchemist's self-sacrifice and centreless movement. The variations on the sublime discussed in this section have suggested a subversive figuration of the visual which turns inward and allows the visual to implode in infinite space. Zénon's abandonment of attempts to control his surroundings gains him access to the wonder and power of the world. He has to lose colour in order to find it again; the alchemical transformation is supported by the mystical and negative path through the visual which he experiences. The text of Zénon's disappearance endeavours to operate its mediation of the visual by comprising the fragmentary and the disruptive—patches of colour, interspersed with blank, spectral white, of uncertain definition and weight—into his abandonment to the materiality of his fate. This sublime spectacle undoes all the presumptions lingering inside Zénon.

Studying the Yourcenar–Piranesi dialogue has led us to look at Piranesi's engravings, involving confrontations with corporeal erosion and surprising doubles which stage, in terms of the visual dynamics in operation, many of the difficulties experienced by Zénon in his search within himself and in the world. His retreat within leads to a struggle with his will to reason, which he finally loosens to permit engagement with otherness, although this does not include other people. The passage through the labyrinth of spectral blankness, which may be understood as the irruption of Piranesi's etchings onto the text, is undertaken alone. When Yourcenar's essayistic procedures risk closing off inquiry, a recourse to the fiction, to *Denier du rêve* and *L'Œuvre au noir*, as in *Mémoires d'Hadrien* earlier, permits the reader to pursue links with the artist and, returning to the essays, to develop Yourcenar's positions. This critical method provides a 'royal road' for reading Yourcenar's texts. In the final chapter, the juxtaposition of painting and writing will question the permanence of both art forms, and in so doing, it is hoped, involve new readings of the texts under discussion.

## Notes to Chapter 3

1. The most accessible edition of the series of engravings and etchings of Rome entitled *Vedute di Roma* (*Views of Rome*) and the series of etchings of imaginary prisons entitled *Carceri d'invenzione* (*Prisons*) is John Wilton-Ely, *The Mind and Art of Giovanni Battista Piranesi* (London: Thames & Hudson, 1978). All references to plate numbers for the *Views* and *Prisons* are to this book; the second series of the *Prisons* (1761) is used by Wilton-Ely.

2. The section devoted to the *Prisons* was written for a full-size edition published by the Club International de Bibliophile in 1961 and also published in the *Nouvelle Revue Française* in the same year.

3. John Wilton-Ely, *Piranesi as Architect and Designer* (New Haven and London: Yale University Press, 1975), 4.

4. See the analysis by Rudolf Wittkower, 'Piranesi's Architectural Creed' and 'Piranesi as Architect' in *Studies in the Italian Baroque* (Boulder, Col.: Westview Press, 1975), and Wilton-Ely, *Mind and Art of Piranesi*, 73–7.

5. See Wilton-Ely, *Mind and Art of Piranesi*, pl. 15.

6. John Summerson explains the significance of the orders of architecture in his study *The Classical Language of Architecture* (London: Thames & Hudson, 1980).

7. Mitchell, *Picture Theory*, 57.

8. Didi-Huberman, *Ce que nous voyons*, 118.

9. Christine Buci-Glucksmann, *La Folie du voir: de l'esthetique baroque* (Paris: Galilée, 1986), 32.

10. Germaine Bazin, *Baroque and Rococo*, trans. Jonathan Griffin (London: Thames & Hudson, 1985), 6–7.

11. 'Dis', in 'Glossary', *The Comedy of Dante Alighieri the Florentine. Cantica I: Hell (L'Inferno)*, 318.

12. Jennifer Bloomer, *Architecture and the Text: The S(crypts) of Joyce and Piranesi* (New Haven and London: Yale University Press, 1993), 82.

13. On the *mundus*, see R. Sennett, *Flesh and Stone: The Body and the City in Western Civilization* (London and Boston: Faber and Faber, 1994), 108.

14. Jacques Derrida, *La Vérité en peinture* (Paris: Champs/Flammarion, 1993), 32.

15. Luzius Keller, *Piranèse et les romantiques français—le mythe des escaliers en spirale* (Paris: José Corti, 1966).

16. Georges Poulet, 'Piranèse et les poètes romantiques français', *NRF* 161 (May 1966), 860.

17. Bonnefoy, *Rome 1630*, 37.

18. Immanuel Kant, *The Critique of Judgement*, trans. James Creed Meredith (Oxford: Clarendon Press, 1952), §26 (p. 99) and §27 (p. 108).

19. The phrase 'lines of visual flight' is adapted from the English translation of Gilles Deleuze and Félix Guattari, *A Thousand Plateaus, Capitalism and Schizophrenia*, trans. Brian Massumi (London: Athlone Press, 1988), 21.

20. Aldous Huxley, *Prisons* (London: Trianon Press, 1949), 24.

21. Max-Pol Fouchet, *Jean-Baptiste Piranèse: Les prisons imaginaires* (Paris: Club

français du livre, 1970), 14. Fouchet was one of the judges who awarded *Sous bénéfice d'inventaire* the 'Prix Combat' in 1963: Savigneau, *Marguerite Yourcenar*, 290.

22. The link between Paul Valéry and *L'Œuvre au noir* was first proposed by John Weightman in 'Falling towards Death', *Times Literary Supplement*, 22 July 1983, 767–8.

23. Frank Kermode, 'Poet and Dancer before Diaghilev', in *Modern Essays* (London: Collins, 1971).

24. Quoted by Vera J. Daniel, 'Introduction', in P. Valéry, *Eupalinos ou l'architecte. L'Ame et la Danse*, ed. V. J. Daniel, 37.

25. Weightman, 'Falling towards Death', 768.

26. Valéry, *Léonard de Vinci*, 89.

27. Valéry, *Léonard de Vinci*, 89.

28. Pierre-Yves Bourdil, '*L'Œuvre au noir* de Marguerite Yourcenar. Portrait de Zénon', *L'Ecole des Lettres II* 1 (1988–9), 26.

29. The name 'Zénon' was found by Yourcenar in documents relating to her paternal ancestors: *Lettres*, 300; *LYO*, 157; and *Bulletin de la SIEY* 19 (1998), 19–20. Yourcenar also refers to the philosophers Zeno of Elea (the sceptic who denied the existence of movement, mid-5th Cent. BCE) and Zeno of Citium (founding Stoic, 334?–262 BCE), as well as St Zeno (Bishop of Verona, d. *c*.372 CE).

30. For the context of aesthetic ideas in the 16th cent., see E. Panofsky, *Idea: A Concept in Art History*, trans. Joseph J. S. Peake (Columbia: University of South Carolina Press, 1968).

31. Louis Aragon and Jean Cocteau, *Entretiens sur le musée de Dresde* (Paris: Cercle d'Art, 1957), 14.

32. Didi-Huberman, *Devant l'image*, 189.

33. For the symbols associated with St Bartholomew, see *Hall's Dictionary of Subjects and Symbols in Art*. This literal, physical incorporation of a tree works against Nadia Harris's symbolic reading of trees in Yourcenar's work: Nadia Harris, *Marguerite Yourcenar: Vers la rive d'une Ithaque intérieure* (Saratoga: ANMA Libri, 1994), ch. 2.

34. 'St. Bartholomew', in *The Concise Oxford Dictionary of the Christian Church*, ed. Elizabeth A. Livingstone (Oxford: Oxford University Press, 1980).

35. Keller, *Piranèse et les romantiques français*, 43–5; for other references to Yourcenar, see 32–3 and 35–6.

36. 'Entretien avec Léo Gillet', 66. For a comparison between Yourcenar's essay on Mishima and *ON* see Patricia de Feyter, 'Zénon ou la vision du vide', in '*L'Œuvre au noir*' de Marguerite Yourcenar, ed. A. Y. Julien, *Roman 20–50* 9 (1990), 89–94.

37. See *Hall's Dictionary of Subjects and Symbols in Art*, rev edn. (London: John Murray, 1979).

38. Claude Soulès, '*Lecture d'un chapitre*—La promenade sur la dune', in '*L'Œuvre au noir*', ed. Julien, *Roman 20–50* 9 (1990), 95–107.

39. Geneviève Spencer-Noël, *Zénon ou le thème de l'alchimie dans 'L'Œuvre au noir' de Marguerite Yourcenar* (Paris: Nizet, 1981), 98.

40. Didi-Huberman, *Devant l'image*, 282–5.

41. C. Mettra, 'Les explorations de Marguerite Yourcenar', 3; quoted by Spencer-Noël, *Zénon*, 119–20.

42. G. Bachelard, *La Poétique de la rêverie* (Paris: Quadrige/PUF, 1993), 9–18, 128–31, 145.

43. Roger Caillois discusses the difference between 'rêve' and 'rêverie': R. Caillois, *L'Incertitude qui vient des rêves* (Paris: Gallimard, 1956), 90–1.

44. Kandinsky, *Du spirituel dans l'art*, 165 (author's italics).

45. Hugo von Hofmannsthal, *Lettre de Lord Chandos et autres textes*, trans. Albert Kohn and Jean-Claude Schneider (Paris: Gallimard, 1992), 152–3.

46. In his contribution to *Hommage de la France à Thomas Mann à l'occasion de son quatre-vingtième anniversaire* (Paris: Flincker, 1955), Blanchot registers 'la sphère heureusement fermée de la narration' ('La rencontre avec le démon', 41). A shorter version of Yourcenar's essay on Mann appears in the same volume.

47. R. M. Rilke, *Duino Elegies*, 2nd edn., trans. J. B. Leishman and Stephen Spender (London: Hogarth Press, 1942), 18.

CHAPTER 4

❖

# Still Lives:
# *Un homme obscur* and
# '*Deux Noirs* de Rembrandt'

The novel *Un homme obscur* (1982) and the essay '*Deux Noirs* de Rembrandt' (1986) are the most explicit examples in Yourcenar's work of the negotiation of the status and permanence of representation. Engaging with the possibilities and challenges offered by Yourcenar's incorporation of the visual arts into the project of writing, this last chapter couples text and picture in ways that assist the unravelling of the processes of the visual. The discussion in this chapter of the visual–verbal interface comprises the following aspects: the representation or position of Nathanaël in the context of the textual pictures in *Un homme obscur*; Nathanaël's encounter with the two paintings owned by Van Herzog; the fantasia on Piranesi's *Prisons*, with recollections of the essay 'Le cerveau noir de Piranèse'; the 'dehors–dedans' dialectic in the first part of the essay on Rembrandt and in the novel;[1] the vision of 'l'intolérable' in Rembrandt's painting *Deux Noirs*; and the dissolution of Nathanaël into the landscape of the Friesian island, together with the disappearance of the slaves into the sea at Dunbar Creek, as related in the legend which closes '*Deux Noirs* de Rembrandt'.[2] The surprising range of pictorial reference that can be found in *Un homme obscur* tests and challenges critical accounts of the novel to date.

## Preliminary

The novel and the essay are the culmination of Yourcenar's writings on the visual and of her admiration for Rembrandt. The 'postface' to *Un homme obscur* tells us that the first published version of the story was called 'D'après Rembrandt'.[3] This had previously been known as 'Nathanaël', forming part of *Remous*, the ambitious project of Yourcenar's early years (*OR*, 1037). '*Deux Noirs*' provided her with an opportunity to offer an account of a lifetime's experience of looking at Rembrandt.

When Yourcenar came to revise the early stories in *La Mort conduit l'attelage*, she was particularly dissatisfied with the titles. In the 'Note de l'auteur' which follows *L'Œuvre au noir*, she observes: 'Le titre du premier récit dans le volume paru en 1934 avait le tort, comme d'ailleurs ceux des deux autres nouvelles du même recueil, de présenter ces récits comme imitant systématiquement l'œuvre de trois peintres, ce qui n'était pas le cas' (838). Although we always have to be cautious when reading Yourcenar's retrospective accounts of her early work, it is true that the use of pictorial sources for some of the scenes in 'D'après Rembrandt' often resulted in derivative transcriptions. This is particularly the case in the scene when Nathanaël addresses the crowd at the tavern, where Yourcenar conflates etchings by Rembrandt of Christ preaching (*La Mort conduit l'attelage*, 200). Yourcenar realized that she had sometimes imitated artists far too simplistically, copying the 'details' of scenes and the 'expression' of figures. Her early stories had not done justice to her knowledge of Dutch painting, nor to her appreciation of the possibilities available to the writer responding to painting.

The new versions of the tales are far removed from derivative presentations of the lives of pictorial heroes. The writing has enormously altered since *La Mort conduit l'attelage* and, as Maurice Delcroix has noted in 'Parcours d'une œuvre', all the major texts precede the re-writing of 'D'après Rembrandt'.[4] Yourcenar offers the reasonable explanation that 'D'après Rembrandt' revealed her general naïveté about life and her insufficient knowledge of the period and the place involved. Although she had been able to draw on her knowledge of Dutch painting, she realized in retrospect that at the time this limited knowledge restricted her to a lifeless view of the period: 'Tout cela restait gris sur gris comme l'est bien souvent une vie vue de dehors, jamais une vie vue de dedans' ('Postface', 1038). The interplay between 'dehors' and 'dedans' is precisely the concern of the two later texts. Yourcenar is acknowledging that her approach to painting in *La Mort conduit l'attelage* was simplistic and that she had not thought through how best to employ painting in fiction.

Nevertheless, it would be wrong to write off *La Mort conduit l'atte-lage* altogether. The preface has disappeared from the later versions of the stories and from the accounts of the book in other prefaces and 'postfaces'. It shares the bold and vibrant rhetoric of the prefaces from the 1930s. In the case of the prefaces to *La Mort conduit l'attelage, Feux* and *Les Songes et les Sorts*, we have brief texts happily lacking the ponderous tone that can inhabit the later revised prefaces.[5] Her purpose had been to sketch out the lives of certain portraits that had appealed to her:

A Vienne, au Louvre, en Hollande, dans ces musées qui sont aussi des cimetières, mais des cimetières où l'on voit les morts, tels portraits inconnus, dont quelques-uns sont illustres, fixent pour nous ces élans et ces retombées d'ardeur, cette fureur de vivre et cette peur de mourir. Mettre sur les visages, non seulement un nom, mais une vie, c'est l'ambition des chercheurs. On m'excusera, j'espère, d'avoir tenté ici ces trois esquisses après trois peintres. (*MCA*, 9)

In the context of her three stories, this passage voices her desire to bring the dead back to life in her historical fiction, to match the passion and vigour of painting and to face death with the active engagement of the writer. However, in view of the artists concerned, the stories were comparable to the preparatory trials of sketches, since they lacked the more substantial work of the artists' paintings.

In the context of her later works, the above quotation may be given an additional interpretation. The experience of life and death available to the spectator in this visual cemetery is relevant for the interaction between the body of the painting and the body of the spectator: this is the subject of the opening of Yourcenar's essay on Rembrandt and will be discussed in this chapter. Also, what Yourcenar calls 'l'ambition des chercheurs', appropriate for the emphasis on the active involvement of the eyes of the spectator, may also have hidden the need on the writer's part to fix and control the content of the painting ('fixent pour nous ces élans') and to strengthen this hold by ascribing a biography to the figures depicted. By contrast, *Un homme obscur* and 'Deux Noirs de Rembrandt', which both engage with this issue of the life and lives of painting, endeavour to bring about a positive restoration of unfixed anonymity to the 'portraits inconnus' discovered in the museums of Europe.

## Representing Nathanaël: Textual Pictures in *Un homme obscur*

Once Nathanaël makes it onto the staff in Van Herzog's house, he experiences his habitual distance from other people, surprised that the members of the household have such an impact, albeit temporary, on his life. He reflects that some people are encountered very briefly, 'croisés seulement l'espace d'un clin d'œil' (966). Others become companions, but then soon disappear into thin air. Nathanaël recognizes that he is recalling acts of seeing and of remembering others: 'On ne comprenait pas pourquoi ces gens s'imposaient à votre esprit, occupaient votre imagination, parfois même vous dévoraient le cœur, avant de s'avouer pour ce qu'ils étaient: des fantômes. [...] Tout cela était de l'ordre de la fantasmagorie et du songe' (966). Past and present are engaged in this remembrance of others. Their evanescent presence in Nathanaël's mind reflects his own status in the narrative of *Un homme obscur*, a story written as a flashback after the introductory first paragraph.[6] The passage quoted above therefore makes the reader think about the way the passage of Nathanaël through the story is traced in the text. Looking out for Nathanaël's appearances, as well as his 'disappearances', from the text is one way of approaching the remark in the 'postface' that Nathanaël somehow exists outside the world of words: 'Nathanaël est de ceux qui pensent presque sans l'intermédiaire des mots' (1041). *Un homme obscur* requires the reader to look carefully in order to establish Nathanaël's status in the text; it also invites the reader to look away from the hero (and from Yourcenar's directions) at the other areas of the text which he eludes.

The 'postface' acknowledges that the historical background to Nathanaël's story is vague, although, as Christiane Guys has argued in 'Le porteur d'eau' it can be fixed in terms of reference to historical events to the period 1609–48.[7] In terms of cultural reference, the story extends beyond the first half of the seventeenth century. By moving away from the connection with one artist and his period, Yourcenar is able to extend her range of pictorial reference. The number of artists whose paintings have been employed for the narrative reflects the diversity of seventeenth-century Dutch painting. This open frame of reference emphasizes the freedom available to the reader. Also, the later version of this story invites the application of recent interpretations of the ways of looking that characterized Dutch culture at the time of Nathanaël's discreet life.

In *The Art of Describing*, Svetlana Alpers argues that Dutch art in the seventeenth century celebrated the visible world in paint by representing its infinite variety. Alpers contrasts this art with the Italian tradition of painting theory, derived from Alberti, that presented 'significant' human actions based on a narrative text (history painting). For Alpers, when Dutch art represents the world on the surface of a canvas, it describes the world but does not tell a story about the world. She discusses artists who tested this culture of seeing to its extremes (e.g. Vermeer) and who subverted it (e.g. Rembrandt). For the purposes of this discussion, Alpers's book suggests differences between the descriptive and the narrative which may be applied to the question of how Nathanaël's story of looking at the world is told. The Dutch model as explained by Alpers helps us to recognize the status of Nathanaël in the narrative. Both narrative and description are employed to situate him in the novel, since he is both engaged in the world and detached from it, on the surface of society and separate from it. We follow Nathanaël in the web of the text acting as spectator and agent. The reader is always aware of the ways in which this experience of the world is mediated by Nathanaël's vision and by the narrative of the text. As Louis Marin remarks in 'Eloge de l'apparence', Alpers's achievement was to make people aware of representation in Dutch Art and think about its methods and its limitations (250).[8]

The use of paintings to represent Nathanaël looking at a particular situation commences once he has returned from his journey to the New World. The surreptitious way in which Nathanaël looks at the world makes the pictorial references easy to spot, even if there is no specific painting involved as a textual referent.[9] On his return from 'L'Ile Perdue', Nathanaël visits his mother in the asylum. The description of the humble room sets the scene of a still life or genre painting (even if the scene is set in England): 'Celle où résidait sa mère était miraculeusement propre: le cuivre du bougeoir et de la bouillotte brillait. C'était l'heure du repas; un bol de gruau et une assiette de hareng fumé étaient posés sur une nappe très blanche. [...] Mais une partie de son attention était distraite par son chat, qui se dressait contre ses genoux, tirant sur son tablier, alléché par le hareng sur l'assiette' (935–6). Nathanaël's mother, a Calvinist, has ennobled modest surroundings. But this order is threatened by the cat and the idea of consumption. Were this a painting, the comical disruption of the scene would draw the Calvinist spectator's attention to the idea of *vanitas*, the illusion of the material world. As Norman Bryson has

argued, when investigating the ideological context in his study of
Dutch still life,[10] the Calvinist distrust of images made the genre
problematic, since visual display had to be aware of its own flaws. In
*Un homme obscur*, the reader senses the fragility of the existence of
Nathanaël's mother, since she cannot live on cleansed surfaces alone.
The fragility of the scene lies in the fragility of the way in which his
mother's world presents itself, represented in the text by means of the
pictorial arrangement.

   Nathanaël nurtured his critical approach to society when he read
Latin literature while a proof-reader at Elie Adiansen's bookshop.
Hence the description through Nathanaël's eyes of the wealth of Van
Herzog contains an analysis of the sources of the wealth. Nathanaël's
status as a servant enhances his awareness of how the objects of wealth
become detached from the circumstances of their acquisition and take
their place in the rich veneer of the house's existence: 'Cette fortune
déjà vieille donnait à l'ancien bourgmestre les prérogatives et les loisirs
d'un homme né riche; les pertes en vies humaines, les exactions et les
astuces, inséparables de toute opulence, dataient d'avant son temps et
d'autres que lui en étaient responsables; son luxe et celui de sa fille en
recevaient une sorte de douce patine' (966). When the objects in Van
Herzog's house are seen for what they represent, their owners are
envisaged acquiring a surface gloss, as if they too are set in the picture
representing this display: we read their lives as representations.
Nathanaël's status as observer of this process is grounded in his ability
to detach himself from his surroundings, although this can only be
temporary, since he is implicated in the fragility of this particular
narrative for as long as he is part of Amsterdam society, even if he
seems to try to keep himself from being implicated.

   These two examples see pictorial representation or artificial display
employed in the text to tell the story of Nathanaël's existence through
the description of his observation of fragility at his mother's lodging
and through the account of his pretended detachment from the story
of the background to the Van Herzogs' wealth. A third aspect of the
function of painting in the novel is seen in the way the attention to
detail disrupts any attempt to provide a clear account or description of
the world. Nathanaël is unimpressed by those of his master's friends
who only dabble in scientific experiments because it is fashionable. The
proper reception of the world is again at issue: 'Nathanaël avait entendu
louer, comme une qualité spéciale aux Pays-Bas, l'esprit d'égalité
régnant dans les mœurs et dans les coutumes, dont la sobriété rejetait

les galons et les rubans français. Mais il y a bien des nuances de ton et de qualité dans le simple drap noir' (971). Yourcenar may here be adapting a celebrated remark by Van Gogh that there are 'no less than twenty-seven blacks' in the paintings of Frans Hals.[11] The reader complements Nathanaël's awareness of the scene, reading what Nathanaël later realizes about the limits to possible interpretations of his world, since the difference in moral worth is enlarged to represent the difficulty of finding any overall system with which to comprehend the world.

### The Sacred and the Profane: Picturing Love and Prince Aldobrandini's Joke

As was noted above, the historical framework for the story can be specified as 1609–48. This dating is relevant for the two paintings described in *Un homme obscur*. About thirty years before Nathanaël's time in his service, Gerrit Van Herzog bought two paintings from one of the Aldobrandini princes (975–6). We can speculate that this means they were bought in about 1600, possibly from a prince happy to sell paintings which had become dated. One painting is a *Judith* and the other represents Titus and Berenice. It is only because he has to dust the pictures owned by Van Herzog that Nathanaël has a chance to look at them closely. The element of chance in his encounter is indicative of the unorthodox views he then takes both of the pictures and of their reception among Van Herzog's friends. The paintings provide unexpected elaborations upon the story and structure of *Un homme obscur*, one of which Nathanaël is keen to overlook, while another escapes both him and the owner. Whether intended or not by Prince Aldobrandini, we will see that if we speculate further on the sale of the paintings, it is possible that a joke was made at the youthful Van Herzog's expense at the time of the purchase, a trick repeated on the French Ambassador when he comments on the paintings during a visit to Van Herzog's house.

Nathanaël's reaction to the paintings is initially a simple matter of reaction to the colours and stories depicted before him. He responds to the different tones of white in the *Judith* and considers how the artist would have arrived at this effect. He also mentions the sword and the lighting. He is told later that the painting is a masterpiece of chiaroscuro, but his account suggests that he does not need to know this technical term. He displays similar independence in his suspicion about the lack of integrity in the gestures and sentiments depicted in the *Titus and Berenice*. He is also surprised that Van Herzog and his friends rarely pay much attention to the figures and stories in these representations of violence and passion.

Nathanaël's comments are not supposed to be sophisticated. After considering the comments from the French Ambassador on the perspective and proportion in the pictures, Nathanaël regrets that the artisanry evident in them is overlooked: 'Il semblait toutefois à Nathanaël que ces louanges sophistiquées ne tenaient pas compte de l'humble tâche de l'artisan occupé de ses brosses, de ses pinceaux, de ses couleurs à broyer et de ses huiles. Il devait y avoir comme toujours, pour ces tâcherons comme pour tous les autres, des cheminements imprévus et des gaffes tournées en aubaines. Les riches amateurs simplifiaient ou compliquaient tout' (976). The activity of picture-making is brought down to earth after the overblown praise from the Ambassador. Educated criticism seems to follow pre-arranged rules, here deriving directly from the concepts of chiaroscuro and perspective, rules which then have to be found in the paintings. Nathanaël suspects that the course of painting must be more complicated, involving mistakes and surprises.

Earlier in the story, when Nathanaël takes galley proofs of the *Prolégomènes* to Léo Belmonte, he recalls an adage about how comments on a painting should be appropriate to the knowledge the observer has of the things represented; the adage is a version of the anecdote about the ancient painter Apelles and the shoemaker: 'Mais il se souvint de l'adage qui veut que le cordonnier, en présence d'un portrait, doit se borner à juger, non de la ressemblance ou de la beauté du modèle, mais du bien-rendu de la chaussure' (955). The consideration of the grinding of the colours in the passage quoted above uses and modifies another story about Apelles, from the same part of Pliny's *Natural History*. This concerns Alexander the Great: 'When in Apelles' studio, Alexander talked often about painting although he had no specialist knowledge, and Apelles used to advise him politely to keep quiet, saying that the lads who ground the colours were laughing at him' (XXXV, 332). Nathanaël also prefers the artist and the spectator to be freed from excessive reliance on received views or rhetoric. His reference to 'cheminements imprévus' corresponds to his own admiration and engagement with the landscapes of the islands on which he happens to live and to his desire to be receptive to their wonders.

The phrase 'gaffes tournées en aubaines' is another reference to a story about Apelles, who was once unable to depict the detail of the lather around a horse's nostrils: 'A la fin, pris de dépit, il saisit l'éponge imbibée de toutes les couleurs, qui se trouvait à portée de sa main, et le lança contre le tableau, pour anéantir son œuvre. Le hasard dirigea l'éponge droit vers les naseaux du cheval et obtint l'effet que le peintre cherchait. Ainsi, ce que l'art avait été impuissant à produire, le hasard se chargea de le représenter.'[12] For Nathanaël, art requires the assistance of chance or of some other power. The reader may also take this as an invitation to find independent paths in pictures and in Yourcenar's text. Although this element is not easy to quantify in terms of the making of the two Van Herzog pictures, the reception and function of the paintings in the story does lead in unexpected directions. In terms of his 'quest', Nathanaël is voicing his desire to restore a sense of wonder to the way the world is represented. This is only achieved in part away from society, on the islands, particularly on the Friesian island where he dies.

The two paintings which Nathanaël dusts and considers at length are history paintings. They come from the Italian tradition of portraying dramatic moments from classical narratives: the *Judith* is based on the Old Testament story about the Jewish heroine; the *Titus* is based on Suetonius' *Lives of the Caesars*. We are reminded that Nathanaël has sufficient knowledge of these texts to reflect on the content of the narratives and their representation on canvas. In contrast to our discussion of the uses of Dutch seventeenth-century painting above, here Nathanaël stands back and looks at these stories. His comments indicate that he relates to some aspects of these paintings and ignores other correspondences with his own story.

To take the *Titus and Berenice* first, Nathanaël is unimpressed by the theatrical gestures of the figures depicted. Although he cannot be aware of the tradition of depicting the gestures of great human dramas in history painting, Nathanaël objects to the excessive rhetoric of the picture. His comments are sufficient to lend support to the suggestion above that the painting comes from the Mannerist period, in the latter part of the sixteenth century. His concern for accuracy leads him to question the veracity of the alleged love between Titus and Berenice. He suspects the motives of the lovers sully the purity of the ideal love that they are supposed to represent. Yet he allows some room for artistic licence, as long as it does not distort: 'A coup sûr, l'histoire n'avait pas à être reproduite point par point sur des toiles bordées d'or.

Mais il lui semblait qu'au faux des sentiments répondait le faux des gestes' (975). Nathanaël's concern for purity means that he demythologizes the story of Titus and Berenice by reflecting on the content of the story and the way it is being told. He is drawing on his own experience of love; he has been made fully aware of falseness in feeling. It is not surprising that the *Titus*, praised by connoisseurs, is considered a piece of superficial display compared with the poignant hopelessness of his love for Madeleine d'Ailly.

Nathanaël's lessons in looking derive from Yourcenar's use of the Racinian version of the story of Titus and Berenice. Maurice Delcroix, in 'Mythes de l'obscur', has pointed to the echoes of Racine in the text, concentrating in this context on the use of the adjective 'pur' in Nathanël's critique of the painting.[13] However, the particular nuance applied by Yourcenar is in her adaptation of Racine's 'Préface', a satirical and didactic exercise in dressing down critics of his version of the story. The right combination of artistry and reserve is discussed by Racine, who adopts an anecdote from classical literature to support his argument, citing a musician's response to Philip of Macedon when the latter criticized the rendition of a song: 'A Dieu ne plaise, Seigneur, que vous soyez jamais si malheureux que de savoir ces choses-là mieux que moi!' (*Bérénice*, 34). Yourcenar's use of such anecdotes carries comparable satire and the desire to couple modest learning and mystery when looking at the creations of art. In *Un homme obscur* this mode of looking is extended, experimentally, to both society and the natural world.

Nathanaël is unconsciously recuperating the myth of pure love in his comments on the *Titus*. At this point in the story, he is becoming enamoured of Madeleine d'Ailly. The passage concerning the paintings follows the music party and the last solitary note played by Madeleine on the harpsichord. Nathanaël objects to the indiscreet farewells of Titus and Berenice; he replaces their myth with his own idealized love affair with Madeleine. His departure from her is extraordinarily discreet, as Maurice Delcroix demonstrates in 'D'une rhétorique de la discrétion'. For Nathanaël the farewell is also a visitation and he lingers momentarily on the threshold of this ideal world before leaving for the island. He decides that he ought not to presume to kiss her hand: 'Pendant qu'il se le disait, elle s'approcha et l'embrassa sur les lèvres d'un baiser si léger, si rapide et cependant si ferme qu'il recula d'un pas, comme devant la visitation d'un ange. Ils se tenaient sur le seuil de la porte. Madame lui dit adieu de son beau

regard qui ne souriait pas et referma sur lui le battant' (994). The
reference to pictorial representations of the Visitation organizes the
space in this scene with Nathanaël and Madeleine according to the
distance that exists between them physically and socially. Madeleine
may become 'un ange' but she remains 'Madame'. The scene also
presents the idea of the two characters standing on a threshold, in
terms of encountering the Other in space and by sight.

In *Ce que nous voyons, ce qui nous regarde*, Didi-Huberman
incorporates Kafka's parable about the doorkeeper at the gates of the
Law, from the penultimate chapter of *The Trial*, [14] into a discussion of
the act of looking in terms of a threshold: 'Regarder, ce serait prendre
acte que l'image est structurée comme un *devant-dedans*: inaccessible
et imposant sa distance, si proche soit-elle—car c'est la distance d'un
contact suspendu, d'un impossible rapport de chair à chair. Cela veut
juste dire—et d'une façon qui n'est pas seulement allégorique—que
*l'image est structurée comme un seuil*.'[15] The threshold between Nathanaël
and Madeleine is only transgressed during two brief moments of
erotic contact, during the kiss just mentioned and during the joint
stroking of the spaniel Sauvé: 'Pour lui, le contact de cet épiderme
délicat lui fit l'effet d'une douce brûlure. Nulle femme ne lui avait
paru si tendre ou si pure' (991). In the scene above, Nathanaël returns
almost immediately to the position of observer at the threshold. Both
events are moments of sacred communion for him.

Otherwise, he stands apart and when he looks at Madeleine it is
with reverence and awe. In Madeleine's bedroom hangs a painting on
the subject of Diana at her toilet: 'On voyait [...] un petit tableau qui
scandalisait fort les servantes. Le peu qu'il avait retenu d'Ovide lui fit
deviner une Diane au bain' (974–5). This reference to the painting
owned by Madeleine invites us to consider the spectator again, on this
occasion Nathanaël as Actaeon in the painting, as suggested by this
textual allusion. In his worship for his goddess, Nathanaël is protected
by his lowly position from the sight of the naked Diana or private
world of Madeleine, but he is daily involved in a process of looking
that shares the dramatic danger and sacred taboo of Actaeon's discovery of Diana. Delcroix only comments on the *Diane au bain* in
order to compare the reported reactions of the servants to the
reactions of Van Herzog's friends to his paintings and to note that
Nathanaël does not see the painting, since he only hears about it
(Delcroix, 'Mythes de l'obscur', 133–4). However, what operates here
in the text is a symptom of the taboo about seeing the goddess; despite

literally not seeing the picture, Nathanaël does not perceive this representation of his situation. He has a habit of remembering selectively and of suppressing disturbing memories: here he does not recall what happened to the male character in Ovid's *Metamorphoses*.[16]

On the encounter with the painting of the Old Testament story of Judith and Holofernes, Nathanaël observes that the obscene decapitated body and bloodless head are disturbing and he is reminded of the violence contained in Biblical stories. In his initial description of the painting, we read of the two sources of light in the *Judith*: 'Un lumignon dans un coin faisait luire un glaive d'où gouttait du sang. Un peu d'aube entrait par une embrasure' (975). We are reminded of an earlier scene in the story when Nathanaël makes a surprise visit to Mevrouw Loubah's shop where his wife Saraï has been living since two months before the birth of their son, Lazare. He notices light coming from the back of the dark shop: 'Un peu de lumière provenait d'une lampe dans la petite pièce du fond, à travers l'entrebâillement d'une tenture. [...] Il était ignoble d'épier; il s'avança pourtant sans bruit jusqu'au seuil de la chambrette éclairée comme une scène' (955). Again the sight and space of contact with the beloved is figured by a threshold. Chiaroscuro has been associated with Saraï since her appearance in the story: 'C'était une fille plus toute jeune, au beau visage doré comme une pêche. Juive sans doute, car il ne connaissait qu'aux Juives ce teint chaud et ces yeux sombres' (943). Then her presence illuminates his shabby and murky lodging: 'Et pourtant, depuis qu'elle était là, tout semblait doré comme par la lumière d'une lampe' (945). Maurice Delcroix detects the use of Rembrandt here for this glorification of love, but the question of the adaptation of paintings and of Nathanaël's position as spectator is perhaps more complicated than in Delcroix's reading of a general reference to Rembrandt ('Clair de femme', 647). In terms of the structure of the narrative, Nathanaël stands before a painting that uses these devices of light and dark. He is not aware of the connection between Saraï and Judith that the chiaroscuro motif invites us to make.[17]

This light–dark motif is developed in the story. They are not balanced evenly, since this would be artificial and restrictive. Nathanaël remains 'un homme obscur', preferring the night on l'Ile Perdue and at sea: 'Mais, ce qu'il préférait, c'étaient les ciels tout noirs mêlés à l'océan tout noir. Cette nuit immense lui rappelait celle qui emplissait les combles de la hutte, et qui lui avait semblé immense elle aussi' (934). The 'lights' of Amsterdam colour the experience of the

city, during his life at the printing press, with Saraï and at the house
of Van Herzog. Then, on an island again, Nathanaël is free to indulge
his preference for the night:

il continuait d'aimer passionnément la nuit. Elle semblait ici illimitée, toute-
puissante: la nuit sur la mer prolongeait de tous côtés la nuit sur l'île. Parfois,
sorti de la maison, dans le noir, où l'on n'apercevait indistinctement que la
masse molle des dunes, et, dans l'entrebâillement, le blanc moutonnement de
la mer, il enlevait ses vêtements, et se laissait pénétrer par cette noirceur et ce
vent presque tiède. Il n'était alors qu'une chose parmi les choses. Il n'aurait
su dire pourquoi, ce contact de sa peau avec l'obscurité l'émouvait comme
autrefois l'amour. A d'autres moments, le vide nocturne était terrible.
(1004–5)[18]

The night absorbs man, island and sea. Nathanaël's union with the
night provides him with a simpler and more direct path to union with
the landscape than Zénon experiences on his way out of Bruges at the
start of 'La promenade sur la dune'. We will come to the idea of the
sight and touch of landscape and the body later in this chapter. The
skin's immersion in the darkness of night contrasts with the discreet
contact with the pale skin of Madeleine d'Ailly. The glimpse of white
('dans l'entrebâillement...') attenuating this dark picture provides an
erotic variation on the light–dark motif in Yourcenar's text. The
sacred status of communion with Madeleine is represented by the
penetration of Nathanaël by the night, since their exchanges are
established in terms of the visual, located at the site of threshold. The
sexual intercourse has to be figured by displacement. We will return
to the method of representation here: it is precisely the negotiation of
the question of artifice and the figuration of the body which is
addressed in the essay on Rembrandt.

In Renaissance depictions of the story of Judith and Holofernes,
the story was read as an allegory of man's downfall at the hands of a
scheming woman, sometimes forming a companion-picture to representations of the story of Samson and Delilah.[19] We know that the
picture employs the technique of chiaroscuro and that it was bought
in Italy c.1600: it is certainly pre-Counter-Reformation, when,
according to Hall's Dictionary, the subject comes to represent victory
over sin. The 'somptueux seins nus', for example, contrast with the
austerely dressed Judith in Caravaggio's Judith and Holophernes of
1598–9, now in the Galleria Nazionale (Palazzo Barberini) in Rome.
Delcroix discusses the way the description of the painting makes us

think of Saraï as a mythical female figure, who drags Nathanaël into a world of deception and vice. Bérénice, as a Jewish queen, was deeply resented by the Romans and seen as a threat to custom; hence they obliged Titus to give her up. In the case of the *Judith*, Delcroix argues that the demythologizing of the grand narratives represented on canvas is supported by the way Nathanaël is able to see his relationship with Saraï as part of the randomness of his existence: 'Il fit un long somme. Cette année de passion et de déconvenue tombait au gouffre, comme tombe un objet qu'on lance par-dessus bord, comme étaient tombés, à son retour à Greenwich, ses craintes paniques d'avoir tué le gros négociant amateur de chair fraîche, ses longs mois de vagabondage avec le métis, ses deux années d'amour et de pénurie avec Foy. Tout cela aurait pu n'avoir jamais lieu' (956). Delcroix also argues that the restrained destruction of some crockery and the cradle made for Lazare contrasts with the extreme violence of the *Judith*.

Meanwhile, Delcroix does not discuss the absence of any realization on Nathanaël's part that the *Judith* may speak to him personally. This may be read as suppression of the power possessed by Saraï, from which Nathanaël endeavours to free himself. His approach to art is to demythologize, but this has to involve some inner distancing which may again be read as the suppression of personal memories. He does not think of Foy when he sees the severed head of Holophernes, although she inhabits his memory by association with the act of severing: 'Le vieux s'était distrait de son chagrin en creusant la fosse: au cours de son travail, il aperçut une taupe dérangée dans son gîte souterrain et la coupa sauvagement en deux d'un coup de pelle. Sans que Nathanaël sût pourquoi, la mémoire de Foy et celle de cette bestiole assassinée restèrent à jamais liées l'une à l'autre' (931). Arguing from the basis of Nathanaël's general naïvety about life would only add to the covering of the narrative reflected in his interpretation of the *Judith*. He is certainly not ready to face such an explicit representation of the private emasculation and public scandal he risked when with Saraï. The text carries his encounter with disturbing memories by focusing on his response to the patches of white or blanks in the painting: 'L'artiste s'était sûrement plu à opposer le blanc livide de cette tête sanguinolente au blanc doré de cette poitrine. Le corps tronqué gisait sur le lit; il était nu, lui aussi, sauf pour les plis discrets d'un linge, qui, avec ceux du drap froissé, offraient à l'œil un autre effet de blancheur. Le peintre avait dû reculer d'un pas pour mieux juger du contraste' (975). The text responds, of course, to the variation on white in what is called 'un chef-d'œuvre de clair-obscur', but the function of this passage may also be understood in terms of the particular impact of the colour white on Nathanaël. The 'blancs'/blanks mark the trace of pain and fear. White figures, for the reader, both disturbing absence and unavoidable presence. The visualized memory of Saraï is too painful and she is only discussed again when he has to remember her following the scene when he hears of her death; on the island he can only cry out her name repeatedly (995–8). At this point in *Un homme obscur*, the reader has to place Nathanaël in the narrative represented in the painting, just as it was necessary to take up the hint offered by the painting of Diana.

To conclude this section on Nathanaël's encounter with the two history paintings, it is worth speculating further on the original purchase of them by Van Herzog. The text satirizes the owner and his guests for their scant attention and pre-prepared praise. No doubt it was easy for Aldobrandini, or one of his staff, to persuade Van Herzog that the *Titus* was intrinsically valuable in view of the noble subject; Van Herzog himself tells Nathanaël that the subject of the painting is elevated. As suggested above, the style of the painting may well have been out of fashion and this could have prompted the sale: this is therefore a typical example of a purchase of a work of art as part of a tour of Italy undertaken by a wealthy young Northerner. The *Judith* is more suggestive. For a young bachelor abroad for his tour prior to his return to marriage and a comparatively enclosed existence, the sale of a painting of a scheming dangerous woman with the severed head of a deceived man shows no little humour. More amusing still is the implication of the suggestion made by René Wilenski that in the Low Countries artists portrayed the story of Judith in order to celebrate the resistance against the Spanish army of occupation.[20] Although Wilenski provides no documentary evidence that this meaning was either intended by artists or found by spectators of such paintings at the time, the idea of a historical allusion offers an intriguing alternative to the reaction of Van Herzog and his friends.[21] No mention is made of their detecting any historical allusion, but then their leisured lives as dilettantes are wilfully ignorant of so much of the outside world. Nathanaël does speculate on the place of Van Herzog's household in society and is of course unaware of the specifics of a historical interpretation. Van Herzog had real reason to be the proud owner of the painting and might have noticed the irony in the situation when the French Ambassador restricted his praise of the picture to a reference to its diagonal perspective, since France was becoming the next great power in Europe and would later be challenging the borders of the Low Countries.

In terms of references and allusions within Yourcenar's text and in the field of Yourcenar studies, it is also necessary to consider one painting which has been associated with *Un homme obscur*. Jan Metsijs's *Judith* in Antwerp, chosen for the cover of *Nathanaël pour compagnon*, the special issue of the *Bulletin de la Société Internationale d'Etudes Yourcenariennes* devoted to *Un homme obscur*. In his article in the volume, Maurice Delcroix explains that the Metsijs is chosen because it shows a use of chiaroscuro that is more appropriate for the story than Rembrandt's (even though there is no known *Judith* by Rembrandt). The fact that Delcroix passes from the text to the painting without any explanation for this transposition suggests that we are supposed to find exact parallels.[22] In Yourcenar's text, Judith is holding the head in both hands and the sword can be seen in one corner; in the Antwerp picture she holds the head in her left hand and the sword in her right. The Assyrian tents in the background of the Metsijs are not mentioned in Yourcenar's text; there is no sign in the picture of the 'petite négresse' mentioned in the text. The text does refer to the contrast between Judith's breast and the severed head: 'L'artiste s'était sûrement plu à opposer le blanc livide de cette tête sanguinolente au blanc doré de cette poitrine' (975); also to 'le ventre à demi voilé de gaze' (975). The most obvious reason for choosing this *Judith* is that the Antwerp group of Yourcenar scholars, whose articles are collected in the volume, could not resist using the example in the Musée Royal des Beaux-Arts in their city. Although it is not necessarily relevant which particular *Judith* Yourcenar may have had in mind, and there is nothing automatically wrong with using this painting for the cover illustration, the way the allusion is proposed by Delcroix is problematic. The possibility of a contemporary historical allusion, suggested by Wilenski's study, is not considered by the Antwerp group. We have to recognize that we need at least to discuss the implications of possible pictorial references.

Whether the joke about the historical allusion was intended or not, on the part of Van Herzog or Yourcenar, the powerful image of Judith has several layers of relevance for the Van Herzog household. This discussion of the function of the two history paintings has shown that they act as alternative versions for considerations of the structure and content of the story being told in front of the pictures. This story concerns conscious and unconscious ways of looking at the self, other people and the world. The paintings are sites of the disruption of the imagination and stand as a hinge between various parts of the story. Their status as history paintings remind us that we need to keep in mind the way Nathanaël and the other characters are represented looking in *Un homme obscur*. The diverse perspectives opened up by a discussion of this part of the novel were provoked by the symptomatic allusions to anecdotes about Apelles. We turn now to an artist already discussed at some length, but who makes an unexpected appearance in *Un homme obscur* and hopefully a not unwelcome re-appearance in this book.

## Piranesi and the Sinking of the Printing Press

The reappearance of characters and historical figures in Yourcenar's texts is frequent. In the case of unnamed referents, this depends on the reader's readiness to respond to the text. In *Un homme obscur* the most dramatic resurgence is Piranesi's, directly in the form of borrowings from the essay 'Le cerveau noir de Piranèse' and more originally in adaptations of the plates of the *Prisons*. This section looks at the way the adventures of Nathanaël are recounted around a series of vertical motifs and then discusses the sublime constructions of Belmonte's discourse about philosophical and physical experimentation. The metaphorical dissolution of words in the narrative restores the horizontal perspective by forcing the verbal accounts inspired by Piranesi underground and underwater. Nathanaël comments on the over-neat mind of Van Herzog: 'Le cerveau de ce vieillard faisait au jeune domestique l'effet d'une chambre meublée avec soin et correctement rangée. Rien ne s'y trouvait de sale ou de laid, rien non plus de rare ou d'unique, qui eût compromis la belle symétrie du reste' (969). He suspects that there may be a secret compartment somewhere, although he realizes that it may well be empty. The 'cerveau noir' of Piranesi offers more challenging perspectives.

In the conversation between Belmonte and Nathanaël, echoes of the Piranesi essay abound. We are given a brief indication of what is to follow when Van Herzog calls Belmonte's published work '"Ces sublimes Prolégomènes"'; Yourcenar's essay refers to 'ces *Carceri* sublimes': 'sublime' is a word used sparingly in Yourcenar's work. Nathanaël's speech is the first to make an explicit echo of the etchings: '"je crois bien m'être dit que je marchais dans vos *Prolégomènes* comme sur des

ponts-levis ou des passerelles à claire-voie... A une hauteur qui donnait
le vertige. [...] Mais on se sentait mal à l'aise sur ces ponts volants qui
pliaient sous vous, et ne rejoignaient entre eux que des sommets nus
où il faisait froid...'" (982). The drawbridges and walkways abound in
the etchings, especially plates VI-VIII (figs. 15–16). One of the strengths
of Yourcenar's essay is to suggest ways in which we might study Piranesi's
'pre-sublime' or method of attaining the sublime. Saying that the *Prisons*
are sublime means that the task is to show how Piranesi's etchings lead
to the infinite.

Nathanaël's comments, cited above, can be read as bridges or
ladders helping us to gain access to Belmonte's discourse, via Piranesi's
constructions:

"Ces myriades de lignes, ces milliers, ces millions de courbes par lesquelles,
depuis qu'il y a des hommes, l'esprit a passé, pour donner au chaos au moins
l'apparence d'un ordre... Ces volitions, ces puissances, ces niveaux d'existence
de moins en moins corporalisés, des temps de plus en plus éternels, ces
émanations et ces influx d'un esprit sur l'autre, qu'est-ce, sinon ce que ceux
qui ne savent pas ce dont ils parlent appellent grossièrement des Anges?" (982).

It is the infinite in space and time that concerns Belmonte. Providing
an order to the trajectories of the human mind is his ambition, assisted
by algebra and words. Belmonte acknowledges that the network of
passages he constructs leads to nothing: 'Les passerelles des théorèmes
et les pont-levis des syllogismes ne mènent nulle part, et ce qu'ils
rejoignent est peut-être Rien. Mais c'est beau' (983). 'Le cerveau noir
de Piranèse' also plots the path from walkway to the infinite (106–8).
The arrival at Nothing after the pursuit of the mathematical infinity
is considered decisive by Annelies Schulte Nordholt. For her, it is the
moment when Belmonte prefigures Pascal, for whom infinity is 'le
signe de notre impuissance à saisir l'univers comme vestige signifiant',
rather than the Spinoza of the earlier part of Belmonte's discourse,
meaning the logic and algebra ('Soif de connaissance et désir du bien
dans l'œuvre de Marguerite Yourcenar').[23] Belmonte then proceeds to
suggest how he tried to extricate himself from this beautiful but
redundant framework.

In *Confessions of an English Opium-Eater*, De Quincey writes,
recalling Coleridge's description of the 'Dreams': 'follow the stairs a
little further, and you perceive it come to a sudden abrupt term-
ination, without any balustrade, and allowing no step onwards to him
who had reached the extremity, except into the depths below' (70).

Belmonte, from the dizzying heights of his beautiful mountain, finds himself back on the ground, on his backside, 'me revoilà le cul sur la terre nue' (983), like Montaigne: 'Si, avons-nous beau monter sur des échasses, car sur des échasses encore faut-il marcher de nos jambes. Et au plus élevé trône du monde, si ne sommes assis que sus nostre cul'.[24] Belmonte's search for a way forward employs abysses, holes and curves; his search for a centre leads him to dig within himself. This return to within the body after the imaginary flights across the outer world locates the position shared by Montaigne, Belmonte and Nathanaël. Thus when Nathanaël later distances himself from Belmonte's discourse, he neglects to acknowledge the embodied self that Belmonte envisages: 'Mais il n'allait pas, comme Léo Belmonte, s'inquiéter jusqu'au bout d'on ne sait quel axe ou quel trou qui était Dieu ou bien Soi-même. Il y avait autour de lui la mer, la brume, le soleil et la pluie, les bêtes de l'air, de l'eau et de la lande; il vivrait et mourrait comme ces bêtes le font. Cela suffisait' (1009).

Belmonte's comments on exploring the body will be developed further after we have looked at Rembrandt's *Deux Noirs*, but here it is worth recalling our discussion in Chapter 3 of Georges Poulet's account of the way the Romantics turned Piranesi's etchings into figures of inner self-exploration. The flight to the sublime has led us back to the brain and body of the source and the reader/spectator. It is not surprising that Nathanaël has to let the torrent subside: 'Ce torrent de mots qui sur le moment l'avait jeté bas semblait rentré sous terre' (985). Again we find Nathanaël needing to bury experience within himself, as if that is the place where an alchemical process can be worked upon these strange words. The water functions doubly because it alerts the reader to the way the text has prepared us for this dissolution of discourse, which here is salvaged within the body of writing. It remains to be seen for how long. The earlier passage of dissolution occurs when Cruyt's printing press is destroyed by men in the pay of the French Ambassador.

Nathanaël's reservations about pictorial rhetoric reiterate his doubts about the various genres of Latin literature that he encounters when working for his uncle. Any dogmatic approach to culture is rejected: the value of words seems to have been debased by culture and society. When Nathanaël arrives at Cruyt's printing press to ask for lodgings, he finds the presses and cranks destroyed: 'une grande flaque d'encre s'étalait sur le comptoir et en dégoulinait en longues traînées. La mare luisante et noire lui rappela celle dont Mevrouw Loubah, toutes portes fermées, se servait pour dire la bonne aventure. Mais le plus étrange encore était le sol jonché de caractères d'imprimerie sortis des tiroirs béants; des milliers de lettres s'enchevêtraient en une sorte d'alphabet insensé' (957). The letters are in disorder and are separated from the ink which allows us to read their sense when printed. The third ingredient is mentioned a little further on: 'le courant d'air faisait voleter çà et là des mains de papier déchiquetées sorties de leurs sacs ouverts' (957). The letters of language, having been detached from the sea of ink, will disappear into it; here too water displays its spatial diversity in its appearance as a surface and, when it falls, as a substance of depth. Nathanaël realizes that Cruyt's oaths do not reflect reality. He will come to appreciate the visual chaos inflicted upon the alphabet, the foundation of verbal discourse, in a later manifestation. The prurient publications of Cruyt's press have reduced language to insignificance: Patricia de Feyter suggests that the Cruyt episode sees the defeat of an attempt to express the truth, but misses the point that it is a debased 'truth' that was being printed.[25]

The later incidence of this surface-depth figure occurs when Nathanaël returns to Belmonte's apartment. The disappearance of the man and all the contents, not least the new philosophical work, is related in the brief sentence: 'Le dedans était vide' (986). Nathanaël learns that 'ces bouts de papier-là' ended up in the canal. The pool of ink expanding, almost in revenge, towards the letters, here takes the form of the canal, swallowing the text. The threat has been realized:

Nathanaël regarda l'eau lourde. Depuis que ce canal avait été creusé, on avait dû y jeter bien des choses, des déchets de nourriture, des fœtus, des charognes d'animaux, peut-être un ou deux cadavres. Il pensa à ce trou qui était Rien ou Dieu. [...] Il rentra à la maison plus assombri que surpris. Il pensait à cette écriture délayée par l'eau et à ces feuillets ramollis et flasques coulant dans la vase. Ce n'était peut-être pas pire pour eux que l'imprimerie d'Elie. (987)

The heavy water replaces the thick pool of ink, except that 'flasque' is now associated with the paper. The canal absorbs things and words. The outlook that has been darkened by the abandonment of Belmonte's papers to the water brings three elements of Yourcenar's texts to mind: the 'don sombre' motif of death from *Mémoires d'Hadrien* and other texts; the collection of Negro Spirituals entitled *Fleuve profond, sombre rivière*; and the phrase used by Yourcenar in *Les Yeux ouverts*, 'sombrer au large' (329). As we saw in Chapter 1, water threatens to destabilize discourse from as early on in Yourcenar's work as the essay on Poussin. In *Un homme obscur*, the principal tale in *Comme l'eau qui coule*, the danger is more marked, but the text endeavours to confront what this might mean for verbal and visual investigation.

His last philosophical utterance concerns his desire to inject chaos into the ordered structures of the *Prolégomènes*: 'Le chaos sous l'ordre, puis l'ordre sous le chaos, puis...' (984). The metaphor of the depth of water is relevant here, since Zénon uses the same metaphor to suggest ways of seeing the complexity of the appearance of human understanding in the cancelling out of contrary wave movement. Then he considers the depth of the sea as a way of seeing through successive layers of theses and antitheses during his meditations in 'L'abîme': 'Zénon regardait fuir ce flot désordonné, emportant comme des épaves le peu de vérités sensibles dont nous nous croyons sûrs. Parfois, il lui semblait entrevoir sous le flux une substance immobile, qui serait aux idées ce que les idées sont aux mots. Mais rien ne prouvait que ce substratum fût la dernière couche, ni que cette fixité ne cachât point un mouvement trop rapide pour l'intellect humain (687).[26] Zénon then descends into an exploration of his own body, where water is the dominant force. Water's function in the inner and outer world is one site of the 'dehors–dedans' dialectic.

The words that have found their way to the bottom of the canal have been drawn in by the element that is more than a match for the vertical movement of the Piranesian adventures, the sublime flights of philosophical inquiry and the subterranean passages of self-exploration. The decay of words accompanying the decay of things in the story is figured in the revenge of ink and the abyss of the canal. In the concluding section of *Un homme obscur*, water will again, in different ways, demonstrate its flat calmness and its hidden power. One brief and discreet moment at the end of the music party given by Madeleine d'Ailly, drawing on Vermeer's *Music Lesson*, encapsulates the way the drift from culture to nature is visualized in the story: 'avant de refermer le clavecin, elle posait parfois un doigt distrait sur une touche. Ce son unique tombait comme une perle ou comme un pleur. Plein, détaché, tout simple, naturel comme celui d'une goutte d'eau solitaire qui choit, il était plus beau que tous les autres sons' (974). The simile hesitates between a bodily emission and a prized natural object. For Maurice Delcroix, the similarities in sounds and meanings (he also mentions the mirror that appears in the text a few lines before the above quotation) are signs of the persistent sorrow for an impossible love: the unconsolable that remains the unsaid.[27] However, the apparent simplicity of the action is deceptive, since the passage involves considerable complexity and problems.

Madeleine's absent-minded touch of the keyboard involves the descent of her finger onto the key and downward pressure to make the note, which is released after the plucking of two strings on the instrument; the movement of the sound is figured by reference to the pearl–tear cliché. By contrast, rather than as a simile, the droplet of water first descends to the surface of the water, then makes its impact on the surface and its sound, before bouncing back slightly and finally fading away. Unfortunately the commonplace pearl–tear simile does not work here: a tear does not fall in one way and it is not clear from where the pearl might fall. The picture is not quite convincing; the text gets confused trying to picture a sound falling. In this parallel the seeing is made needlessly more complicated than the hearing. Previously, Nathanaël had equated the mirages of the eyes to those of the ears (973); the learning process continues for him and for the reader. In spite of the awkward phrasing, in a radical subversion of music's traditional time, organization and reception, here water is the ideal musical form as well. The elusive sound that language tries to represent points out the limits of the possibilities of representation. Looked at closely, we cannot hear the sound because the words make us see too much; the brief presence on the surface of a passing note is as ungraspable as Madeleine in *Un homme obscur* and the woman in Vermeer's *Music Lesson*. In terms of the representation attempted, we encounter, according to Louis Marin, 'un procès de différenciation infinie au cours duquel le réel en vient à manquer au dispositif mimétique'.[28] In both cases, the mirror, the man and the words only take us to the threshold of grasping the woman represented.

### Rembrandt's Vision: The Secrets of Painting

Reading Yourcenar's essay on Poussin, we are made aware of the tradition of written commentary on the artist. The same is true of the essay on Rembrandt and his painting *Deux Noirs* (fig. 17). In a letter to me in 1994, H. R. Hoetink stated that the Rembrandt Research Project may well reject the attribution of the painting to Rembrandt; they have yet to publish their verdict. Yourcenar believed it to be by Rembrandt and the points she makes will be seen not to rely significantly on the question of attribution. In other circumstances,

Fig. 17. Rembrandt, *Two Negroes* (1661)
Oil on canvas, 78×64·5 cm
Mauritshuis, The Hague

for example if a case were being made for Rembrandt's sympathy for slaves, a change in attribution would be relevant. By the time Yourcenar gets to this specific painting, she has moved away from her general consideration of Rembrandt to look at the figures represented in the picture. The consistencies in her argument discussed here would not be undermined by a change in attribution, since her essay always remains independent of fixed, harmonized interpretations of the artist.

The essay is divided into three sections: the two general opening paragraphs which discuss Rembrandt's work as a whole; the response to the one painting, *Deux Noirs*; and the account of the Dunbar Creek Legend. The purpose of the present discussion is to look at the opening part of the essay, which addresses the secret life of a painting by Rembrandt. Where words have failed Nathanaël, in the essay Yourcenar attempts to use the visual to help her verbal account present a persuasive commentary which could exist alongside Rembrandt's vision.

Paul Claudel focuses on the 'dehors–dedans' motif when referring to the *Portrait of Jan Six*: 'J'y vois comme une figure du peintre lui-même qui appartient à la fois à deux mondes, celui du dedans et celui du dehors, et qui se sert de la réalité pour déchiffrer le grimoire.'[29] Yourcenar's essay opens with this motif, an idea common in writing on Rembrandt. In her version, it is applied explicitly across Rembrandt's work: 'Rembrandt a eu peut-être plus que tout peintre sa vision, son rêve si l'on veut, du monde qu'il portait en lui et du monde où il a vécu' (227). Both the inside of the mind and body, on the one hand, and the world external to him, on the other, are represented in Rembrandt's work. His vision presents both worlds and the passage between them, operating as a fluid surface. Bachelard's analysis of the exchanges between the inner and outer is relevant here: 'Précisément, la phénoménologie de l'imagination poétique nous permet d'explorer l'être de l'homme comme l'être d'*une surface*, de la surface qui sépare la région du même et la région de l'autre.'[30] We may adapt Bachelard's idea and consider a painting as a surface of being. The life of the painting, the surface of being, exists thanks to the vision of the artist; this vision positions the picture between the two worlds, inner and outer, attempting to represent the exchange between them.

It is the inner world to which, in Yourcenar's view, we most readily respond, even if this reponse is not a simple issue. The body of the painting, its texture and artifice, engages the spectator's body, both at the surface and within. Merleau-Ponty discusses this call from the painting to the spectator: 'Qualité, lumière, couleur, profondeur, qui sont là-bas devant nous, n'y sont que parce qu'elles éveillent un écho dans notre corps, parce qu'il leur fait accueil.'³¹ For Yourcenar, this engagement is private, secret and physiological: 'On sent bientôt que chaque tableau, chaque dessin, est un fragment d'un univers rembrandtesque auquel nous appartenons, mais secrètement et le plus souvent inconsciemment, comme aux nerfs, aux artères, aux globules blancs et rouges qui circulent dans la nuit du corps' (567). Though concerned primarily with painting in the essay, Yourcenar does include the drawings in her account of Rembrandt's visual appeal. The essay passes from the general to the body, emphasizing the depiction of the outer and inner world, and the link between painting and the spectator.

Moving on to list some examples, Yourcenar starts with *David playing the harp before Saul*: 'Le vieux Saül cachant derrière un rideau toute la douleur humaine' (567).³² This world within remains a secret, unspecifiable to the individual or to others. Molecules and blood also feature in Elie Faure's account of Rembrandt: 'les palpitations lumineuses et les mouvements instinctifs qui sont inappréciables pour les autres, réduisent pour lui l'univers à une circulation ininterrompue de molécules animées dont il fait partie lui-même. [...] Il suit notre marche à la mort aux traces de sang qui la marquent.'³³ In 'Deux Noirs de Rembrandt', the darkness of this inner world of blood, nerves and arteries is a way of introducing the celebrated darkness of Rembrandt's pictures early in Yourcenar's discussion, by shifting our attention to the dark inner world of the spectator. When this unconscious awareness irrupts or is released then the life of the painting becomes even more engaging and powerful; this contrasts with the way Nathanaël was seen to suppress aspects of his response to the *Judith*.

The essay moves on to discuss artifice in Rembrandt, especially his use of chiaroscuro. This analysis complements the preceding discussion of chiaroscuro in *Un homme obscur*. Yourcenar notes how the question of the balance of light and dark has been interpreted as either artifice or mystery; many writers on Rembrandt start with the first and link this to the second, but Yourcenar is concerned to simplify the subject and to contrast the positions.³⁴ Her tone is sceptical: 'Artifices, disent les uns, symboles d'une mystérieuse pénétration au dedans des choses, diront les autres' (568). The difference is indicated by the

denigration of the term 'symboles', which she considers inadequate
when applied to an artist's or writer's practice. Also, she is uncertain
about saying, simplistically, that Rembrandt's *mystery* is best described
by his ability to get inside objects.

The essay responds to Eugène Fromentin's discussion of Rembrandt's
*Night Watch* in *Les Maîtres d'autrefois*, the book on Dutch and Flemish
painting which set the agenda for writers for the next century: 'On y
cherche des mystères qui n'y sont pas. Le seul mystère que j'y découvre,
c'est l'éternelle et secrète lutte entre la réalité telle qu'elle s'impose et
la vérité telle que la conçoit un cerveau épris de chimères.'[35] Fromentin's
enthusiasm for 'l'éternelle et secrète lutte' is developed in Yourcenar's
treatment of secrecy in the visual, although it does not follow
Fromentin's psycho-biographical reading of Rembrandt's work.[36]
Yourcenar's version of the 'dehors–dedans' recurs briefly in the way she
sees artifice and naturalness presented in *The Anatomy Lesson of Dr Tulp*:
'un amphithéâtre en plein jour groupe des médecins en vêtements
bourgeois, mais la chaleur de la vie imprègne leur corps, alors que le
cadavre qu'ils dissèquent est froid. L'artifice équilibre exactement le
manque d'artifice' (568). Fromentin's avoidance of the notion of
mystery, preferring instead an interaction between physical reality and
the artist's personal vision, has proven to be influential. Yourcenar's use
of the idea involves more emphasis on the physical involvement of the
spectators in the pictures, just as the animate bourgeois faces, figuring
surface pulse (surface of the picture) and inner life are spectators, readers
and listeners at Dr Tulp's lesson.[37]

For Yourcenar, therefore, Rembrandt's paintings are 'alive'. She
locates her discussion of secrecy and the visual in Rembrandt's
portrayals of the human head, mainly the self-portraits. This way of
approaching the works by Rembrandt which have received as much
attention as any, except perhaps the *Night Watch*, might be considered
as a corporeal or incarnate variation of the 'dehors–dedans' and of the
verbal–visual. She approaches the self-portraits by pursuing her
'visage–chaleur de la vie' symbiosis. Pondering the faces, she finds
further visual complexity, since it is a superficial sense of hesitation
about their identity that causes the feeling of strangeness, in contrast
to Focillon, who observes a 'kind of family likeness' in the portraits;[38]
it is not a matter of a secret that could be explained as something
specific, hidden or disclosed: 'Ils ne cachent ni ne livrent un secret'
(568). Here Bachelard's 'dialectique du dehors et du dedans' is
relevant, although, as is often the case with so-called Bachelard–

Yourcenar parallels, the link requires some nuance on the part of the reader: 'Alors, à la surface de l'être, dans cette région où l'être *veut* se manifester et *veut* se cacher, les mouvements de fermeture et d'ouverture sont si nombreux, si souvent inversés, si chargés aussi d'hésitation que nous pourrions conclure par cette formule: l'homme est l'être entr'ouvert.'[39] Multiplicity, movement and openness are all concepts Yourcenar is about to employ in her discussion of the surface and depth of Rembrandt's self-portraits. The half-open depicted figure on the surface of the painting is the most sensitive way, for Yourcenar, of speaking about Rembrandt's mysterious chiaroscuro.

In *Un homme obscur*, Belmonte abandons his cosmic meditations and investigates his body, describing his cough as 'cette boule d'eau et de boue qui monte et descend dans ma poitrine et m'étouffe' (984). The microcosmic bodily 'boule' recurs in Yourcenar's analysis of the subject of the self-portraits: 'Cette boule d'os et de chair, cette physionomie tantôt vulgaire et tantôt pathétique, [...] il a pu suivre ce quelqu'un au cours de la vie, depuis la ferme et charnue enveloppe de la jeunesse jusqu'à la substance avachie du vieil âge' (568). We have the little globe of flesh and bone as the bold surface and textured substance of the self-portraits. As the style of Rembrandt changes in the physical application of paint, so the body's progress is recorded.

What interests Yourcenar above all is that this progress is seen to involve the continuous transformation and passage that constitutes the life of a man, as well as the presence of an elusive self. Yourcenar again differs from Henri Focillon, and many others, who interpret the self-portraits as revelations of the artist's personality.[40] In '*Deux Noirs* de Rembrandt', the language of Belmonte's infinite speculations is recuperated in the witness to the passage of an elusive self: 'C'est ainsi qu'il a prouvé, comme personne avant ou après lui, l'incessant changement et l'incessant passage, les séries infinies qui constituent chaque homme, et en même temps ce je ne sais quoi d'indéniable qu'est le *Soi*, presque invisible à l'œil, facile à oublier ou à nier, cette identité qui nous sert à mesurer l'homme qui change' (568). Yourcenar concludes her general discussion of Rembrandt's pictorial vision with an attempt at defining the secret of his appeal. The spectator finds the infinity of the external world and a finite but almost invisible identity or inner world before him on the surface and in the flesh of the paintings. Thus it is the finite scale of the human figure to which near invisibility is applied, the visually secret world barely perceptible; the alchemy achieved by colour, paint and surface carries the body of the spectator with it throughout Rembrandt's work. The secret is in the limits of representation of verbal experience and the enormous range available to the artist for the representation of the passage of life, in the viewer, subject and artist. Paul Claudel voices a retrieval of metaphors similar to the last words of the dying philosopher Belmonte:

Ce chemin qui a servi autrefois à entraîner l'*Enfant Prodigue* et à le dissiper du côté de l'horizon, le *Philosophe* de Rembrandt l'a replié en lui-même, il en a fait cet escalier cochléaire, cette vis qui lui sert à descendre pas à pas jusqu'au fond de la méditation.[41]

The inner staircase reappears. We turn now to Nathanaël's experiments with this corporeal meditation in *Un homme obscur*.

## The Anatomy Lessons of Existence

Et pourtant, après tant d'années, passées à anatomiser la machine humaine, il s'en voulait de ne pas s'être hasardé plus audacieusement dans l'exploration de ce royaume aux frontières de peau, dont nous nous croyons les princes, et où nous sommes prisonniers. (*L'Œuvre au noir*, 689)

This section brings together the novel and the essay, so far discussed separately. It looks at how the corporeal investigations suggested by Belmonte are developed in *Un homme obscur* and how the idea of the body of the painting is explored in the extreme case of Rembrandt's painting *Deux Noirs*.

Nathanaël and the two figures in the painting could be read as representations of Everyman. Helen Watson-Williams considers that the anonymity and impassive life of Nathanaël make him an archetypal Everyman: 'Like another Everyman he moves forward to his end, accepting whatever chance or opportunity brings him and recognizing the finality of each phase as it closes'.[42] In his essay on Rembrandt, Jean Genet mentions how thinking of a pictorial Everyman might allow him to de-eroticize himself.[43] Nathanaël may be elusive to others, but the physical stays at the centre of his life on the island. Indeed, erotic response is still relevant in his fusion with the landscape. While the 'slaves' in the painting are visibly reduced to wrecks of their former bodies, the physical charge remains very strong.

Belmonte's wild discourse, which overwhelms Nathanaël, is one of the decisive moments in the story. In *Un homme obscur*, the revelatory moments tend to occur before Nathanaël realizes their significance, if he does so at all. So we read how it is possible to find an axis inside the body of the thinking being. The dark inner galaxy of the following passage has the near invisibility of the secrecy of identity discussed by Yourcenar at the end of the first part of the essay:

Car le secret, c'est que je creuse en moi, puisqu'en ce moment je suis au centre: ma toux, cette boule d'eau et de boue qui monte et descend dans ma poitrine et m'étouffe, mon dévoiement d'entrailles, nous sommes au centre... Ce crachat qui roule en moi strié de sang, ces boyaux qui me tourmenteront comme ne me tourmenteront jamais ceux d'un autre, et qui pourtant sont la même chair que les siens, le même rien, le même tout... Et cette peur de mourir, quand je sens néanmoins la vie battre avec passion jusqu'à la pointe de mon gros orteil... Quand il suffit d'une bouffée d'air frais venant de la fenêtre pour me gonfler de joie comme une outre... Donne ce cahier. (984)

Belmonte suspects that Nathanaël is able to comprehend his ideas because he is fatally ill: 'Vous crèverez comme moi dans environ deux ans' (980). Illness and vitality are continually allied in *Un homme obscur*. However, what matters in our present context is that the stoical attitude adopted by Belmonte requires the darkly lit invisible inner world. This is the human, bodily perspective on vision as constructed in the story. The intestinal labyrinth is a centreless world within this frame: the sea of bloody spittle; the pains that make Belmonte an individual, his alone and yet also the common lot; and the balance of blood circulating and the air rushing in. The passage explains how man is the place or axis where these inner and outer worlds meet.

Nathanaël later considers that the world before his eyes is his own body and this provides him with his text for study, although as we noted earlier he does not recognize how Belmonte had also spoken of such a text, albeit in the discourse of metaphysics: 'il pensait en tout cas qu'il eût été mal de ne pas s'absorber exclusivement dans la lecture du monde qu'il avait, maintenant et pour si peu de temps, sous les yeux et qui, pour ainsi dire, lui était échu en lot. [...] Plus ses sensations corporelles devenaient pénibles, plus il lui semblait nécessaire, à force d'attention, d'essayer plutôt de suivre, sinon de comprendre, ce qui se faisait ou se défaisait en lui' (1007). Reading the coverage of Rembrandt's painting in the essay and reading the world in the novel come together in this passage. The phrase 'sous les yeux' signifies the near invisibility mentioned above in the context of the secret inner life of the spectator of Rembrandt's paintings.

During the conversation with Belmonte, Nathanaël thinks of the effect of the philosophical constructions of Belmonte on ordinary objects. He recalls the slaves he saw when his ship stopped in Jamaica:

—Sauf le respect dû à Monsieur, il me semble que les choses ainsi enchaînées meurent sur place et se détachent de ces symboles et de ces mots comme des chairs qui tombent...
      Il pensait à une bande de captifs noirs à demi pourris dans leurs chaînes qu'il avait vus à la Jamaïque. (981)

In the context of Nathanaël's story, the image of objects casting themselves adrift from human interpretation transforms Nathanaël's ice-pack metaphor for his understanding of his own life. Now the parts that are detached are the residue, the basic remaining limbs of human beings. Yourcenar's essay on Rembrandt's two figures who were probably slaves complements Nathanaël's memory by changing the perspective and considering how the slaves experienced a life of physical hardship. If we ask whether they share the fate that befalls objects when suffocated by writing (as happens, in Nathanaël's view, in Belmonte's discourse), then we are seeing the text confront the question of how to represent this idea.

      In her powerful and sensitive attempt to describe the experience of looking at this painting, Yourcenar considers the two young men as remnants of their lives, reduced by experience to anonymity, frailty and unknown status—'inconnus, maladifs et déshérités' (568). They differ from other representations of Blacks in the tradition of history painting and Dutch painting, a tradition of representation which Yourcenar discussed in a long letter of November 1967 to Dominique de Ménil (*Lettres*, 260–9). In the essay, Yourcenar suggests where Rembrandt, like Nathanaël, might have encountered Blacks: 'Rembrandt dans les rues d'Amsterdam a sûrement rencontré des Noirs, esclaves à n'en pas douter, ou, pis encore, débris abandonnés d'esclaves; peut-être a-t-il vu amarré le long d'un quai un vaisseau négrier' (569). These slaves are reduced to debris, 'comme des chairs qui tombent', and transformed into different matter in *Un homme obscur*; it is simply fortunate that we do not have a more pitiful sight here. For Yourcenar, it is not a question of artificially representing the fact of the real wretchedness of slaves in that period; she demonstrates that these figures present sufficient hardship, spelling out how they are 'si visiblement dévastés' (569). The absence of artifice is also signalled by Roland Barthes in his discussion of a photograph of a freed slave: 'il certifie que l'esclavage a existé [...] le fait était établi sans méthode'.[44]

To empathize with the fate of the two figures, Yourcenar considers this physical and individual sight against the background of a fate that might have befallen anyone. These figures are debris and their eyes are one side of the evidence: 'Ceux-ci sont maigres, émaciés presque, et leurs yeux exorbités ou creux, aux paupières rosâtres, sont d'hommes qui ont connu les coups et la fièvre, en tout cas l'*intolérable*' (569). The costumes do not hide the frailty. To concentrate on the eyes is to present the idea of witness and the activity of looking at a picture as one of seeing a half-open surface, as we discussed earlier in this chapter. In another instance of adapting Bachelard's topos, Yourcenar has the external movement and reference in the adjective 'exorbités' and the look inside the body in the word 'creux'. Faded life causes the eyelids to be a pale form of bodily red, 'rosâtres'. Yourcenar sticks close to the picture's terms, without ignoring the visual evidence for the sake of expressions of pity: the empathy has to be handled via the picture. Hence her distinction between this image and later polemical representations: 'Pas même plaintifs ou visiblement craintifs, pas même bonassement accablés ou revendicateurs, comme les eussent représentés à partir du XVIIIe siècle les peintres à bons sentiments. Plus humains que Noirs, plus hommes qu'esclaves, soumis seulement plus encore que la plupart de nous à l'outrage d'exister' (229–30). For Yourcenar, the later approach would have diminished the corporeal power of the painting.

The essay may be supplemented if we consider the direction in which the eyes of the two figures tentatively look, seeming in fact to remain open-eyed without projecting much of a gaze at all, as if trying to look outside the frame of the painting but not managing to cross this distance. Their gazes set off in wholly different directions, the left figure looking down and across to the right, the right figure looking slightly upwards and to the left. Pascal Bonafoux's considers the look of Rembrandt's *Self-Portraits* to be the sight of solitude:

Le regard n'exprime pas ce qu'il possède, il révèle sa quête. Ses portraits interrogent une solitude.
Inquiète parce qu'elle est face à l'irrémédiable. Seule la métamorphose qu'est la peinture conjure le désespoir.[45]

The transformation of the story 'D'après Rembrandt' into *Un homme obscur* and this essay suggests an uncanny visual reference, since one of the principal pictorial sources for 'D'après Rembrandt' was the Berlin *Head of Christ*, where Christ is represented looking slightly upwards to the left.[46] The horizontal angle between the two sets of eyes differs, but the motif of the half-open eyes is repeated, linking the painting of the Saviour to the painting of the two slaves. Bonafoux refers to the *Head of Christ*: 'C'est par le seul portrait d'un Christ qui n'est ni torturé ni pantocrator, qui ne souffre, ne règne ni ne pardonne, qu'il tente d'atteindre le sacré. Par ce portrait d'un dieu incarné qui n'est qu'un homme.'[47] The idea of the figure incarnate in paint and flesh supports the comparison suggested here. The three figures are all presentations of existence in the form of the bodily life of painting.

Yourcenar then combines the idea of 'les séries infinies' and the '*Soi*', as she did when concluding her general remarks on Rembrandt. The experience depicted by Rembrandt could have occurred to anyone and could have been different; Yourcenar suggests that in the past the two figures have shown dignity, courage and even gentleness. She returns to the surface of the painting for evidence to support these observations. She finds fear in the expressions and maltreatment in the lips and shoulders, but contrasts these features with their apparent response to their condition: 'L'homme de gauche, qu'on dirait le plus robuste des deux, paraît s'appuyer sur son camarade, et en dépendre pour exister. L'autre, qui se tient très droit, si noble dans sa force usée, a l'indifférence royale des races fières. Rien de ce qu'il a été ne l'empêche d'être ce qu'il est' (569–70). As we will see, the Yourcenarian view of indifference, allied to secrecy, is applied to men, animals and landscape. The debris that have fallen away from the originals through abuse still show this, but there is strength in the detachment. The figure on the right retains his dignity, his 'forme maîtresse', according to Montaigne's formulation: 'Regardez un peu comment s'en porte notre expérience: il n'est personne, s'il s'écoute, qui ne découvre en soi une forme sienne, une forme maîtresse, qui lutte contre l'institution, et contre la tempête des passions qui lui sont contraires.'[48] The secret inner life of the two figures is detectable at the surface of Rembrandt's painting. The visual presentation of endurance also figures in the costume of the man on the right, especially around the stomach. The 'pentimenti' (areas retouched by Rembrandt), the subject of so much recent attention amongst specialists, give depth to the surface of the garment: behind the vigorous vertical lines lie a few transversal ribs and patches of white against a dark background which may represent either clothing or flesh.[49]

A means of passage down into the inner world of the figures

represented by Rembrandt was proposed in Belmonte's discourse. Nathanaël stands as observer of this process, listening to Belmonte, witnessing scenes on his travels, experiencing the anatomy lessons himself. In the painting *Deux Noirs*, the figures are discussed according to the body of the picture, their condition and the ways they are looking, in order to grasp the weight and corporeality of their pictorial presence. Yourcenar finds that they retain their dignity despite adverse circumstances; Nathanaël also manages to assert his humble, silent complaint at the text of the world. He does so by concentrating on the world immediately before him and the world within.

### Seascape and the Blues

One of the definitions of indifference in Yourcenar's writing comes in a letter to Nathalie Barney where she writes about how various buildings and certain stories concerning the island where she lives have left no trace: 'Ici, l'homme ne laisse pas de trace; la terre se refuse au souvenir humain. [...] Ces grands paysages se reformeront peu à peu, imperturbés, avec seulement au fond de leur indifférence un secret de plus' (*Lettres*, 189, 190). In *Un homme obscur* and 'Deux Noirs de Rembrandt', the secrets of the lives of Nathanaël and the two figures are absorbed into their respective backgrounds in the painting and on the island. Yourcenar achieves this conclusion in the novel by reviving painting and in the essay by using a legend about slaves making their escape by sea. Writing and painting enact disappearance.

The opening paragraph of 'Deux Noirs de Rembrandt' contains brief references to a number of paintings, etchings and drawings. One painting receives almost as much attention as all the other works put together: *Landscape with the Good Samaritan*. Yourcenar notes how the central human figures of the landscape are threatened by a hostile natural world and how the hero of the story is reduced to dark insignificance: 'où la sauvagerie de la mer démontée et des bois automnaux permettent à peine d'apercevoir, filant le long d'une plage dangereuse, le carrosse de l'homme riche qui ne s'est pas arrêté pour porter secours (et aura peut-être bientôt lui-même besoin d'aide), et moins visible encore, insignifiant, perdu dans un coin d'ombre, le Bon Samaritain qui soigne le blessé' (567). The painting has been cleaned since Yourcenar's visit to Cracow, revealing that the Samaritan is not quite lost in the corner, but certainly faces an awesome landscape ahead, in a painting that has been recently interpreted as hesitating between applauding action (the hunters) and the saving of a life (the Samaritan), on the one hand, and depicting submission to an ominous natural world, on the other.[50] Nathanaël's experience of the island is open to both interpretations: we read of Nathanaël's position in the canvas; we also read of the sea and the trees.

Painting has not been abandoned just because of the pictures in Van Herzog's house. We have seen how Yourcenar uses painting in her narrative. In the final part of *Un homme obscur*, there is a reference to her early story 'La tristesse de Cornélius Berg'. In this story, in the 1938 collection *Nouvelles orientales*, the disillusioned artist agrees that the colour of flowers reveals God to be the supreme artist, regretting that He had done a poor job on man (*OR*, 1218). Nathanaël comes across some shells that remind him of those collected by Van Herzog. He responds to objects that lack artifice and mention is made of a curious object he discovers on the beach: 'Ces babioles si prisées dans la grande maison semblaient un peu moins futiles, puisqu'elles se rapprochaient des formes que le temps, l'usure, et la lente action des éléments donnent aux choses. Il ramassa une fois une sorte de galette oblongue faite de sable durci et concrétisé, qu'une indentation pareille à l'empreinte d'un pouce faisait ressembler à la palette d'un peintre. La nature, comme l'homme, fabriquait de beaux objets inutiles' (999). The strange object leads Nathanaël to assert an equivalence between the prized objects of society and the useless works of nature. Unlike the grand theme of transhistorical indifferentiation between forms discussed in connection with Piranesi and *L'Œuvre au noir*, on this occasion the comparison concerns utility and value of the object. On the island he does not think that an artist could add anything to his vision of the world. However, the reader may recall that Rembrandt, working at the time of Nathanaël's demise, was testing the possibilities of representation in ways which relate to Nathanaël's criteria. Even if Nathanaël is unaware of it, the natural world of the island can be seen to have its narrator-artist, aware of the transience and futility of artificial constructions. Nature as artist assists, paradoxically, in illustrating the pervasive and unavoidable mediation of representation.

As long as he cannot sense worthless human involvement, the natural habitat of the island is a source of wonder for Nathanaël. Maurice Delcroix has argued that the conventional range of natural elements, described in commonplace terms, is an attempt on the part of the text to restore a sense of communion and reverence for the landscape and the sea. As applied to the last two sections of *Un homme obscur*, Delcroix's argument is persuasive,[51] while the less successful uses of commonplaces earlier in the story, as in the *perle–pleur* episode discussed above, are not rescued by his account.

Nevertheless, throughout the text nature is privileged over culture, especially on the island: 'Le matin, les vanneaux exécutaient dans le ciel leur vol nuptial, plus beau qu'aucune figure des ballets du roi de France' (1000). Another art form is downgraded. However, some human constructions are different and are retained for parallels. In a Bachelardian picture of the refuge found in the plantation (see the chapter 'Les coins' in *La poétique de l'espace*) the metaphor of the space and music of a church salvages the meagre human arrangement of the trees: 'On était là abrité comme à l'intérieur d'une église. Tout d'abord le silence semblait régner, mais ce silence, à l'écouter, était tissu de bruits graves et doux, si forts qu'ils rappelaient la rumeur des vagues, et profonds comme ceux des orgues de cathédrales; on les recevait comme une sorte d'ample bénédiction' (999–1000). Nathanaël is a nomadic figure registering the dissolution of human concepts about the external world and the impact of the natural world on himself, both within and without.

A brief remark in the narrative when he comes across a dead seagull suggests, albeit vaguely, a parallel with Diogenes: 'Nathanaël la retourna du bout de son bâton' (1012). Diogenes, always represented with his staff, also once wandered around in daylight shining a lantern in search of a wise person, as represented in Caesar van Everdingen's *Diogenes looking for an Honest Man* (Mauritshuis).[52] As Nathanaël comes to accept his lot, he seems to acquire an inner light: 'A mesure que son délabrement charnel augmentait, comme celui d'une habitation de terre battue ou d'argile délitée par l'eau, on ne sait quoi de fort et de clair lui semblait luire davantage au sommet de lui-même, comme une bougie dans la plus haute chambre de la maison menacée' (999–1009). Here the position of the human brain in the picture of the landscape is more specific than in the comparable figuration in the last two sentences of the essay on Bede. The mind is the last human light in the landscape and is transformed into a mountain besieged by the water flooding the earth. During the equinox storms, the threat that the sea will engulf the island is recognized, if not imminent. Landscape is to become seascape, but the inner light of the body's mind and eyes lives on for the time being.

The colour of Nathanaël's experience of impending death passes from pink to colourless clouds. The end of *Un homme obscur* is painted

Fig. 18. Poussin, *Vénus et Adonis* (c.1630)
Oil on canvas, 75×100 cm
Museum of Art, Rhode Island School of Design, Providence

less brilliantly than the end of *L'Œuvre au noir*, since the former is not a text of investigation but one of passive observation. As Elie Faure said of Rembrandt, 'l'individu suprême ne se sépare plus du monde'.[53] At the end he moulds himself into the landscape, but only accompanied by internal pain: until his death he retains his dark inner kingdom. Nathanaël is lying on the substance out of which nature had forged the painter's palette. He closes his eyes and that is the end of his story. The position of Nathanaël at the end of the text may be discussed with reference to the work of Louis Marin. Marin tests the limits of theories of representation, fascinated by the way theory's knowledge of its own limitations is in fact a strength. Inquiry is therefore open to the intelligible and the unknowable. On the encounter with the visual, Marin posits, with necessary hesitation, a searching 'Je', a subject always open to challenge and change. The hesitant Nathanaël proceeds as just such a fallible subject.

Interpretative hesitation and transformation are topics discussed in Marin's article 'A l'éveil des métamorphoses', which pursues his work on representations of the body and his investigation into the interaction of word and image in seventeenth-century theory.[54] He speculates on the crossing of the threshold between dreams and waking, between the seen and the unseen, between silence and speech: here, he suggests, we have a way of getting beyond the question of the desiring gaze by positing the activity of the subject as arrival or appearance. 'A l'éveil des métamorphoses' argues that in Poussin's *Vénus et Adonis* both the spectator and the river god have access to the world of desire hidden by the figures while they sleep and forgotten as soon as they wake (fig. 18).[55] In Marin's view, we see their dreams represented in the actions of the figures around them. On the question of desire, he considers that the sleeping bodies also represent a strange powerlessness, the illusory command of representation shared by spectator and picture-maker alike.[56]

This is relevant for the nature of Nathanël's perception and limitations. For Marin, the discovery of a balance between insight and impotence seems also to be the revelation of a secret. This secret concerns the status of the looking and speaking subject as it contemplates the painting. The subject watches the figuration of life and death in the sleeping bodies, of *still life*; of a system of representation holding in equilibrium the looking and the afterlife. Thinking about the bodies in Poussin's representations of the stories of metamorphosis, Marin turns to the Louvre *Echo et Narcisse* (see above, fig. 5). Here Marin comes to clarify the relationship between language and sight during the act of coming into visual contact. The three figures in the painting present muteness awaiting the poise and voice of the spectator, whose words will only repeat the scene depicted, provide an echo to its text. Marin goes on to locate this emerging subject: 'Et c'est ainsi que parfois, par une grâce qui est la beauté dans ses effets sensibles, il advient entre sommeil et éveil, silence et parole, que le regard trouve sa fin dans une voix et celle-ci, à son tour, dans un visible, par une incessante métamorphose où s'ouvre l'espace du sujet et d'où émerge de sa réserve endormie le moi.'[57] The dynamics of looking activated between spectator and painting are included in the recognition of the status of the subject in language and visibility; this awareness incorporates a dangerous fluidity of notions of the self and takes risks in the encounter with the visual. The systems of signs encountered by the subject both locate and transform it, or rather make it aware of these processes, involving it in a secret operation. Nathanaël shares this status of the constricted spectator in his encounters with the signs and sights in *Un homme obscur*. As a subject he experiences a succession of 'births'. These take the form of his successive appearances, or rather disappearances, when he passes through a series of openings in the text.

Nathanaël's escapades include regular acts of vanishing: from Greenwich after the accident with the voyeur; from one galley ship to another; from L'Ile Perdue; from Saraï's life; from human contact in the months before his death. His disappearance from L'Ile Perdue occurs when he finds out about a ship at anchor nearby and jumps into the messenger's canoe: 'Nathanaël sut de lui qu'un bâtiment anglais avait jeté l'ancre à l'entrée de leur crique, cachée à la vue, du point où l'on se trouvait, par des saillants de rocher. [...] Un éperon rocheux les cacha bientôt' (933). The limited perspective from the island onto the outside world is suddenly exposed, as if the island were bound by the frames of a painting. Nathanaël rows from one picture to another, disappearing from the spectators' line of sight. The incident recapitulates the events at the end of Yourcenar's story 'Comment Wang-Fô fut sauvé': 'Enfin, la barque vira autour d'un rocher qui fermait l'entrée du large; l'ombre d'une falaise tomba sur elle; le sillage s'effaça sur la surface déserte, et le peintre Wang-Fô et son disciple Ling disparurent à jamais sur cette mer de jade bleu que Wang-Fô venait d'inventer' (OR, 1153).[58] Wang-Fô has orchestrated his own escape and survival, under the gaze of the emperor who is looking at the painting as it traces their disappearance, shortly after his praise for the pictorial kingdom mastered by Wang-Fô: 'Le seul empire sur lequel il vaille la peine de régner est celui où tu pénètres, vieux Wang, par le chemin des Mille Courbes et des Dix Mille Couleurs' (*OR*, 1150). The decision to alter the perspectives radically is still available to Nathanaël and his choice of his manner of death is another form of this action. The novel ends with dissolution, although Paul Joret sees this *tabula rasa* as reconstructive[59] and indeed acts of disappearance have been interpreted by Paul Virilio as an attempt to gain mastery over time.[60]

Disappearance is a frequent motif in writing on Rembrandt. This concerns the momentary appearance of the figures in a painting in the shapes represented prior to their disappearance from our sight, when the configurations change and the pigments of paint decay. Fromentin provided the classic account of this passage before and after the stasis of the canvas's surface: 'Son idéal, comme dans un rêve poursuivi les yeux fermés, c'est la lumière: la nimbe autour des objets, la phosphorescence sur un fond noir. C'est fugitif, incertain, formé de linéaments insensibles, tout prêts à disparaître avant qu'on ne les fixe, éphémère et éblouissant.'[61] As ever, Fromentin is taken up and modified by later writers, since the idea of a painting as an ephemeral creation is not his drift. The capture of light by the artist is interpreted by others as a temporary defiance of dissolution. For Paul Claudel, the Dutch masters present a time of silence after and before the noise of the language of intellectual analysis:

ainsi il ne faudrait pas me presser beaucoup pour avancer que l'entreprise de l'art hollandais est comme une liquidation de la réalité. A tous les spectacles qu'elle lui propose, il ajoute cet élément qui est le silence, ce silence qui permet d'entendre l'âme, à tout le moins de l'écouter, et cette conversation au-delà de la logique qu'entretiennent les choses du seul fait de leur coexistence et de leur compénétration. Il délie les êtres du moment, et, lavés dans l'essentiel, il les congèle sous le glacis, du seul fait de ce regard qui les envisage ensemble, en un rapport qui suspend leur droit à la disparition.[62]

Claudel considers the relationship between the objects represented and between the surface of water and the surface glaze of a painting. The spectator resumes the work of the artist's look in retaining the objects represented in view. Yourcenar's contribution to the elaborations upon the idea of disappearance, or 'liquidation de la réalité', as Claudel has it, occurs in the conclusion to her essay which takes the form of telling a story that reworks the Wang-Fô sea-escape once again.

In the land/seascape of the legend, the writer presents a linear development via narrative time, sound in its three variations, the movement away and disappearance of the human figures, and the shift back to the painting. The feelings of the anonymous group of captured men who have survived the voyage are imagined and reasons why they set off back to Africa on foot are proposed. The actions of the group are described from the perspective of their guards and the modern reader: they walk away into the sea; they sing a long strange chant: 'on vit cette petite troupe d'hommes entrer dans la mer comme pour s'y rafraîchir, en chantant inexplicablement une de ces longues complaintes de leur pays, ponctuées de cris ou prolongées par de profonds murmures à bouches closes, et qui font pleurer' (231). Writing responds to painting with reference to a third medium that is as elusive to them as they are to each other, as we saw in the use of Vermeer's *Music Lesson*. Yourcenar has the interruptions of the cries and the continual flow of the murmur; our reaction is also suggested. In *Blues et Gospels*, Yourcenar gave a brief account of the legend and commented on the sea journey–song link: 'Depuis des siècles, le destin noir semble lié à ces notions de traversées marines ou de remontées ou de descentes de fleuves, symbolisés eux-mêmes par la houle du chant' (9). The association between blues and water, the place of the birth of the blues, is reversed and now the association leads to death, although here this may be something accepted or as yet unimagined. By their song they affirm an experience that extends to everyone; Yourcenar's preface to *Fleuve profond, sombre rivière* commented on the way the song identifies with our experience, though she does not claim to extend the specific suffering of slavery to everyone: 'Par-delà l'expérience de l'individu, ou même celle de la race, par-delà la ferveur chrétienne elle-même, le chanteur noir s'y élève à l'affirmation d'une expérience tragique et mystique qui est à nous tous' (49). Earlier in the essay, the common experience of the painting was discussed. Yourcenar returns to the painting and imagines that in the course of time the two companions will also disappear into the distance.

In 'Le retour de Hollande', a text largely about Descartes and Rembrandt, Paul Valéry discusses how Rembrandt carefully conceals his artifice. Valéry then ponders the difficulty of this strategy in writing; he wonders about ways of developing writing's inner resources: 'C'est là construire un art à plusieurs dimensions, ou organiser, en quelque sorte, les environs et les profondeurs des choses explicitement dites. [...]

Je m'assurais, peut-être trop facilement (mais, à tout dire, je m'en assure encore), que l'art d'écrire contient de grandes ressources virtuelles, des richesses de combinaisons et de composition à peine soupçonnées, si ce n'est inconnues'.[63] Yourcenar's essay is one of many attempts by writers to respond to Rembrandt. The visual experience of looking at *Deux Noirs* registered in her commentary is complemented by the legend in a way that illustrates and celebrates the potential of writing. The tale tries to present a picture that will go some way to matching the painting that commands the commentary. The two art forms head for dissolution at the end: they represent the gradually disappearing group, the two companions and the solitary Nathanaël. As in the self-portraits, we witness the passage of these beings.

Reading the visual in *Un homme obscur* and in '*Deux Noirs* de Rembrandt' has led to an awareness of the nature and function of the pictorial appearances in the narrative, to new interpretations of Yourcenar's texts and to an attempt to examine the capacity of writing to encounter the body and the world. The issues involved in the stories and the reception of the pictures in Van Herzog's house suggest new readings of these specific passages and of others. Instability and fragmentation indicate that cultural productions are not watertight, as figured in the episode of the sinking of the alphabet. The transfer from culture to nature effects the movement from exterior to interior represented by the act of looking at the body of the painting. This process involves a two-way flow and culture is not subsumed wholly by nature: writing and painting both disappear and enact disappearance, both represent time and elude it.

At the same time, the dignity presented in Yourcenar's reading of the painting is a respect for public and private domains of experience. We have followed Nathanaël's observations, visualized him on the threshold of contact with the Other and considered the surface of the painting as a threshold, surface and momentary sight of fixed presence: these are all fruitful ways of reading *Un homme obscur*. These aspects of the text all supplement and sometimes challenge recent critical response. The application of the visual/textual inquiry has led to an opening up of the text to these new interpretations. While the overall schema of the story cannot carry all the visual complexities with it and the detachment achieved by Nathanaël means an inevitable and unresolvable lack of involvement with the world, the text has none the less succeeded in operating the challenges to representation posed by the circumstances of Nathanaël's life. Nathanaël is liberated from textual enclosure by such a reading. It is when Nathanaël gives up representing the world that he is closest to the threshold between the text and the reader, since we vacillate and disappear from the surface with him.

## Notes to Chapter 4

1. The phrase 'dehors-dedans' is adapted from 'La dialectique du dehors et du dedans', a chapter in Bachelard's *La Poétique de l'espace* (Paris: PUF/Quadrige, 1994).
2. In this chapter, with the exception of the caption for the reproduction of the painting (fig. 17), *Deux Noirs* will be used as the title of the painting. The Mauritshuis and many books on Rembrandt translate the Dutch title as *Two Negroes*, while Gary Schwartz gives *Two Black Africans* and notes that this painting is probably the one referred to as 'Two Moors' in the artist's inventory (*Rembrandt—his life, his paintings* (Harmondsworth: Viking, 1985), 315, no. 365).
3. 'D'après Rembrandt', *MCA*. 'D'après Dürer' became *L'Œuvre au noir* and 'D'après Greco' became *Anna, Soror....* The short tale 'Une belle matinée', which follows *Un homme obscur*, came from the ending of 'D'après Rembrandt'.
4. Maurice Delcroix, 'Parcours d'une œuvre: Marguerite Yourcenar et l'Histoire de Nathanaël', in *Il Confronto Litterario*, ed. Giorgetto Giorgi (Pavia: Schena, 1986), 44.
5. See C. Gaudin, 'Marguerite Yourcenar's Prefaces: Genesis as Self-Effacement', *Studies in Twentieth Century Literature* 10/1 (1985), 31–55. The original preface to *Les Songes et les Sorts* is preserved in its current edition: *EM*, 1533–41.
6. On the flashback, see Paul Joret, '*Un homme obscur* de Marguerite Yourcenar: un «traité du vain combat»?', in *Nathanaël pour compagnon*, ed. M. Delcroix, *Bulletin de la SIEY* 12 (1993), 95.
7. Christiane Guys, 'Le porteur d'eau', in *Nathanaël pour compagnon*, ed. M. Delcroix, 7–8.
8. For a response that expresses grave reservations about Alpers's book, focusing on problems similar to those Marin mentions in passing, see Didi-Huberman's comments in *Devant l'image*, 'Appendice'.
9. See David Scott, 'La structure picturale du sonnet parnassien et symboliste: Hérédia et Baudelaire', in *Ecrire la peinture*, ed. Philippe Delaveau (Paris: Editions universitaires, 1991), 45.
10. Norman Bryson, *Looking at the Overlooked: Four Essays on Still Life Painting* (London: Reaktion Books, 1990).
11. From a letter to his brother Théo of Oct. 1886; quoted by Frances S. Jowell, 'The Rediscovery of Frans Hals', in *Frans Hals*, ed. Seymour Slive (London: Royal Academy of Arts, 1990), 77.
12. A. J. Reinach, *Recueil Milliet. Textes grecs et latins relatifs à l'histoire de la peinture ancienne* (Paris: Macula, 1985); quoted by Didi-Huberman, *La Peinture incarnée*, 10–11.
13. Maurice Delcroix, 'Mythes de l'obscur,' in *Nathanaël pour compagnon*, ed. M. Delcroix, *Bulletin de la SIEY* 12 (1993), 109–60.
14. In his film of *The Trial*, Orson Welles reads the parable in a 'voice-off' prologue.

15. Didi-Huberman, *Ce que nous voyons*, 192.
16. See Malcolm Bowie's discussion of the Actaeon myth in Lacan and Proust: *Freud, Proust and Lacan*, 168–78.
17. For a comparison between Saraï and Judith as Jewish women, see Delcroix, 'Mythes de l'obscur', 137.
18. For Nathanaël's experiences of the night, see Helen Watson-Williams, 'Memento mori: Marguerite Yourcenar's *Un homme obscur*' in *European Relations: Essays for Helen Watson-Williams*, ed. Bruce Bennett and John Hay (Perth: University of Western Australia Press, 1985), 141–50. In Yourcenar's *Quoi? L'Eternité*, the sexual power ascribed to the night incites Jeanne to walk naked on Texel island, including the night she loses her virginity: *EM*, 1243–4.
19. *Hall's Dictionary*, 181.
20. René Wilenski, *Flemish Painters* (London: Faber and Faber, 1960), i. 118.
21. My thanks to Elizabeth McGrath for her comments on Wilenski and on representations of Judith.
22. Delcroix, 'Mythes de l'obscur', 136, 139.
23. Annelies Schulte Nordholt, 'Soif de connaissance et désir du bien dans l'œuvre de Marguerite Yourcenar', *Neophilologus* 70 (1986), 357–71. Schulte Nordholt also discusses aspects of the link between *Un homme obscur* and 'Le cerveau noir de Piranèse'.
24. Michel de Montaigne, 'De l'expérience', *Essais III*, ed. Pierre Michel (Paris: Librairie Générale Française, 1980), 416.
25. Patricia de Feyter, 'Nathanaël ou la désinvolture', in *Nathanaël pour compagnon*, ed. Delcroix, 74.
26. Yourcenar is close here to Foucault's notion of the strata of the 'epistème' as put forward in *Les Mots et les choses* and as it is seen at work in the argument of *L'Archéologie du savoir*.
27. Maurice Delcroix, 'D'une rhétorique de la discrétion: le personnage de Madeleine d'Ailly', in *Marguerite Yourcenar et l'art*, ed. Castellani and Poignault, 371–9.
28. Louis Marin, 'Mimésis et description', in *De la représentation*, 264.
29. Paul Claudel, *L'Œil écoute* (Paris: Gallimard, 1991), 44.
30. Bachelard, *La Poétique de l'espace*, 199.
31. Merleau-Ponty, *L'Œil et l'Esprit*, 22.
32. See Schwartz, *Rembrandt*, 321–31, for matters of attribution and interpretation concerning this painting. Until it was suggested that Saul is contemplating revenge on David, the painting was thought to represent Saul being consoled by David's music and drying his tears. Interpretation fell into the trap of psychological readings of facial expression; Yourcenar is also caught here.
33. Elie Faure, *Histoire de l'Art. L'Art Moderne I* (Paris: Librairie Générale Française, 1976), 105, 109.
34. For the former approach see e.g. Henri Focillon, 'Introduction', in Ludwig Goldscheide, *Rembrandt* (London: Phaidon, 1960), 8–11.
35. Eugène Fromentin, *Les Maîtres d'autrefois* (Paris: Plon, 1910).
36. See Albert Thibaudet, 'Fromentin', in *Intérieurs* (Paris: Plon, 1924), 142–8, for a discussion of this problematic area in Fromentin's book.
37. Claudel, *L'Œil écoute*, 24.
38. Focillon, 'Introduction', 14.

39. Bachelard, *La Poétique de l'espace*, 200.
40. Focillon, 'Introduction', 7. An antidote to literal readings is found in Alexander Korda's film *Rembrandt* (1936) when Charles Laughton makes faces at a mirror in order to create an imposing image for a self-portrait.
41. Claudel, *L'Œil écoute*, 136–7.
42. Watson-Williams, 'Memento Mori', 147.
43. Jean Genet, 'Ce qui est resté d'un Rembrandt déchiré en petits carrés bien réguliers, et foutu aux chiottes', *Œuvres complètes*, vol. 4 (Paris: Gallimard, 1968).
44. Roland Barthes, *La Chambre claire—Note sur la photographie* (Paris: Gallimard/Seuil, 1980), 125.
45. Pascal Bonafoux, *Rembrandt, Autoportrait* (Geneva: Albert Skira, 1985), 137.
46. See Michael Kitson, *Rembrandt* (London: Phaidon, 1982), pl. 45.
47. Bonafoux, *Rembrandt*, 134.
48. Montaigne, 'Du repentir', *Essais III*, 33.
49. See Ernst van de Wetering, 'Rembrandt's Manner: Technique in the Service of Illusion'. The research team at the Mauritshuis examined our painting in the 1970s and discovered extensive areas that were retouched: A. B. De Vries, M. Tóth-Ubbens and W. Froentjes (eds.), *Rembrandt in the Mauritshuis* (The Hague: Alpen aan de Rijn, 1978), 146.
50. Cynthia P. Schneider, *Rembrandt's Landscapes* (New Haven and London: Yale University Press, 1990), 124–7.
51. Delacroix, 'Mythes de l'obscur', 157.
52. See the reproduction in the Mauristhuis volume for which Yourcenar's essay was written: H. R. Hoetink (ed.), *Gezicht op het Mauritshuis* (The Hague: Meulenhoff/Landshoff, 1989), 103, ill. no. 25.
53. Faure, *L'Art Moderne I*, 110.
54. Marin, 'A l'éveil des métamorphoses', 161–74, in *Sublime Poussin*.
55. See Wright, *Poussin*, cat. no. 21, and Blunt, *Poussin: Text*, 106–8 and *Poussin: Catalogue*, no. 185.
56. Marin's argument here represents a development of his thinking after the discussion about narcissism and the spectator at the 1981 Colloque de Cérisy: 'Les fins de l'interprétation', 200–3, in *De la représentation*.
57. Marin, *Sublime Poussin*, 174.
58. In Claudel's much shorter version of the story, the artist steps into the canvas: 'Aegri somnia', *L'Œil écoute*, 110–11.
59. Paul Joret, 'Un homme obscur', 96–7.
60. Paul Virilio, *Esthétique de la disparition* (Paris: Galilée, 1989), 28–35.
61. Fromentin, *Les Maîtres d'autrefois*, 384.
62. Claudel, *L'Œil écoute*, 33–4.
63. Paul Valéry, 'Le retour de Hollande', in *Variété II* (Paris: Gallimard, 1956), 39.

# CONCLUSION

❖

I hope that this book has shown that the study of the visual provides fresh and original access to Yourcenar's essays and fiction. The issues involved in the selection and treatment of various works of art in her essays lead to a more general reflection on her views on pictorial representation. This inquiry in turn yields an approach to the strategies of representation in her fiction which can then be considered through the study of the dynamics of the principal visualized encounters. These encounters—sightings of objects and people, memories, mirror images and dreams—have been seen to comprise the following elements: alluring appeal and enticement; the figuration of desire and repression; a consideration of memory and oblivion; and the construction of the space of encounter. Throughout we have witnessed how these issues open up the inquiry into Yourcenar's work.

Studying confrontations with images and exploring networks of vision in the texts supplies the reader with ways of approaching the persistent solitude of the human figure in Yourcenar's work. Paintings and other images provide models for thinking about the spatial and temporal focus given to the encounter between searching selves, on the one hand, and between these selves and the world, on the other. This book has attempted to illustrate what is at stake in these acts of communication by sight: the division of the self into twenty images in *L'Œuvre au noir*, discussed in Chapter 3, is symptomatic of the bold confrontation with disorder and loss in Yourcenar's writing.

Reading the texts with these considerations in mind therefore involves a constant negotiation with questions of stability and function. Images oblige their interpreters to declare their interest in the process of looking. The encounters studied here, both within and between texts, have been, in part, struggles for supremacy. The unsettling impact of the visual on the essayist in 'Une exposition Poussin à New York' and on the characters of *Mémoires d'Hadrien*, *L'Œuvre au noir* and *Un homme obscur* has taken this inquiry in two directions: investigating the stakes and strategies of the encounter between writer and painting or between character and image; and questioning whether any resolution of these visual confrontations is ever possible. The emergence of Hadrien from melancholic repetition and of Zénon from the fear of alterity has been traced as the course of a conflict whose troubles are not simplistically harmonized at the end of their stories, but are rather shown to be persistently acts of struggle and transformation. At the respective ends of these stories, the characters are still changing radically. Conclusion is continuation.

The reader's ability to explore and supplement the dynamics and limitations of representation, both alongside and independently of Yourcenar's projects, has also been investigated. The ways in which the visual arts may be read alongside the written texts have been crucial, specifically involving the positioning together of essay, novel and image. The connections indicated have sometimes been between texts, as in the case of Yourcenar's essay on Piranesi and the character Belmonte's discourse in *Un homme obscur*. Then there have been links between text and image where the visual referent, as in the case of the etchings of Hadrian's Villa and the end of *Mémoires d'Hadrien*, specifically locates the link which was read as a clue given in the 'Carnets', where Yourcenar stated that Piranesi was a regular source of inspiration for her project. The relationship between text and image detected here by the reader worked around both media's play of light and shade, spatial arrangement and the passage into darkness. In the case of the 'parallel' between the enclosed spaces of *L'Œuvre au noir* and the *Prisons*, we saw that the attempt to gain a visual hold over an image may in fact be seen to be staged within the image. This versatile method of inquiry into the conjunction of text and image has provided new readings of the essays and novels discussed.

In *Un homme obscur*, impoverished discourses of representation compete for Nathanaël's attention. He is read as the spectator of his world, positioned in mobile relationship to the world which he confronts and which confronts him. Considering Nathanaël as a spectator and continuing the cross-gazing which we detected in Rembrandt's *Deux Noirs* provides us with a way of assessing the end of the text. This proposes to regenerate the visual and the textual just at the point of dissolution. Following Louis Marin, we read Nathanaël's perpetual and subtle transformation as a subject, experienced as a series of rebirths or returns to the world.

An 'alchemy of the visual' emerges as the formulation which might draw together both Yourcenar's reflections on the visual and some of the ideas employed in this book in order to open up the debate concerning her work. The phrase derives in part from the novel *L'Œuvre au noir* and the reading given here of its treatment of the visual. It is used in this conclusion to refer to the complex and problematic processes involved in looking at images: articulating the work of the picture via its structures of narrative, memory, place, contemplation; the power of images over their spectators; the incorporation of the spectator into the contact with colour; the challenge to structures of looking to acknowledge their interests and to open themselves up to exchange with different systems; and the inevitable dangers which face the subject open to metamorphosis. All these aspects involve a searching, hesitant but bold confrontation with the challenge of the visual: we have explored Zénon's experiments and investigations into how to represent the world, as well as the series of disappearances performed by Nathanaël. The term 'alchemy' is adopted to convey the material measure and mystery of looking at a work with the aim of addressing the visual. It therefore covers the continual frustration of possession and the brutal obligation to accept transience which characterize the nature of representation in the work of Yourcenar.

How the structure of the exceptional locates the strategies and limits of a theory is the challenge which emerges here. Reading the visual in the work of Yourcenar involves the constant confrontation with limitation, desire, transformation and death. The strange and unsettling in all the works discussed obliges the reader to consider how these events challenge the structure of the texts; we have seen that this challenge leads to the detection of another more complex structure of desire, defeat, patience and survival in her work. At the same time, images have not been complacently absorbed into the discussion of texts, nor have they been assumed to be easier to interpret. This book has attempted to find an organizing structure which brings together the discourse of the texts, the role of the reader and the visual frame of reference. These are held in equilibrium, since otherwise the inquiry into the visual would focus excessively on Yourcenar's avowed aesthetics, instead of capturing her work's engagement with the visual and its meditation on the dynamics and durability of representation.

# BIBLIOGRAPHY

❖

## Works by Yourcenar

### (1) Primary sources

#### (a) Fiction

*Alexis ou le Traité du vain combat* (1929), suivi du *Coup de grâce* (1939) (Paris: Gallimard, 1978).

*La Mort conduit l'attelage* (Paris: Grasset, 1934).

*Denier du rêve* (Paris: Grasset, 1934; rev. edn. Gallimard, 1971).

*Feux* (Paris: Grasset, 1936; rev. edn. Plon, 1957).

*Nouvelles orientales* (1938) (Paris: Gallimard, 1978).

*Mémoires d'Hadrien* (1951), suivi des 'Carnets de notes des *Mémoires d'Hadrien*' (Paris: Gallimard, 1977).

*Mémoires d'Hadrien*, illustrated edn. (Paris: Gallimard, 1971).

*L'Œuvre au noir* (Paris: Gallimard, 1968).

*Un homme obscur* (Paris: Gallimard, 1981).

*Comme l'eau qui coule* (Paris: Gallimard, 1982).

*Œuvres romanesques* (Paris: Gallimard, Bibliothèque de la Pléiade, 1982).

*Conte bleu. Le premier soir. Maléfice* (Paris: Gallimard, 1993).

#### (b) Essays, memoirs, translations, correspondence and sources

*Les Songes et les Sorts* (Paris: Grasset, 1938).

*Sous bénéfice d'inventaire* (Paris: Gallimard, 1978).

*Mishima ou la Vision du vide* (Paris: Gallimard, 1980).

*Le Temps, ce grand sculpteur* (Paris: Gallimard, 1983).

*En pèlerin et en étranger* (Paris: Gallimard, 1989).

*Le Tour de la prison* (Paris: Gallimard, 1991).

*Souvenirs pieux* (1974) (Paris: Gallimard, 1988).

*Archives du Nord* (1977) (Paris: Gallimard, 1982).

*Quoi? L'Eternité* (1988) (Paris: Gallimard, 1990).

*Essais et Mémoires* (Paris: Gallimard, Bibliothèque de la Pléiade, 1991).

*Fleuve profond, sombre rivière—Les «Negro Spirituals»*, ed. and trans. M. Yourcenar (Paris: Gallimard, 1964).

*La Couronne et la Lyre*, ed. and trans. M. Yourcenar (Paris: Gallimard, 1984).
*Blues et Gospels*, trans. M. Yourcenar, ed. M. Yourcenar and Jerry Wilson (Paris: Gallimard, 1984).
*La Voix des choses*, ed. M. Yourcenar (Paris: Gallimard, 1987).
*Lettres à ses amis et quelques autres*, ed. M. Sarde and J. Brami (Paris: Gallimard, 1995).
*Sources II*, ed. Elyane Dezon-Jones and M. Sarde (Paris: Gallimard, 1999).

*(c) Uncollected texts—essays, original versions and others*

'Abraham Fraunce traducteur de Virgile: Oscar Wilde', *Revue bleue* 20 (1929), 621–7.
'L'improvisation à Innsbruck', *Revue européenne* 12 (1930), 1013–25.
'Mythologie', *Lettres françaises* 11 (1944), 41–6.
'Mythologie II: Alceste', *Lettres françaises* 14 (1944), 33–40.
'Mythologie III: Ariane-Electre', *Lettres françaises* 15 (1945), 35–45.
'L'écrivain devant l'histoire', *Publications du Centre national de la documentation pédagogique*, 1954.
'Le cerveau noir de Piranèse', *Nouvelle Revue Française (NRF)* 67 (Jan. 1961), 63–78.
'André Gide Revisited', *Cahiers André Gide 3—Le Centenaire* (Paris: Gallimard, 1972), 21–44.
'Réponse au questionnaire sur le "Roman noir"', in *Le Romantisme noir*, ed. Liliane Abensour and Françoise Charras (Paris: L'Herne, 1978), 161–2.
'Lettres à Mlle S.', *NRF* 327 (Apr. 1980), 181–91.
'Les 33 noms de Dieu', *NRF* 401 (June 1986), 101–17.
'Carnets de notes de *L'Œuvre au noir*', *NRF* 452 (Sept. 1990), 40–53, and 453 (Oct. 1990), 54–67.
'Lettre-préface de Marguerite Yourcenar', in Jean Chalon, *Chère Nathalie Barney* (Paris: Flammarion, 1992), 9–14.

*(2) Works and translations also consulted*

*Le Jardin des chimères* (Paris: Perrin, 1921).
*Les dieux ne sont pas morts* (Paris: R. Chiberre, 1922).
*La Nouvelle Eurydice* (Paris: Grasset, 1931).
*Pindare* (Paris: Grasset, 1932).
'Préface' (1936), in Rainer Maria Rilke, *Poèmes à la nuit*, trans. G. Althen and J.-Y. Masson (Lagrasse: Verdier, 1994).
*Discours de réception de Marguerite Yourcenar à l'Académie Royale belge de Langue et de Littérature françaises, précédé du discours de bienvenue de Carlo Bronne* (Paris: Gallimard, 1971).

*Discours de réception à l'Académie Française de Mme Marguerite Yourcenar et réponse de M. J. D'Ormesson* (Paris: Gallimard, 1981).
*Les Charités d'Alcippe*, rev. edn. (Paris: Gallimard, 1984).
*Le Dernier Amour du prince Genghi*, with engravings by Abdallah Benanteur (Paris: C. Lemand, 1989).
*Présentation critique de Constantin Cavafy*, ed. M. Yourcenar, trans. M. Yourcenar and Constantin Dimaras (Paris: Gallimard, 1958).
*Présentation critique d'Hortense Flexner*, ed. and trans. M. Yourcenar (Paris: Gallimard, 1969).
BALDWIN, JAMES, *Le Coin des 'amen': pièce en trois actes*, trans. M. Yourcenar (Paris: Gallimard, 1983).
MISHIMA, YUKIO, *Cinq nô modernes: théâtre*, trans. M. Yourcenar (Paris: Gallimard, 1984).
*Le Cheval noir à tête blanche: conte d'enfants indiens*, ed. and trans. M. Yourcenar (Paris: Gallimard, 1985).

*(3) Interviews*

ROSBO, PATRICK DE, *Entretiens radiophoniques avec Marguerite Yourcenar* (Paris: Mercure de France, 1972).
'Entretien avec Léo Gillet' (1986), *NRF* 507 (Apr. 1995), 50–74.

### Secondary Literature

ALPERS, SVETLANA, *The Art of Describing: Dutch Art in the Seventeenth Century* (Harmondsworth: Pelican, 1989).
ARAGON, LOUIS, and COCTEAU, JEAN, *Entretiens sur le musée de Dresde* (Paris: Cercle d'Art, 1957).
ARLAND, MARCEL, *Le Promeneur* (Paris: Editions du Pavois, 1944).
AURELIUS, MARCUS, *Meditations*, trans. Maxwell Staniforth (Harmondsworth: Penguin, 1962).
BACHELARD, GASTON, *L'Eau et les Rêves*, rev. edn. (Paris: José Corti, 1956).
—— *La Poétique de la rêverie* (Paris: Quadrige/Presses Universitaires de France, 1993).
—— *La Poétique de l'espace* (Paris: Quadrige/Presses Universitaires de France, 1994).
BANN, STEPHEN, *The True Vine: On Visual Representation and the Western Tradition* (Cambridge: Cambridge University Press, 1989).
BARRÈS, MAURICE, 'Le Testament d'Eugène Delacroix', in *Le Mystère en pleine lumière* (Paris: Plon, 1926).
BARTHES, ROLAND, *La Chambre Claire—Note sur la photographie* (Paris: Gallimard/Seuil, 1980).

BASKINS, CRISTELLE L., 'Echoing Narcissus in Alberti's *Della Pittura*', *The Oxford Art Journal* 16/1 (1993), 25–33.

BÄTSCHMANN, OSCAR, *Nicolas Poussin: Dialectics of Painting*, trans. Marko Daniel (London: Reaktion Books, 1990).

BAZIN, GERMAINE, *Baroque and Rococo*, trans. Jonathan Griffin (London: Thames and Hudson, 1985).

BERNIER, YVON, Inventaire de la bibliothèque de Marguerite Yourcenar (unpublished typescript, 1988).

BLANCHOT, MAURICE, 'La rencontre avec le démon', in *Hommage de la France à Thomas Mann à l'occasion de son quatre-vingtième anniversaire* (Paris: Flincker, 1955).

BLOOMER, JENNIFER, *Architecture and the Text: The S(crypts) of Joyce and Piranesi* (New Haven and London: Yale University Press, 1993).

BLUNT, ANTHONY, *The Paintings of Nicolas Poussin*, 3 vols. (London: Phaidon, 1966–7).

BOATWRIGHT, MARY TANNERO, *Hadrian and the City of Rome* (Princeton: Princeton University Press, 1987).

BONAFOUX, PASCAL, *Rembrandt, Autoportrait* (Geneva: Albert Skira, 1985).

BONNEFOY, YVES, *Rome 1630: l'horizon du premier baroque* (Paris: Flammarion, 1970).

BOURDIL, PIERRE-YVES, 'L'Œuvre au noir de Marguerite Yourcenar. Portrait de Zénon', *L'Ecole des lettres* 2/1 (1988–9), 15–29.

BOWIE, MALCOLM, *Freud, Proust and Lacan: Theory as Fiction* (Cambridge: Cambridge University Press, 1987).

BRETON, ANDRÉ, *Les Vases communicants* (Paris: Gallimard, 1970).

BROWN, CHRISTOPHER, KELCH, JAN, and VAN THIEL, PETER (eds.), *Rembrandt: The Master and his Workshop. Paintings* (New Haven and London: Yale University Press, 1991).

BRUNEL, PIERRE, *Transparences du roman: Le romancier et ses doubles au XX$^e$ siècle* (Paris: José Corti, 1997).

BRYSON, NORMAN, *Looking at the Overlooked: Four Essays on Still Life Painting* (London: Reaktion Books, 1990).

BUCI-GLUCKSMANN, CHRISTINE, *La Folie du voir: de l'esthétique baroque* (Paris: Galilée, 1986).

CAILLOIS, ROGER, *L'Incertitude qui vient des rêves* (Paris: Gallimard, 1956).

CAMERON, KEITH, *Henri III: A Maligned or Malignant King? (Aspects of Satirical Iconography of Henri de Valois)* (Exeter: University of Exeter Press, 1978).

CARDANO, GIROLAMO, *The Book of my Life*, trans. Jean Stoner (London: J. M. Dent & Son, 1931).

CARRIER, DAVID, 'Poussin's Self-Portraits', *Word & Image* 7/2 (1991), 127–48.

CASTELLANI, JEAN-PIERRE, and POIGNAULT, RÉMY (eds.), *Marguerite Yourcenar et l'art. L'art de Marguerite Yourcenar* (Tours: SIEY, 1990).

CLAUDEL, PAUL, *L'œil écoute* (Paris: Gallimard, 1991).

*The Concise Oxford Dictionary of the Christian Church*, ed. Elizabeth A. Livingstone (Oxford: Oxford University Press, 1980).

DANTE, *The Comedy of Dante Alighieri the Florentine. Cantica I: Hell (L'Inferno)*, trans. Dorothy L. Sayers (Harmondsworth: Penguin, 1949).

DELAVEAU, PHILIPPE (ed.), *Ecrire la peinture* (Paris: Editions Universitaires, 1991).

DELCROIX, MAURICE, 'Parcours d'une œuvre: Marguerite Yourcenar et l'*Histoire de Nathanaël*', in *Il Confronto Litterario*, ed. Giorgetto Giorgi (Pavia: Schena, 1986), 31–45.

—— 'D'une rhétorique de la discrétion: le personnage de Madeleine d'Ailly', in *Marguerite Yourcenar et l'art. L'art de Marguerite Yourcenar*, ed. J.-P. Castellani and R. Poignault (Tours: SIEY, 1990), 371–9.

—— 'Mythes de l'obscur,' in *Nathanaël pour compagnon*, ed. M. Delcroix, *Bulletin de la SIEY* 12 (1993), 109–60.

—— (ed.), *Nathanaël pour compagnon, Bulletin de la SIEY* 12 (1993).

DELCROIX, SABINE, and DELCROIX, MAURICE (eds.), *Roman, histoire et mythe dans l'œuvre de Marguerite Yourcenar* (Tours: SIEY, 1995).

DELEUZE, GILLES, and GUATTARI, FÉLIX, *A Thousand Plateaus, Capitalism and Schizophrenia*, trans. Brian Massumi (London: Athlone Press, 1988).

DEPREZ, BÉRENGÈRE, and MEDEIROS, ANA DE (eds.), *Marguerite Yourcenar: Ecritures de l'exil* (Louvain-la-Neuve: Academia Bruylant, 1998).

DE QUINCEY, THOMAS, *Confessions of an English Opium-Eater*, ed. G. Lindop (Oxford: Oxford University Press, 1985).

DERRIDA, JACQUES, *Marges: de la philosophie* (Paris: Minuit, 1972).

—— *La Vérité en peinture* (Paris: Champs/Flammarion, 1993).

DESJARDINS, PAUL, *La Méthode des Classiques Français: Corneille, Poussin, Pascal* (Paris: Armand Colin, 1904).

DESPORTES, PHILIPPE, 'Les amours d'Hippolyte', in *Poètes du XVI$^e$ siècle*, ed. Albert-Marie Schmidt (Paris: Gallimard, 1964).

DE VRIES, A.B., TÓTH-UBBENS, M., and FROENTJES, W., *Rembrandt in the Mauritshuis* (The Hague: Alpen aan de Rijn, 1978).

DIDI-HUBERMAN, GEORGES, *La Peinture incarnée* (Paris: Minuit, 1985).

—— *Devant l'image: question posée aux fins d'une histoire de l'art* (Paris: Minuit, 1990).

—— *Fra Angelico. Dissemblance et figuration* (Paris: Flammarion, 1990).

—— *Ce que nous voyons, ce qui nous regarde* (Paris: Minuit, 1992).

ERLANGER, PHILIPPE, *Diane de Poitiers: déesse de la Renaissance* (Paris: Perrin, 1976).

*L'Esotérisme d'Albrecht Dürer II*, in *Hamsa* (1977).

FAURE, ELIE, *Histoire de l'Art. L'Art Moderne I* (Paris: Librairie Générale Française, 1976).

FAVERZANI, CAMILLO, 'Marguerite Yourcenar et la culture italienne', Ph.D. thesis (Paris: Université de Paris III/Sorbonne Nouvelle, 1990).

—— '...*non sendo in loco bono, né io pittore*: Quelques notes comparatives entre les *Rime* de Michel-Ange et *Sixtine* de Marguerite Yourcenar', in *Roman, histoire et mythe dans l'œuvre de Marguerite Yourcenar*, ed. S. and M. Delcroix (Tours: SIEY, 1995), 177–88.

FEYTER, PATRICIA DE, 'Zénon ou la vision du vide', in *'L'Œuvre au noir' de Marguerite Yourcenar*, ed. A.-Y. Julien, *Roman 20–50* 9 (1990), 89–94.

—— 'Nathanaël ou la désinvolture', in *Nathanaël pour compagnon*, ed. M. Delcroix, *Bulletin de la SIEY* 12 (1993), 71–80.

FOCILLON, HENRI, 'Introduction', in Ludwig Goldscheide, *Rembrandt* (London: Phaidon, 1960).

FOUCAULT, MICHEL, *L'Archéologie du savoir* (Paris: Gallimard, 1969).

—— *Les Mots et les choses* (Paris: Gallimard, 1990).

FOUCHET, MAX-POL, *Jean-Baptiste Piranèse: Les prisons imaginaires* (Paris: Club français du livre, 1970).

FREUD, SIGMUND, *On the History of the Psycho-Analytic Movement, Papers on Metapsychology and Other Works* [*Standard Edition vol. XIV*] (London: Hogarth Press, 1957).

FRIEDLÄNDER, WALTER, 'America's First Poussin Show at Durlacher brothers', *Art News* 38/1 (Mar. 1940).

FROMENTIN, EUGÈNE, *Les Maîtres d'autrefois* (Paris: Plon, 1910).

FRY, ROGER, *Transformations* (London: Hogarth Press, 1926).

—— *Vision and Design* (Harmondsworth: Pelican, 1937).

FUMAROLI, MARC, *'L'Inspiration du poète' de Poussin* (Paris: Réunion des musées nationaux, 1989).

GAUDIN, COLETTE, 'Marguerite Yourcenar's Prefaces: Genesis as Self-Effacement', *Studies in Twentieth Century Literature* 10/1 (1985), 31–55.

—— *Marguerite Yourcenar: A la surface du temps* (Amsterdam and Atlanta, GA: Rodopi, 1994).

GENET, JEAN, *Œuvres complètes*, iv (Paris: Gallimard, 1968).

GENETTE, GÉRARD, *Palimpsestes: la littérature au second degré* (Paris: Seuil, 1982).

GIDE, ANDRÉ, 'L'enseignement de Poussin', in *Poussin* (Paris: Au Divan, 1945).

GOETHE, J. W. VON, 'Ruisdael the poet', in *Goethe on Art*, ed. and trans. John Gage (London: Scolar Press, 1980), 210–15.

GREENBLATT, STEPHEN, *Learning to Curse: Essays in Early Modern Culture* (New York and London: Routledge, Chapman and Hall, 1990).

GYS, CHRISTIANE, 'Le porteur d'eau', in *Nathanaël pour compagnon*, ed. M. Delcroix, *Bulletin de la SIEY* 12 (1993), 7–22.

HALL, JAMES, *Dictionary of Subjects and Symbols in Art* (rev. edn. London: John Murray, 1979).

HARRIS, NADIA, *Marguerite Yourcenar: Vers la rive d'une Ithaque intérieure* (Saratoga: ANMA Libri, 1994).

HIBBARD, HOWARD, *Poussin: 'The Holy Family on the Steps'* (New York and London: Allen Lane, 1974).

*Histoire Auguste: Les empereurs romains des II$^e$ et III$^e$ siècles*, ed. and trans. André Chastagnol (Paris: Laffont/Bouquins, 1994).

HOETINK, H. R. (ed.), *Gezicht op het Mauritshuis* (The Hague: Meulenhoff/ Landshoff, 1989).

HOFMANNSTHAL, HUGO VON, *Lettre de Lord Chandos et autres textes*, trans. Albert Kohn and Jean-Claude Schneider (Paris: Gallimard, 1992).

*Hommage de la France à Thomas Mann à l'occasion de son quatre-vingtième anniversaire* (Paris: Flincker, 1955).

HUXLEY, ALDOUS, *Prisons* (London: Trianon Press, 1949).

JORET, PAUL, '*Un homme obscur* de Marguerite Yourcenar: un "traité du vain combat"?', in *Nathanaël pour compagnon*, ed. M. Delcroix, *Bulletin de la SIEY* 12 (1993), 81–97.

JOWELL, FRANCES S., 'The Rediscovery of Frans Hals', in *Frans Hals*, ed. Seymour Slive (London: Royal Academy of Arts, 1990).

JULIEN, ANNE-YVONNE, '*L'Œuvre au noir*' de Marguerite Yourcenar (Paris: Gallimard, 1993).

—— (ed.), '*L'Œuvre au noir*' de Marguerite Yourcenar, Roman 20–50 9 (1990).

—— (ed.), *Marguerite Yourcenar: Aux frontières du texte* (Lille: Roman 20–50, 1995).

KANDINSKY, WASSILY, *Du spirituel dans l'art, et dans la peinture en particulier*, ed. Philippe Sers (Paris: Denoël, 1989).

KANT, IMMANUEL, *The Critique of Judgement*, trans. with analytical indexes by James Creed Meredith (Oxford: Clarendon Press, 1952).

KELLER, LUZIUS, *Piranèse et les romantiques français—le mythe des escaliers en spirale* (Paris: Librairie José Corti, 1966).

KERMODE, FRANK, 'Poet and Dancer before Diaghilev', *Modern Essays* (London: Collins, 1971).

KERYELL, JACQUES, 'Variations sur Marguerite Yourcenar', *Cahiers du Cerf* 20/5 (1989), 45–68.

KING, KATHERINE CULLEN, 'Achilles on the Field of Sexual Politics: Marguerite Yourcenar's *Feux*', *Literature Interpretation Theory* 2/3 (1991), 201–20.

KITSON, MICHAEL, *Rembrandt* (London: Phaidon, 1982).

KOHN, INGEBORG, 'The Castle and the Prison: Verbal Architecture in the Non-Fiction of Marguerite Yourcenar' (unpublished paper, MLA Convention, New York, 1981).

LACAN, JACQUES, *The Four Fundamental Concepts of Psycho-Analysis*, trans. Alan Sheridan (Harmondsworth: Penguin, 1991).

LEE, RENSSELAER W., '*Ut Pictura Poesis*': *The Humanistic Theory of Painting* (New York: W. W. Allen, 1967).

LEUWERS, DANIEL, and CASTELLANI, JEAN-PIERRE (eds.), *Marguerite Yourcenar: Une écriture de la mémoire, SUD* (1990).

LEVILLAIN, HENRIETTE, *'Mémoires d'Hadrien' de Marguerite Yourcenar* (Paris: Gallimard, 1992).

LOT, FERDINAND, *La Fin du monde antique* (Paris: Albin Michel, 1951).

MADOU, JEAN-POL, 'L'art du secret et le discours de l'aveu', in *Marguerite Yourcenar: Une écriture de la mémoire*, ed. D. Leuwers and J.-P. Castellani, *SUD* (1990), 45–55.

*Marguerite Yourcenar, SUD* 55 (1984), 5–87.

MARIN, LOUIS, *De la représentation* (Paris: Gallimard/Seuil, 1994).

—— *Sublime Poussin* (Paris: Seuil, 1995).

MAROGER, NICOLE, '*Le Changeur d'or*: un essai d'histoire économique?', *Bulletin de la SIEY* 10 (1992), 23–34.

MARROU, HENRI-IRÉNÉE, *Décadence romaine ou antiquité tardive?—III^e–VI^e siècle* (Paris: Seuil, 1991).

MERLEAU-PONTY, MAURICE, *L'Œil et l'Esprit* (Paris: Gallimard, 1993).

METTRA, CLAUDE, 'Les explorations de Marguerite Yourcenar', *Les Nouvelles littéraires* (27 June 1968), 3.

—— 'La dernière vision du Maître de Nuremberg', in *L'Esotérisme d'Albrecht Dürer II, Hamsa* (1977), 46–51.

MICHELET, JULES, *Renaissance et Réforme: Histoire de France au XVI^e siècle*, with a preface by Claude Mettra (Paris: Robert Laffont, 1982).

MITCHELL, W. J. T., *Picture Theory* (Chicago: University of Chicago Press, 1994).

MONTAIGNE, MICHEL DE, *Essais III*, ed. Pierre Michel (Paris: Librairie Générale Française, 1980).

MONTESQUIEU, *Œuvres complètes II*, ed. Roger Caillois (Paris: Gallimard, 1951).

*Le Nouvel Observateur* (16–22 Dec. 1983).

NYSENHOLC, ADOLPHE, and ARON, PAUL (eds.), *Marguerite Yourcenar, Revue de l'Université de Bruxelles* 3–4 (1988).

OVID, *Metamorphoses*, trans. Mary M. Innes (Harmondsworth: Penguin, 1955).

PACALY, JOSETTE, 'Les Songes et les Sorts. Préface et "dossier"', in *Marguerite Yourcenar: Aux frontières du texte*, ed. A.-Y. Julien (Lille: Roman 20–50, 1995), 31–42.

PANOFSKY, ERWIN, *Albrecht Dürer*, 2 vols. (Princeton: Princeton University Press, 1945).

—— *Idea: A Concept in Art History*, trans. Joseph J. S. Peake (Columbia: University of South Carolina Press, 1968).

—— *Meaning in the Visual Arts* (London: Peregrine, 1970).

PAOLUCCI, ANTONIO, *Ravenna*, trans. Simon Dally (London: Constable, 1978).

PAULHAN, JEAN, 'La peinture moderne et le secret mal gardé', *Fontaine* 35 (1944), 527–30.

PIRANESI, GIAN-BATTISTA, *Carceri d'Invenzione: Les Prisons imaginaires* (Monaco: Jaspard, Polus & Cie; Club International de Bibliophile, 1961).

PLINY THE ELDER, *Natural History: A Selection*, trans. John F. Healy (Harmondsworth: Penguin, 1991).

POIGNAULT, RÉMY, 'Alchimie verbale dans *Mémoires d'Hadrien* de Marguerite Yourcenar', *Bulletin de l'Association Guillaume Budé* 3 (1984), 295–321.

—— 'Du soleil de Lambèse aux boues du Nil', in *Voyage et connaissance dans l'œuvre de Marguerite Yourcenar*, ed. C. Biondi and C. Rosso (Pisa: Libreria Goliardica, 1988), 195–206.

—— 'Chronologie historique et chronologie du récit dans *Mémoires d'Hadrien*', in *Marguerite Yourcenar*, ed. A. Nysenholc and P. Aron, *Revue de l'Université de Bruxelles* 3–4 (1988), 19–31.

—— 'Antinoüs: un destin de pierre', in *Marguerite Yourcenar et l'art. L'art de Marguerite Yourcenar*, ed. J.-P. Castellani and R. Poignault (Tours: SIEY, 1990), 107–19.

—— 'Images de l'Empereur Hadrien d'après l'*Histoire Auguste* relue par Marguerite Yourcenar', *Revue des études latines* 69 (1991), 203–18.

—— *L'Antiquité dans l'œuvre de Marguerite Yourcenar. Littérature, mythe et histoire*, 2 vols. (Brussels: Latomus, 1995).

—— (ed.), *Bulletin de la Société Internationale d'Etudes Yourcenariennes* 1–19 (1987–98).

POTTS, ALEX, *Flesh and the Ideal: Winckelmann and the Origins of Art History* (New Haven and London: Yale University Press, 1994).

POULET, GEORGES, 'Piranèse et les poètes romantiques français', *NRF* 160 (Apr. 1966), 660–71, and 161 (May 1966), 849–62.

PRIMOZICH, LOREDANA, 'L'empire de l'esprit: sources et variantes dans l'œuvre de Marguerite Yourcenar', *Bulletin de la SIEY* 13 (1994), 25–37.

PROUST, MARCEL, *A l'ombre des jeunes filles en fleurs*, in *A la recherche du temps perdu I* (Paris: Laffont, 1987).

*Prud'hon ou le rêve du bonheur*, text by Sylvain Laveissière (Paris: Réunion des musées nationaux, 1997).

REINACH, A. J., *Recueil Milliet. Textes grecs et latins relatifs à l'histoire de la peinture ancienne*, ed. Agnes Rouveret (Paris: Macula, 1985).

RILKE, RAINER MARIA, *Duino Elegies*, trans. J. B. Leishman and Stephen Spender (2nd edn. London: Hogarth Press, 1942).

ROSENBERG, PIERRE, *Nicolas Poussin 1594–1665* (Paris: Réunion des musées nationaux, 1994).

ROZIÉ, FABRICE, 'Reflets de l'entre-deux-guerres dans le paratexte de Marguerite Yourcenar', in *Marguerite Yourcenar: Aux frontières du texte*, ed. A.-Y. Julien (Lille: Roman 20–50, 1995), 113–21.

RYSSELBERGHE, MARIA VAN, *Les Cahiers de la Petite Dame 3* (*Cahiers André Gide 6*) (Paris: Gallimard, 1975).

SARDE, MICHÈLE, *Vous, Marguerite Yourcenar* (Paris: Laffont, 1995).

SARTRE, JEAN-PAUL, *L'Imaginaire: Psychologie phénoménologique de l'imagination* (Paris: Gallimard, 1948).

SAVIGNEAU, JOSYANE, *Marguerite Yourcenar: L'invention d'une vie* (Paris: Gallimard, 1990).

SCHNEIDER, CYNTHIA P., *Rembrandt's Landscapes* (New Haven and London: Yale University Press, 1990).

SCHULTE NORDHOLT, ANNELIES, 'Soif de connaissance et désir du bien dans l'œuvre de Marguerite Yourcenar', *Neophilologus* 70 (1986), 357–71.

SCHWARTZ, GARY, *Rembrandt—His Life, His Paintings* (Harmondsworth: Viking, 1985).

SCOTT, DAVID, 'La structure picturale du sonnet parnassien et symboliste: Hérédia et Baudelaire', in *Ecrire la peinture*, ed. Philippe Delaveau (Paris: Editions universitaires, 1991).

*The Scriptores Historiae Augustae*, with an English translation by D. Magie, 3 vols. (London: W. Heinemann, 1921–32).

SENNETT, RICHARD, *Flesh and Stone: The Body and the City in Western Civilization* (London and Boston: Faber & Faber, 1994).

SHURR, GEORGIA H., 'Yourcenar et Piranèse: une relation artistique', in *Marguerite Yourcenar et l'art. L'art de Marguerite Yourcenar*, ed. J.-P. Castellani and R. Poignault (Tours: SIEY, 1990), 175–86.

—— 'Narcisse: le mythe caché chez Yourcenar,' in *Roman, histoire et mythe dans l'œuvre de Marguerite Yourcenar*, ed. S. and M. Delcroix (Tours: SIEY, 1995), 411–18.

SLIVE, SEYMOUR, *Frans Hals* (London: Royal Academy of Arts, 1990).

—— and HOETINK, H. R. (eds.), *Jacob van Ruisdael* (New York: Abbeville Press, 1981).

SMITH, JEFFREY CHIPPS, *German Sculpture of the Later Renaissance c.1520–1580: Art in an Age of Uncertainty* (Princeton: Princeton University Press, 1994).

SOULÈS, CLAUDE, 'Lecture d'un chapitre—La promenade sur la dune', in *'L'Œuvre au noir' de Marguerite Yourcenar*, ed. A.-Y. Julien, *Roman 20–50* 9 (1990), 95–107.

SPENCER-NOËL, GENEVIÈVE, *Zénon ou le thème de l'alchimie dans 'L'Œuvre au noir' de Marguerite Yourcenar* (Paris: Nizet, 1981).

STAAL, FRITS, *Exploring Mysticism* (Harmondsworth: Penguin, 1975).

STEIN, GERTRUDE, *The Autobiography of Alice B. Toklas* (Harmondsworth: Penguin, 1983).

STILLMAN, LINDA KLIEGER, 'Marguerite Yourcenar and the Phallacy of Indiff-erence', *Studies in Twentieth Century Literature* 9/2 (Spring 1985), 261–77.

SUARÈS, ANDRÉ, *Xénies* (Paris: Plon, 1923).

SUMMERSON, JOHN, *The Classical Language of Architecture* (London: Thames and Hudson, 1980).

SYME, RONALD, *'Historia Augusta' Papers* (Oxford: Clarendon Press, 1983).

—— *Fictional History Old and New. Hadrian* (Oxford: Somerville College Publications, 1986).

TERNEUIL, ALEXANDRE, 'Le thème de l'exil dans quelques essais de Yourcenar', in *Marguerite Yourcenar: Ecritures de l'exil*, ed. B. Deprez and A. de Medeiros (Louvain-la-Neuve: Academia Bruylant, 1998), 191–201.

THIBAUDET, ALBERT, *Intérieurs* (Paris: Plon, 1924).

TOURNIER, MICHEL, 'Gustave et Marguerite', in *Marguerite Yourcenar, SUD* 55 (1984), 68–77.

VALÉRY, PAUL, *Variété II* (Paris: Gallimard, 1956).

—— *Œuvres II*, ed. Jean Hytier (Paris: Gallimard, Bibliothèque de la Pléiade, 1960).

—— *Eupalinos ou l'architecte. L'Ame et la Danse*, ed. Vera J. Daniel (London: Oxford University Press, 1967).

—— *Introduction à la méthode de Léonard de Vinci* (Paris: Gallimard, 1992).

VERDI, RICHARD, 'Poussin's Critical Fortunes', Ph.D. thesis (London, 1976).

—— *Nicolas Poussin 1594–1665* (London: Royal Academy of Arts, 1995).

VEYNE, PAUL, *Comment on écrit l'histoire* (Paris: Seuil, 1979).

—— 'Préface', in Peter Brown, *Genèse de l'antiquité tardive*, trans. Aline Rousselle (Paris: Gallimard, 1983).

—— '*Humanitas*: les Romains et les autres', in *L'Homme romain*, ed. Andrea Giardina (Paris: Seuil, 1992).

—— 'Les fonctions des empereurs romains', Collège de France seminar, 1993–4.

VIRILIO, PAUL, *Esthétique de la disparition* (Paris: Galilée, 1989).

VOLTAIRE, *Essai sur les mœurs*, ed. René Pomeau (Paris: Garnier Frères, 1961).

WALFORD, E. JOHN, *Jacob van Ruisdael and the Perception of Landscape* (New Haven and London: Yale University Press, 1991).

WATSON-WILLIAMS, HELEN, 'Memento mori: Marguerite Yourcenar's *Un homme obscur*', in *European Relations: Essays for Helen Watson-Williams*, ed. Bruce Bennett and John Hay (Perth: University of Western Australia Press, 1985), 141–50.

WEIGHTMAN, JOHN, 'Falling towards Death', *Times Literary Supplement* (22 July 1983), 767–8.

WELLS, COLIN, *The Roman Empire* (2nd edn. London: Fontana, 1992).

WETERING, ERNST VAN DE, 'Rembrandt's Manner: Technique in the Service of Illusion', in *Rembrandt: The Master and his Workshop. Paintings*, ed. C. Brown, J. Kelch and P. van Thiel (New Haven and London: Yale University Press, 1991), 12–39.

WILENSKI, RENÉ, *Flemish Painters*, 2 vols. (London: Faber & Faber, 1960).

WILTON-ELY, JOHN, *The Mind and Art of Giovanni Battista Piranesi* (London: Thames and Hudson, 1978).

—— *Piranesi as Architect and Designer* (New Haven and London: Yale University Press, 1993).

WITTKOWER, RUDOLF, *Studies in the Italian Baroque* (Boulder, CO: Westview Press, 1975).

WRIGHT, CHRISTOPHER, *Poussin, Paintings: A Catalogue Raisonné* (London: Jupiter Books, 1984).

YATES, FRANCES A., *The Art of Memory* (London: Ark Paperbacks, 1984).

# INDEX

❖

194 INDEX

# BRITISH COMPARATIVE LITERATURE ASSOCIATION

The British Comparative Literature Association aims at promoting the scholarly study of literature without confinement to national or linguistic boundaries, and in relation to other disciplines. Through its regular publications *New Comparison* and the yearbook *Comparative Criticism*, conferences, workshops, a translation competition and other activities, the BCLA encourages research along comparative, intercultural and interdisciplinary lines; fosters the exchange of critical ideas; informs its members of developments in the study of literature; and provides a forum for academic contacts within Britain and in other countries. Membership is open to academic members of universities and other institutions of higher learning, to graduate students and others having appropriate scholarly interests in Britain and abroad.

President: Professor Malcolm Bowie (Oxford)
Secretary: Mrs Penny Brown (Manchester)
Treasurer: Dr Stuart Gillespie (Glasgow)

*Enquiries:*
Mrs Penny Brown
Department of French
University of Manchester
Manchester M13 9PL
E-mail: Penny.Brown@man.ac.uk